Blood of a Savage

The Savage Series – Book 2

Zachary Shadoan

Copyright © 2024 by Zachary Shadoan
All rights reserved.

For Lilly, my sprekelia

Prologue

✣ Creed of the Blooded ✣

I am Blooded, and this is my creed.
I am warrior, and this is my sword.
I am shadow, and this is my cloak.
I am darkness, bringer of light.
The whisper in the wind.
The order in the chaos.

I am son to my father.
Daughter to my mother.
Bane of the wicked.
Guardian of the innocent.

My blood is strength from weakness.
Bravery from cowardice.
Hope from despair.
Truth from illusion.
Life from death.

I commit my blood to the earth.
Not for myself.
But for those whose blood has been shed unwillingly.
For those whose sacrifices have been ignored.
For those whose mortal lives have been stolen.

I am the blood, and the blood is me.
From this breath until my last.
I am Blooded, and this is my creed.

❀ The Savage Reborn ❀

I rest my eyes upon the trickle of blood that drips from my savage hands. Just as the people of this land have bled for a cause long seen as lost, I too now bleed. I do not spill my blood just for the land, though. I do not bleed for the trees, the grass, or the rolling mountains that plaster across the countryside as though they were painted by God himself.

No, I bleed for a cause far greater.

As the blood of the innocent stains the whole of this world, my brothers and sisters shed their own blood in service to them, for there are no others that will. It is for *them* we bleed. It is for *them* we fight.

What else can a man do who has seen what we have seen? Will the screams ever stop? Will the nightmares ever escape my restless mind?

I think I will carry these visions for the rest of my days. They are a part of me. They haunt me as I sleep. They fill my heart with sorrow. Even the slightest graze of my hand against the purple flower causes its petals to turn black and wilt away. The darkness shrouds every ray of sunlight that shows any ambition to shine upon this world. I have learned to live without the light...without the warmth.

I embrace the sting of the blade as it slides upon my open palm. I relish the pain as my blood feeds the soil of the earth and cleanses the depths of my soul.

I once feared the shadows, for there was no comfort in the dark. That fear is now gone, replaced with a love of the darkness just as a mother loves her child. The shadows become me, and I become them. I welcome them into my soul. We are one and the same.

Through the sadness in my heart...through the blackness that engulfs my soul, I leave behind any semblance of my former life. I emerge as something more than just a man. I commit myself to the darkness so that others may flourish in the light.

Through my skill with ink and paper, I chronicle my story...my codex...for all those whose voices go unheard. The world will learn what happened in this land on the edge of the world. Future generations will know how fiercely these brave souls fought and died for the ones they love.

It is amongst these writings...amongst this pain that I bear...that my savage heart is molded and shaped. I transform into more than just flesh and blood as I am resurrected into the ranks of the order.

The darkness now fears *me*.

For I am no longer Bernardino de Sahagun, Spanish conquistador, invader of foreign lands.

I am a savage, born anew.

I am Blooded.

✺ The Florentine Codex ✺

Dehumanization. A tale as old as time.

The Romans did it. The Greeks did it. The Chinese. The Egyptians. Countless others as well.

How does one justify murder? How can a man be convinced that ridding the world of another person or group of people is actually beneficial for the advancement of the human race? After all, aren't the people being killed also part of this world, the same species as the killer?

The answer is quite simple: no.

Or at least, that's the justification.

Convince yourself and your followers that the flesh being torn apart with your sword is not that of another human being. Sure, the insertion of the blade will sound the same. It will undoubtedly produce blood from the wound, but it's more akin to skewering a wild boar on a hunt. A man doesn't lose sleep when he sends his arrow into the flesh of an animal, so why should he fret when taking the life of a savage? One might argue that the world is now better without them, right?

The savage man will attack you, the savage woman will produce more men to attack you, and the savage child will grow into a man who will eventually attack you. After all, that's what a barbarian does. He attacks. He attacks without warning. He attacks without cause. He is innately born to reject a civilized manner of being. So kill them all and let God decide which ones to save.

That was the message I learned ever since I was old enough to comprehend the way of the world. That was the education I received throughout my childhood in Spain.

"An Italian explorer has made it to India (we think) and discovered a new race of people. They have land and resources that we want. If we have to kill them to get it, then God will understand. We are human. They are not."

More or less.

The sad part is that I believed it. I believed in my bones that they were inferior to us. Many of them still lived in huts and tents, wearing the fur of animals and shitting in the dirt. And their skin, so dark and coarse, as if tainted and cursed by God for their savagery.

It was nearly impossible to *not* feel the way I did, at least at the time. I don't blame my Spanish countrymen for feeling that way, either. We were indoctrinated and brainwashed. We were forced to believe a dangerous lie, and it took me witnessing our atrocities in person to finally realize that *we* were in fact the true savages, not them.

I was there that day at Cholula when Hernan Cortes ordered the execution of countless innocent Aztecs. Not just the men, but the women and children too, even the babies that were barely old enough to hold their heads up. I watched as Cortes and his nephew, Francisco Pizarro, commanded their men to cut the Aztecs down like cattle who had outgrown their usefulness.

I, Bernardino de Sahagun, vowed to never raise my sword against these people again. In fact, my refusal to march with the army to Tenochtitlan got me thrown into a prison back in Veracruz. I was slated to be hanged for treason, but Cortes never came back to give the order. He took a spear through the heart during the sack of Tenochtitlan, so I suppose it was hard for a dead man to order my execution.

With Cortes gone, I became a forgotten man. Sure, the prison guards fed me and emptied my chamber pot, but I was a ghost. I was no one. Just another traitor to the crown who nobody knew what to do with.

Ironically, it was during this time that I found my true purpose in life. I befriended the most unlikely of individuals, and with his help, I wrote my masterpiece...my Magnum Opus...the same work of art that enters your vision at this very moment.

It is my sincere hope that the following passages will serve as a reminder that the sacrifices of the people of this land have not been in vain. Their blood has not stained the grass and turned the rivers red for no purpose, and I aim to bring that purpose into the light. I chronicle the stories of those who have fought with courage, loved with passion, and died with honor.

Through their tears and with the help of my penmanship, I present the Florentine Codex.

🌀 Maps of the New World 🌀

Vera Cruz
•Spanish Stronghold

Chinquila
•Maya Fishing Village

Tenochtitlan
•Former Capital of the Fallen Aztec Empire

Pacific Ocean

Cuzco
•Capital of the Inca Empire

Atlantic Ocean

Quito
*Imperial Seat of Atahualpa during Inca Civil War

Cajamarca
*City of Thorns

Machu Picchu
*Mountain Fortress of The Blooded

Cuzco
*Imperial Seat of Huascar during Inca Civil War

Atlantic Ocean

Pacific Ocean

Codex Volume I

Arrows, Eagles, and Big Cats

Volume I, Part I
Ashes of a Dying World

"Stop," Acalan whispered to Chimalli in the Nahuatl language as he placed his outstretched arm across the boy's chest and pulled him back to the cover of the crumbled stone building. The presence of a Spanish patrol marching down the adjacent street halted the Aztecs' advance through the burning city of Tenochtitlan.

Only twelve years of age, the frightened Chimalli swaddled his infant nephew, Ohtli, the child of a Spanish father and an Aztec mother, tight in his arms. Ohtli's parents, Rodrigo and Atzi, had just been taken from this world with the rest of the Aztec people, and they left behind the broken stones of their dying city. Where life and beauty had once flourished on this island city in the middle of Lake Texcoco, death and despair now lingered like a plague in Tenochtitlan. The greatest city in the whole of the Mexica land, which the foreign invaders called the New World, crumbled beneath the onslaught of the Spanish conquistadors.

"What are we to do, Acalan?!" Chimalli prodded with desperation as the trio of Aztecs attempted to escape the flames and the swords of the enemy. "Where are we to go?!"

Acalan, who had just saved Chimalli and Ohtli from certain death at the hands of the Spanish soldiers, nervously ran his fingers across the scar on his shoulder where Francisco Pizarro had fired a musket ball into his flesh two years earlier.

"Tenochtitlan and my home of Texcoco are lost," Acalan responded with grief. "We must get off this island and flee to another land."

"Another land?" Chimalli asked with confusion as Ohtli, yet to reach one year of age, rested calmly in his arms.

Acalan wiped the sweat from his brow before replying. "I have heard tales of lands with fresh water and green pastures that have been untouched by the pale-skins' fury...at least for now."

"You mean the land of the Mayans?"

"No, child," Acalan replied as the two Aztecs still whispered to each other. "When I was captured by the Spanish two years ago, I overheard them discussing plans to invade the Mayan lands as well, just as they have done to ours."

The expression on Chimalli's face turned grave. "Where then, Acalan? The Spanish will burn everything and leave no one alive."

"That is why we must travel to a place far from here," Acalan said. "If what I've heard is true, there is a land far to the south that is connected to us by thick jungles and flowing rivers. Our scouts always called it the realm of the Incas, ruled by their old emperor and his two sons. It would take many moons to reach this place, but I fear we have few other choices.

"The Incas?" Chimalli responded as his words tailed off. He peered into the smoke-filled sky in thought. The young boy, battered and out of options, accepted the older Aztec's idea as he shuffled with anticipation. "If you say this is the only way, then we're with you."

Acalan nodded. "We must first escape Tenochtitlan, though, or else a Spanish sword will make this city our final resting place."

Chimalli stood ready and willing to embark as Ohtli, still weak and clinging to life, reached his hand towards his uncle's face and stroked his tiny fingers across Chimalli's cheek. Ohtli's eyes wavered and opened only half-way as the perils of a dying world bore heavily upon the infant.

"Follow me and stay close," Acalan ordered as he peaked around the corner to see if the Spanish patrol had moved out of view. Much to his delight, the route appeared to be clear, and he led Chimalli and Ohtli through the smoke and towards the eastern shore of the giant island where the once-great city of Tenochtitlan stood. The Spanish ships had unleashed the full might of their cannons and reigned down a fury unlike anything ever witnessed in this land. All that remained of the largest and most powerful city in the Aztec Empire was now a heap of rubble and smoldering ash.

"Where are you leading us, Acalan?" Chimalli asked as he placed his trust in the former ruler of Texcoco. Acalan had watched over Emperor Cuauhtémoc of Tenochtitlan for most of his life, and it was only after Acalan and Cuauhtémoc separated that the young emperor met his end at the edge of a Spanish blade...a blade that was wielded by the best friend of Ohtli's father during the battle of Otumba.

"I know of a hidden inlet along the eastern shore that's covered by a dense patch of trees and brush," Acalan replied as the three Aztecs continued to move through the crumbling city. "The thicket hides a small canoe that belonged to Cuauhtémoc. He used to sneak out of the royal palace at night and take it onto the lake. He enjoyed his solitude without the pressure of his bodyguards around him."

Acalan smiled softly as the thought of his best friend, Cuauhtémoc, brought joy to the Aztec's heart.

"That boat will be our way out of the city," Acalan continued.

"I suppose we have no other choice," Chimalli responded with a nervous expression on his face, "but what if it's no longer there?"

Acalan delayed his response while he thought of the words to say to his twelve-year-old friend who held the child from two worlds in his arms.

"If the canoe is gone, pray to Quetzalcoatl for his guidance. Only the will of the gods will save us then, conetl."

Acalan's words frightened Chimalli, but the young Aztec was no stranger to fear and despair. His life had been riddled with it ever since the Spanish had arrived on the shores of their land. Chimalli had accepted his fate long ago and placed his destiny in the hands of Quetzalcoatl, the feathered serpent god. The Spaniards had proclaimed that their now-dead leader, Hernan Cortes, fulfilled the Aztec prophecy and returned to them as a mortal form of Quetzalcoatl. The Aztecs themselves even thought that Ohtli's father, Rodrigo, held this claim. Chimalli knew better than to follow either of these fantasies, though. He knew that Quetzalcoatl had not yet returned and that the feathered serpent god still watched over the last of the Aztecs.

"Stop, get down," Acalan whispered to Chimalli as the screams of an Aztec woman resonated through the air. Acalan and Chimalli had heard similar cries for help during their journey through the city as the Spanish pillaged and raped their way through what was left of the defenseless Aztec people. This was different, though. These screams were not distant or muffled. They sounded close...very close.

The woman's pitiful and stomach-turning squeals were mixed with sounds of commotion and reckless grumblings by her Spanish attackers. A second scream then rang out from the same building, the voice of a young girl emanating through the night.

"Mama! H-help me!" the girl's crackling voice emitted in Nahuatl.

Acalan placed his head against the stone structure at his back. His heart ached at every cry for help that the two female Aztecs bellowed out. He looked at the beleaguered faces of Chimalli and Ohtli as he contemplated his next move.

Leave this woman and her daughter to be raped, tortured, and murdered? Acalan thought in his mind. *Or attempt to save them and risk the lives of Ohtli and Chimalli?*

Chimalli witnessed the predicament that plastered across Acalan's face and knew what his mind was pondering. The young Aztec made no hesitation in assisting his older friend to decide their plan of action.

"We're going in there and saving those people," Chimalli proclaimed. Acalan stared at the young boy for a moment before nodding his head in agreement and forming an eager and angry expression on his face.

"Stay here," Acalan pleaded. "I can't risk losing you and Ohtli."

Chimalli snapped back at Acalan and turned his head abruptly to meet the twenty-four-year-old's gaze. "Quetzalcoatl himself will have to return and stop me from going in there."

Acalan prepared to further plead with Chimalli to stay out of the fight, but he stopped his words when he saw the passion in the boy's eyes. Acalan knew Chimalli was going into that building no matter what words were used to convince him otherwise.

"Strap Ohtli to my back," Chimalli insisted as he untied a piece of cloth from his waist that held his family's broken spear within it.

Chimalli placed Ohtli and the thick piece of cloth in Acalan's hands. Acalan wrapped the cloth around Chimalli's neck and fastened Ohtli tight against his back. The baby remained silent as his swollen eyes still struggled to stay open.

"Hold on, child," Acalan whispered to Ohtli as he made sure the baby was swaddled firmly. "This will all be over soon."

Chimalli grasped his spear in his right hand and held it out in front of him. His brother, who had also been named Ohtli, left the family heirloom to Chimalli upon his death at the hands of Rodrigo two years prior. The spear had been broken about midway down the handle during Chimalli's fight with Francisco earlier that night, but the blade was as sharp as ever. Visions of thrusting the tip of the spear through Cortes's heart just before he could slit Rodrigo's throat flashed through Chimalli's young mind.

"Are you ready, conetl?" Acalan asked as he pulled his bow from behind his back and readied an arrow within its string.

Chimalli nodded and hid the fear in his heart with a mask of anger. This was no time to be afraid, no time for weakness. The lives of this woman and her daughter, who still cried out for help, were now solely in the hands of Acalan and Chimalli.

The two Aztecs raced down the alleyway with haste, and Ohtli bobbed up and down with each step his uncle placed along the ground.

Acalan led the way as he reached the entrance to the building and scanned his surroundings. He peered into the open doorway and saw several fully armored Spanish conquistadors rummaging through the house and terrorizing the helpless Aztec women.

Acalan turned his head around to face Chimalli. "There's a lot of them," he whispered.

"So? What are we waiting for?" the brave Chimalli asked, prompting a smile from Acalan.

"May the war god, Huitzilopochtli, guide our hands on this day," Acalan proclaimed as he and Chimalli both bowed their heads in submission to the will of the gods.

When the two Aztecs raised their heads, Acalan pulled the arrow back against the string of his bow and snapped his body around the corner of the doorway. He released the obsidian-tipped arrow through the air and struck a Spaniard in the side of neck, killing him and collapsing his body to the floor. The two other unsuspecting Spanish guards in the first room jumped up in shock at the sound of the buzzing arrow and the sight of blood spewing from their companion's neck. They scrambled to draw their swords, but before their hands could even grasp the handles, Acalan had already prepared another arrow. The Aztec bolted into the house and released a second arrow at another Spaniard, striking him in the left eye just below the cover of his metal helmet. The last conquistador in the entrance room managed to pull his sword and swing it at Acalan, but the swift and agile Aztec dodged the attack just long enough for Chimalli, wielding the broken spear in his hand and an infant child on his back, to burst through the door and thrust his blade into the man's back.

Three Spaniards laid dead at the Aztecs' feet, but more guards still remained at the back of the house. The screams of the woman and her daughter persisted while Acalan sheathed his bow and pulled his obsidian club from his waistband. As he and Chimalli reached the back of the house, each of them charged into separate rooms.

Acalan barreled into the bedroom where the screams of the older woman had resonated. One Spaniard searched through the furniture for gold and trinkets, while another worked to button his pants back up on the edge of the bed where the Aztec woman laid naked and motionless. Acalan pummeled his club into the first Spaniard's back before switching targets rapidly and bringing his weapon down on the rapist's head, splitting it open and spraying his blood across the room.

Meanwhile, Chimalli charged into the other room where two more Spanish guards attempted to ravish a young Aztec girl. Before they could carry out their heinous act, Chimalli plunged his spear into one of their necks and dropped his body on top of the traumatized girl. The other Spaniard, startled at his friend's death, popped up quickly and struck Chimalli in the face with his fist, careening the boy sideways into the wall. The impact against the stone, while not causing harm to Ohtli, led the baby to welp in fear. The last Spaniard, eager to kill Chimalli, approached the young Aztec and drew his dagger. The girl on the bed grabbed the other blade that belonged to the dead Spaniard on top of her and shoved off his corpse. She rose to her feet just as the conquistador prepared to stab Chimalli and sank her dagger into the man's back. As the Spaniard fell to the ground, she continued piercing his flesh long after the last breath of life left his body. The rage of the young girl, who appeared to be the same age as Chimalli, reminded him of the same rage his sister, Atzi, exhibited when she too was almost raped by the Spanish guards.

When the girl finally finished stabbing her attacker, the bloody knife slipped from her grasp and landed with a loud clanging sound against the floor. Her mind then shifted to her mother, who was now silent in the other room. The young girl yelled out the Nahuatl word for "mother" while she leapt to her feet and raced into the other room.

"Nantli! Nantli!" she screamed with desperation.

When the Aztec girl entered the room, she watched in horror as her mother laid silent on the bed with her eyes wide open and a blank stare covering her face. Acalan, who had just dispatched her attackers, covered the woman's naked, bloodied body with a nearby blanket and ran his fingers across her eyelids to close them one last time.

The woman's daughter let out a gruesome cry of agony when she realized her mother had passed from this world. She ran to the edge of the bed and placed her head on her mother's chest as she continued to weep and shout from the touch of the lifeless body.

"No, Mama! No! Please don't leave me!" the girl bellowed through her tears. Her screams filled the air in and around the house and were sure to be heard by others nearby.

"Conetl, we must go!" Acalan pleaded with the girl. "More Spanish will be here soon! Come with us!"

"Just leave me," the girl said calmly as her screams stopped and she accepted her mother's grisly fate. "I have nothing left to live for."

"We're not leaving you behind!" Chimalli shouted as he placed his hand under the girl's arm and lifted her to her feet. She continued to stare at her mother as Chimalli pulled her limp body out of the room.

The band of Aztecs, who now had a fourth member with them, scurried around the dead Spaniards and out of the house. Ohtli, still attached to Chimalli's back, continued to cry after the fight that had just ensued. Acalan attempted to console the weary infant but failed to do so. Ohtli's screams echoed through the early morning air as the sun made its way over the horizon.

As the Aztecs dashed around the corner of the alleyway, a menacing Spanish voice suddenly rang out from down the street.

"Over there, boys! Run the savages down!" a Spanish commander ordered as the eager shouts of his men rang out towards the fleeing Aztecs.

Acalan and Chimalli glanced in the direction of the voices and saw a group of around ten Spanish conquistadors barreling towards them.

"Go! Now!" Acalan hollered. "To the boat!"

The Aztec girl who they had just rescued still stared off into an empty space with no regard for the approaching danger. Red rings encircled her eyes as she lost almost all desire to move on her own power. Chimalli knew he had to keep pulling her along with them, or else she would have fallen to the ground and joined her mother in death.

The Aztecs sprinted for their lives and made their way through heaps of rubble and debris as the clear blue water of Lake Texcoco emerged into their sight.

"We're almost there!" Acalan shouted to the young Aztecs that followed behind him. "Don't stop!"

At this point, the shouts from their Spanish pursuers had rallied other nearby Spaniards to the chase. The four desperate Aztecs now had twenty or more Spaniards sprinting towards them from multiple directions. Chimalli knew that if they were caught, they would suffer the same brutal death as so many of their Aztec brethren had.

Chimalli's thoughts ran wild in his head as he kept his mind focused on what had to be done.

Left foot. Right foot. Left foot. Right foot. Do not stop, Chimalli. These men will kill you all and drown Ohtli in the lake. Do not stop.

As the Aztecs approached the shoreline, Chimalli spotted a large patch of brush that protruded slightly into the lake. His lips formed a smile as he saw the tip of a small wooden canoe jutting out from the brush.

"There it is!" Acalan shouted in jubilation as he too saw the boat.

As he looked back at the men pursuing them, though, his joy soon faded. The Spanish closed in fast, and Acalan knew they wouldn't have time to pull the boat out and make their escape before being swarmed by the conquistadors.

"They're gaining on us!" Acalan yelled to Chimalli, who still pulled the young Aztec girl alongside him. "You must pull the boat out yourself, Chimalli! I'll hold them off!"

Acalan stopped his forward movement and turned to face the approaching Spanish horde.

"Acalan! No!" Chimalli shouted to his friend. He knew Acalan spoke the truth, though. Without more time, they would surely perish with the rest of the city. Chimalli hesitated for a moment before continuing towards the boat, which was only a few paces away now.

Acalan unsheathed his bow as the flames of the burning city gleamed in his eyes and the spirit of the jaguar growled in his soul. The Aztec warrior from Texcoco strung an arrow and released it with the swiftness of the eagle, piercing a Spaniard and dropping him to the ground. Acalan proceeded to unleash a reign of terror with his arrows as he felled several Spanish conquistadors with devastating strikes. His aim was deadly and consistent as if the gods themselves guided his bow.

As Acalan held off their pursuers, Chimalli, Ohtli, and the Aztec girl reached the boat that was covered in the dense brush. With the help of the young girl, who had now come to her senses about the impending threat, Chimalli tugged with all his strength and dislodged the boat from the thicket of leaves and sticks.

While Chimalli pulled the canoe further onto the lake, he helped the girl climb into the boat before following her.

"Acalan! Let's go!" Chimalli shouted as he looked back to his friend, who was still releasing arrows with a great fury.

As Acalan turned to retreat, a group of Spaniards flanked around him and charged towards the unsuspecting Aztec from the rear.

"Acalan! Behind you!" Chimalli screamed.

The assault of the Spaniards on the flank startled Acalan, forcing him to break his stride and dodge the incoming attacks. Acalan weaved in and out of the Spanish swords as none of them could contend with the agility of the Aztec. He struck down a few more Spaniards with his club, but the force of the dozen or so attackers that remained was too much to bear.

"Chimalli! Get out of here!" Acalan shouted back towards the boat as he climbed a crumbled, nearby structure and continued to evade Spanish strikes that landed all around him.

"Not without you!" Chimalli yelled back.

"There's no time, conetl! You must go now!"

Chimalli looked on as Acalan fought desperately for his life. The reality of the situation sunk into Chimalli's heart when a group of soldiers broke away from Acalan's position and charged the boat. He knew that Acalan would have no chance of escaping with them. With tears in his eyes, Chimalli used the oar to propel them off the last patch of sand that held the boat against the shore.

The canoe floated onto the lake as Acalan and his attackers became smaller and smaller in Chimalli's vision. The young Aztec wept for his friend as the swarm of Spaniards surrounded Acalan and engulfed his position.

Chimalli watched as the rays of the morning sun illuminated a colony of eagles that circled high above the city. Chimalli felt a strange connection to these creatures as they maneuvered out of the smoke and positioned themselves above the spot where Acalan had been fighting.

The boat drifted further from the shore, and the entirety of the city came into Chimalli's view. Tenochtitlan, the city of great kings and mighty heroes that served as Chimalli's home and the foundation of Aztec society for hundreds of years, crumbled and died on that fateful morning in the autumn of 1521. With the collapse of the city, the once-mighty Aztec Empire was no more.

The eagles wept at the fall of the jaguar.

Chimalli wept at the fall of Acalan.

The young boy removed his nephew from the strap on his back and held the baby in his arms. Ohtli still held breath in his lungs and life in his body despite everything they had been through.

Chimalli then glanced at the young girl who sat across the boat from him and stared out towards the burning city.

"W-what is your name?" Chimalli asked as he suddenly felt nervous in her presence.

The battered girl turned to him and stared deep into his eyes before uttering the name that would forever remain in Chimalli's heart.

"Kelia."

Volume I, Part II
The Storm Approaches

The waves dashed against the wooden planks of the large Spanish ships before retreating back to the blue abyss of the Caribbean Sea. The sails of the fleet fluttered in the wind while the sun withdrew behind a set of dark clouds, signaling the arrival of an approaching storm.

At the front of the armada sailed the Santa Ana, the flagship and largest vessel of the Spanish navy. Its cannons protruded menacingly from the hull of the ship, ready to unleash death upon anyone unlucky enough to be caught in its path.

Francisco Pizarro stared blankly towards the boundless sea in front of him from the helm of the Santa Ana before glancing back and grinning sheepishly at the grand fleet that followed behind him. Pizarro, nephew to the conqueror of the Aztecs, Hernan Cortes, set his sights upon the ships that sailed into the heart of a new empire of natives to the south...an empire that had not yet been touched by Spanish influence.

"Papa! Papa!" a squealing Spanish voice called out to Pizarro.

"Yes, Valentino?" Pizarro replied in Spanish. "What is it, my son?"

"When are we getting off this cursed boat, Papa? I grow tired of eating that slop every day and sleeping next to Alejandro. He smells like the pigs."

The twelve-year-old Valentino turned and sneered at his half-brother, Alejandro, a boy also twelve years of age.

"You eat better than every man in this fleet," Alejandro mumbled in response to his brother as he kept his gaze turned towards the sea.

"What was that, dog?" Valentino questioned as he aggressively approached his brother. "I didn't quite hear you."

Alejandro turned and stared into Valentino's eyes as his sniveling half-brother continued to provoke him.

"You want to hit me, don't you?" Valentino whispered. "Well go ahead and do it then, dog. See what father does to you."

Alejandro maintained his glare as Valentino smiled from ear to ear, knowing that Alejandro would not act upon his desires to strike.

"Alejandro, be nice to your brother," Pizarro interjected as he stepped down from the helm of the ship and approached the boys. "Same goes to you, Valentino."

"But why, Papa?" Valentino snapped back at his father. "Why should I? Look at him, Papa. He's no better than the rats in the cargo hold. We should just throw him over now and be rid of him."

Alejandro turned away and gave no response to his brother's incessant whining. The young Spaniard closed his eyes and went somewhere else in his mind...anywhere else but on that ship in the middle of the sea with a brother and father who hated him for being different.

"Valentino, go below deck," Pizarro demanded. "I need a moment to speak with your brother."

"Go below deck while this dog gets to feel the breeze on his face?! Have you gone mad, fa-"

"Now, Valentino! Do as I say!" Pizarro interrupted and shouted at his disobedient son.

The crewmen on the deck of the ship turned to acknowledge Pizarro's shouts before promptly returning to their tasks.

Valentino paused as a look of embarrassment covered his face. He swallowed his pride, though, and the young Spaniard accepted his father's command.

"Yes, father," he replied as he turned and walked in the other direction.

"Out of my way, cabrón!" Valentino shouted at one of the Spanish crewmen after the man accidentally brushed into him while scrubbing the deck. "I'm surrounded by fools!"

Valentino angrily stormed passed the rest of the men and disappeared through the wooden door that led below to the captain's quarters.

Pizarro placed his hand on Alejandro's shoulder and bent down to his level as if to show genuine concern. Alejandro wasn't fooled by Pizarro's caring demeanor, though. He knew of his father's hatred towards him as the man had indicated many times and in many ways.

"Alejandro, you know you can't speak to your brother like that."

It's no more than he deserves, Alejandro thought to himself but never said aloud. Valentino would always be favored by their father, and Alejandro was under no delusion to think otherwise. He found it best not to question Valentino's behavior.

"Yes, father," Alejandro replied with a reluctant sigh.

"Your brother will head up an expedition of his own one day," said Pizarro, "and if you learn to stay quiet and obey orders, you might just earn a spot in his crew."

"But what if I don't want this life, Padre? What if I don't want the life of a conquistador? You've said it yourself. I'm different. I don't fit in with these men. I wasn't born to a Spanish mother as Valentino was."

"I said those things in anger, Alejandro, because you refuse to listen. This may not be the life you want, but it's the life that was chosen for you. All you can do now is make the best of what you have...just like the rest of us."

Alejandro turned his gaze away from his father and stared north from where they first set sail out of Cuba.

"What was my mother like?" Alejandro asked after a short pause.

Pizarro stood up straight and paced across the deck of the Santa Ana, stroking his thick, black beard and contemplating his response.

"Your mother..." he said before pausing again in thought. Alejandro had never mentioned her to his father due to fear of what the response might be, although he thought about her quite often.

"Your mother was nothing but a savage...a common whore from a brothel in Havana that I bedded one night after the ale had dulled my senses. I remember very little of the encounter."

Pizarro's response left Alejandro speechless and ashamed. He looked down at his feet in sorrow as the waves of the sea gently rocked the ship.

"Nine months later," his father continued, "I was called to the same brothel and greeted with a child. The midwife placed you in my arms and told me that your mother had passed away during the birth. I chose to redeem my reckless actions by taking you in and raising you."

"My mother is...dead?" Alejandro asked as a tear fell from his eye and splashed onto the wooden deck. "Why did you never tell me?"

"You never asked, child," Pizarro responded. "Besides, I didn't want you weeping for a dead savage... just as you are now. These people are not worthy of your tears."

"But these people are *my* people, are they not, father?"

Pizarro scowled at his son's question as an expression of anger enveloped his face. "I'll let that comment go just this once, boy, but say it again, and I'll cut your tongue out and throw it in the ocean."

Alejandro remained silent as he didn't know his father to make idle threats. Alejandro had seen him scold and beat his own crewmen for the slightest of errors.

"I was foolish enough in my youth to breed with a whore of this barbaric land," Pizarro continued, "but no son of mine will ever call himself one of *them*...not while I still draw breath in my lungs."

"Yes, father," Alejandro replied. "Forgive me."

Pizarro's heated demeanor cooled as he once again feigned a calming sense of care for his son.

"You still have much to learn, my son, and for that, you are forgiven. Just as my uncle, the great Hernan Cortes, taught me to lead and to be a man, I too will show you what it means to be a true Spaniard."

Alejandro abandoned all genuine notions of truth in his voice and returned his responses back to mirror the false reality that he had been forced to live with his entire life.

"I am honored to serve under you, and one day, I will wear the armor of a conquistador and make you proud."

Alejandro did not believe his own words, but his desperate attempts to seek the approval of his father forced them from his lips.

Pizarro nodded and grinned at his son. "Perhaps this voyage will allow you to kill your first native, my boy. These... Incas...are no better than the Aztecs. When you've seen one savage, you've seen them all."

"I thought we were only going to parley with the Incas, father," Alejandro asked in confusion, "not to fight them."

"Yes, parley," Pizarro sneered and chuckled as he turned back towards the front of the ship and peered off into the distance. "We're simply going to negotiate a trade deal with them."

The young Alejandro stood beside his father and glanced up at him as Pizarro's eyes glimmered. Alejandro could always tell when his father was lying. Pizarro had never been particularly good at it.

Alejandro was not like his father, though. He was not like his brother, Valentino. Born as a half-native, he had no hatred for the people of this land. As he had spent almost all his life in Spain, though, he knew very little about the natives other than what he had heard from his Spanish kinsmen, and he doubted much of what they spewed from their mouths.

Valentino's high-pitched voice rang out from behind Alejandro and poisoned the air once more.

"The only things we should be trading with them are slaves from their own tribes!"

"I thought I told you to stay below deck, Valentino," Pizarro said to his son as he rolled his eyes.

"It stinks in there, father," Valentino replied. "It smells like somebody dumped their chamber pot in my quarters."

"Somebody probably did," Alejandro interjected with a grin.

Judging by how disliked Valentino was amongst the crew, the possibility of this was not far-fetched. Still, Alejandro had heard these ceaseless complaints from his brother many times before, so he figured it was likely to be more of the same.

"Are you saying you were the one to do it, you half-breed son of a savage whore?" Valentino jeered. "Is that what you're saying?"

Upon hearing Valentino's reference to his mother, whose grisly fate he had just discovered, a fire burned inside Alejandro as he gritted his teeth at his half-brother.

"What do you know about my mother?" he asked angrily.

"Nothing other than what I just heard father telling you," Valentino replied with a laugh. "You would be wise to remember what a master of stealth I am, dog. I'm sure I could even disappear if I really wanted to."

Alejandro glanced at his father in hopes that he would rebuke Valentino for eavesdropping on their conversation, but Pizarro continued to stare ahead blankly as he gave no mind to Valentino's insolence.

Alejandro scowled over the smirk on Valentino's face while his brother unsheathed his dagger and waved it through the air while pretending to jab at an invisible target.

"Not that you have skill with that blade," Alejandro commented, "but if you did, I'm not sure how that would relate to you being this 'master of stealth' as you call it."

Valentino chuckled and shrugged off Alejandro's insult, instead choosing to reply with an even greater one.

"I'm preparing myself to carve up savages like your dead mother," the young Spaniard replied.

Alejandro had heard enough this time as his anger boiled over. Before he could stop to consider the consequences of his actions, Alejandro lurched across the deck of the Santa Ana and shoved his brother against the side of the ship, causing Valentino's dagger to fall from his grip.

Pizarro, who had only just now chosen to intervene, perked up when he saw his favorite son pinned against the wooden railing with Alejandro's hands around his neck and half his body hanging over the edge of the ship.

"Enough, Alejandro!" Pizarro yelled. "Release your brother this instant!"

Every voice inside Alejandro's head told him to throw the coward overboard, to rid the world of this filth...this plague.

Alejandro glared into the eyes of his terrified brother as the dashing waves of the deep blue sea lurked below and crashed against the hull of the ship. Alejandro envisioned the joy he would feel at seeing Valentino's body sinking into the dark abyss of the water and never emerging again.

Suddenly, Alejandro felt a strong tug against his shoulder as Pizarro pulled him away from the clutches of Valentino's neck and tossed him to the deck. Valentino let out an exaggerated gasp for air as if his breathing had been restricted for several minutes.

"He tried to kill me, father! You saw it!"

Pizarro said nothing but paced back and forth in thought and bewilderment about what to do with Alejandro.

"Papa! Do something!" Valentino continued in an even higher pitch than his normal voice. "He tried to kill me!"

"Oh, will you shut your mouth for a moment so I can think, boy?!" Pizarro exclaimed.

Valentino widened his eyes as his body shook in fear after being dangled over the side of the ship. He looked at Alejandro with disdain as his brother rose to his feet and stared back at him.

Pizarro's confusion about how to handle the situation was suddenly remedied, though, when a shout came from the sentry in the crow's nest that rested high above them amongst the ship's sails.

"Landfall ahead! Landfall ahead!" the lookout shouted.

Pizarro breathed a sigh of relief as the faint outline of a large mass of land presented itself in the Spaniard's vision ahead of the armada.

"Thank the heavens! I must get off this boat!" he proclaimed while looking up towards the sky. "These children will be the death of me!"

Pizarro then turned to address his sons. "There will be time to deal with this later," he said while glancing primarily at Alejandro. "For now, we must prepare to disembark. Both of you go back to your quarters and gather your belongings."

An expression of derision still smeared across Alejandro's face, but he said nothing and obeyed his father's wishes. He turned and walked away, vanishing into the crowd of Spanish crewmen that scurried around the deck and prepared the ship to run ashore.

Valentino shuffled in his stance.

"B-but –,"

"Now! Valentino!" Pizarro shouted. "I will not repeat myself again."

Valentino pouted and stomped away, sulking and cursing under his breath as he went.

When his sons were safely out of his sight and mind, Pizarro turned his attention back to the vast expanse of coastline that stretched as far as the eye could see and became increasingly clearer as the distant fog parted.

The southern half of the Americas, a land named after the famed Italian explorer Amerigo Vespucci a mere thirty years earlier, now had another European voyager, Francisco Pizarro, ready to disembark on its shores once more.

Just as his uncle, Hernan Cortes, had "parleyed" with the Aztecs, Pizarro sought for his name to live on throughout the ages as the man to tame yet another foreign realm.

The empire of the Incas stood ripe and ready for conquest.

Volume I, Part III
Fangs of the Jungle

An obsidian-tipped arrow soared through the air and found its target, piercing the flesh of a stag and felling it to the ground before the animal could realize it was being hunted. Chimalli, clutching his bow tightly in his steady hand, rose from a crouched position behind the dense brush before pacing slowly towards his kill. The boy reached the dying buck and knelt beside him as his prey writhed in pain.

Chimalli's face remained stoic as he took no pride in watching the stag suffer. The Aztec removed his dagger that rested inside its sheath on his waistband and placed it against the surface of the deer's skin. He thrust the blade into the animal's heart in one clean motion, relieving its misery and offering its soul to Mixcoatl, the Aztec god of the hunt. Mixcoatl accepted Chimalli's kill as the life force of the buck left its body. All that remained was its earthly form, which would now serve a new purpose as sustenance for the host of Aztecs that traveled through thick layers of Mayan jungles in the Yucatan.

Chimalli grabbed the animal's legs and dragged it behind him as the sun made its descent below the tree line, signaling the coming of night. The young boy crossed a stream with his prey and worked his way into a small clearing until he laid his weary eyes on a fire that lightly crackled in the wind and illuminated the evening air.

In front of the flames sat the last remaining parts of his life that kept him breathing. Kelia, the young Aztec girl who had escaped the sack of Tenochtitlan with him six months prior, rested on a log as she bobbed little Ohtli up and down on her knee, causing the baby to smile.

Chimalli witnessed the joy on his nephew's face and emitted a slight grin of his own, which had become increasingly rare these days. The pleasantries of his former life had passed and most of what remained was darkness. Still, he found small bits of comfort in the smiling faces of his Aztec companions.

"I'm glad to see him laughing," Chimalli remarked to Kelia in Nahuatl as he stepped into the clearing and pulled the large deer behind him.

Kelia and Ohtli both perked up upon hearing Chimalli's calming voice. The baby grinned even harder and waved his hands up and down in approval after seeing his uncle, who had become like a father to the child.

"He deserves some happiness after all he's been through," Kelia said as she held Ohtli tight against her face and kissed his cheek.

Chimalli released the dead buck close to the campfire and let out a sigh of relief. Kelia looked on in admiration as Chimalli prepared his knife to skin yet another deer.

"You're becoming quite good at that," Kelia commented with a smile. "It appears that Mixcoatl will make a hunter out of you yet."

Chimalli emitted a slight chuckle. "And you're becoming quite good at that," he replied, referencing her nurturing methods with Ohtli.

Kelia's eyes became teary at hearing Chimalli's compliment.

"I'm just doing what my mother used to do with me," she said as memories of her mother's death at the hands of the Spanish flowed back into her young mind.

Chimalli remained silent for a moment as he allowed Kelia to collect her thoughts. He knew the last memory she had of her mother was the poor woman being raped and murdered in the next room. If not for the actions of Chimalli and Acalan, Kelia would have surely shared her mother's fate.

"You will be a great mother one day, and you will make your own mother very proud," Chimalli finally responded as he broke the silence of the cool evening air. "I know my sister would be honored to have you watching over her son."

"Thank you, ikniutli," Kelia replied as another tear streamed down her face and she stared into Chimalli's eyes.

Kelia's steady glance caused Chimalli to blush from ear to ear, just as he normally did when Kelia looked at him in that manner.

"I want to be more than just a caregiver, though," Kelia continued. "I want to fight for what I love...not just have the men do the fighting for me as I cower in a corner and wait to live or die."

"I know," Chimalli said. "I don't believe that is your fate. You'll probably become a better warrior than me someday."

He only half-jested as he had witnessed Kelia's toughness and determination over the past six months since they had been on the run through the Mayan jungles. She had demonstrated all the characteristics of a true Aztec...courage, resourcefulness, and selflessness, among others.

"Will you teach me?" Kelia asked.

"To be a warrior?"

"Yes."

"I think there are far better trainers that you could learn from."

Kelia looked around sarcastically as she scanned the jungle for someone to teach her.

"I see no one here but us," Kelia said as she shrugged her shoulders and continued to hold the playful Ohtli in her arms. "It's rather hard to get training from someone who isn't here."

Chimalli found it difficult to argue with Kelia's logic as the young boy inserted his knife into the deer that rested at his feet.

"I still struggle to pull the bow string back," Chimalli admitted as he tore the skin from the animal's body. "Rodrigo and Ohtli...my brother, Ohtli...used to make it look so simple."

"Well, they were grown men, Chimalli," Kelia responded. "I think you're doing great for a boy of only thirteen years."

Chimalli jokingly scowled at Kelia before forming a slight grin. "I'm a man, not a boy. And I'm older than you! You're only twelve!"

"Of course, what was I thinking, sir?" she teased with a smile of her own. "I guess your big manly muscles clouded my judgment!"

Chimalli laughed and held his mouth open in awe at Kelia's attempts to mock him.

"Oh, you're going to pay for that one!" he shouted as he darted towards Kelia and Ohtli and playfully wrestled them to the ground.

Kelia screamed in jest as she and Chimalli rolled in the dirt together.

"You're going to get that deer blood all over us, Chimalli!"

Their light-hearted giggles and cries caused Ohtli to belt out in laughter as the baby climbed over the top of them to join in the pile.

The trio of Aztecs wrestled and laughed for a few more minutes, and when their scrum finally ceased, Chimalli and Kelia looked upon each other and the baby with love in their hearts. These were the first moments since leaving Tenochtitlan that they had been able to enjoy life the way children were supposed to.

"I have an idea!" Chimalli shouted as the others listened intently. None of them were ready for the fun to be over just yet. "Let's put Ohtli in the middle of us, and whoever he walks to first...wins the game!"

"Oh, you're on! That child loves his Aunt Kelia! There's no way I would lose that!"

Ohtli moved his head back and forth between the two Aztecs with an anxious and excited look on his face as both of them jokingly bickered with each other.

"He has my blood, silly girl!" Chimalli replied. "You underestimate the bond we share together!"

Kelia hopped up as Ohtli continued to chuckle and smile. Chimalli picked up the baby, who had only been walking for a couple months, and placed him upright on his feet. Chimalli and Kelia both marched a few paces in opposite directions from Ohtli, and the competition commenced.

Ohtli once more looked back and forth at the only two people left in the world that he trusted as they called his name and attempted to coerce him into walking to them.

"Come on, Ohtli, come on!" Kelia shouted softly. Ohtli heard the tone of her gentle voice and started to make his way towards the young girl. "That's it! Come on, conetl!"

Chimalli emitted his own plea to the child, though, and Ohtli stopped in his tracks and questioned his decision upon hearing his uncle's voice.

"Over here, Ohtli, over here! Come to your Uncle Chimalli!"

The baby started pacing towards Chimalli but stopped once again when more cries rang out from Kelia. Still laughing and having one of the best times of his young life, Ohtli planted his feet in the ground right in the middle between Chimalli and Kelia before plopping his bottom in the dirt.

Both Chimalli and Kelia let out an audible "aww" as the sweet child refused to choose between the two Aztecs, who were both part of his family in the infant's mind.

"Well, then it's settled," Chimalli proclaimed as they both walked over and hugged Ohtli. "He loves us both equally."

"Just as *I* love *you* both equally," Kelia replied, changing the mood from silly to sweet and causing Chimalli's cheeks to blush once more. "You two are my family now...the only family I have left."

Chimalli could hardly contain the love in his heart that he had felt for Kelia since the day he loaded her into the boat and helped her escape from Tenochtitlan. Yes, Chimalli's thirteen year old mind thought about her in romantic ways at times, but it was more than just that. His love was pure and genuine, and he cherished every breath that Kelia took. She was his best friend, and he was hers.

"I love you, Kelia, and you, Ohtli," he said as he glanced at his family. "I will protect you both until I join the rest of our people in the next life."

Chimalli and Kelia embraced as their cheeks rubbed against one another. The two Aztecs both lingered in each other's arms for several seconds, not only for the inner comfort it provided from being wrapped around a loved one, but also to shield each other from the cold night air that settled around them now that winter had fallen upon the land.

Soon after, Chimalli finished skinning the deer that he had felled with his bow, and Kelia prepared its meat for supper.

That night, the three young Aztecs laughed and danced and sang merrily amongst each other. For a short period of time, they forgot about how their life was torn from them by the foreign invaders. They forgot about how their families were murdered by Spanish conquistadors and Tlaxcalan warriors. For those few remaining hours on that cool winter evening in January of 1522, they were children once more.

As Chimalli, Kelia, and Ohtli laid down for the night and huddled close to one another, they were blissfully unaware that the harsh reality of their broken world would soon return to haunt them.

Little Ohtli, the half-Spanish and half-Aztec child of both worlds who was midway between the ages of one and two, curled up to Chimalli and Kelia as the three of them formed the most genuine of smiles on their faces before drifting off to sleep.

■■■■■■■■■

A distant shout echoed through Chimalli's ears as it jolted his mind back to consciousness. He sat up abruptly as Kelia and Ohtli remained asleep on the ground beside him. The sun had not yet made its full ascent, but there was just enough light emitting from it so that Chimalli could see his surroundings.

Voices rang out once again through the dewy morning air of the dense jungle. Chimalli quickly rose to his feet and extinguished the remaining embers of the fire that generated a small cloud of smoke around it.

As Kelia and Ohtli continued to rest peacefully, it became clear that the voices resonated from several men, and the Spanish language they spoke sent chills running down Chimalli's spine. Chimalli bent down to wake the others, but he stopped himself when he realized that Ohtli's cries might alert the Spaniards if the baby was forced to wake before he was ready to do so.

Chimalli instead allowed Kelia and Ohtli to keep resting, hoping the men would pass by and not notice the smoke from the fire he had just doused. The young Aztec wrapped his bow string around his neck and across his chest to secure it to his back. He grasped his family's broken spear in his hand as his nerves caused a bead of sweat to stream down the side of his face.

Chimalli slowly crept his way out of the small clearing and through the thick green brush of the jungle. He used his arm and his spear to shield himself from the sticks and thorns as he moved towards the sound of the Spanish voices, hoping to get a better view of the invaders.

When the Spanish torches came into the young boy's vision and illuminated their full plated metal armor, he stopped and slowed his breathing as to not let the conquistadors see his foggy breath that generated from the cold air.

Chimalli counted ten Spaniards in total. They made their way through a small path in the jungle that was used by Mayans and other tribes to navigate the terrain with ease. The conquistadors held their torches high in the air and bantered loudly amongst each other, no doubt disturbing the peace of the wildlife that dwelled within the jungle.

As the men got further from Chimalli's position and began to disappear from his view, the Aztec breathed a heavy sigh of relief. Unfortunately for Chimalli, this relief turned to panic as he heard a loud and sudden shriek ring through the morning air from the direction of their camp. The outburst was followed by the cries of a baby, and Chimalli sprang into action to reach Kelia and Ohtli. He bolted through the jungle with haste, losing sight of the Spanish soldiers and praying to Quetzalcoatl that they didn't hear the screams.

As Ohtli's cries still rang out, Chimalli burst through the last remaining thicket of sticks and leaves to reach the clearing of the camp, but what he saw when he planted his feet on open ground caused him to stop dead in his tracks while fear engulfed his body.

Across the clearing and merely a few paces from where Kelia trembled with terror as she held Ohtli tight in her arms, a full-grown jaguar rummaged through the camp and dug its nose into the dead carcass of the deer that Chimalli had slain the night before. The beast did not seem to be hostile towards Kelia and Ohtli, but when he heard Chimalli enter through the brush, the large animal perked up and snarled his teeth in defense. Chimalli and Kelia both froze their bodies in hopes that the jaguar would leave them alone, but Ohtli's cries continued to echo through the air as he was too young to contain his fear.

Kelia peered at Chimalli with a look of despair as the jaguar abandoned his defensive posture and continued tearing through the remaining flesh of the buck. A whole minute passed as the Aztecs remained in their positions and tried not to move and startle the beast.

The jaguar finally grew tired of picking at pieces of the deer and lifted his nose in the air, which was covered in blood from the carcass. This presented a terrifying sight to the Aztec children as the jaguar lightly pranced his paws on the cold ground and made his way to Kelia and Ohtli. The beast's bloody face struck an even greater fear in Ohtli's little heart, and the baby belted out even louder, this time tugging at Kelia's garments in a desperate attempt for protection.

Chimalli saw the opportunity to unsheathe his bow as he slowly removed it from around his neck. The young boy readied an arrow against the bow string and pulled it back with all his might, holding his draw and waiting for the jaguar's next move.

As the large animal came right over the top of Kelia and Ohtli and looked down upon the terrified Aztecs, Chimalli prepared his hand to release the string and send the arrow straight through the jaguar's heart.

Chimalli stopped himself at the last moment though when his eyes witnessed a true miracle. The hulking cat, which could have probably ripped an adult man's body to pieces in mere seconds, lowered his bloody nose down to Ohtli's head and began licking his cheek.

Ohtli suddenly stopped crying and sat still against Kelia's chest. Kelia herself, with eyes as wide as Lake Texcoco, remained frozen in shock as the beast continued licking the tears from Ohtli's beleaguered face.

Chimalli withdrew the tension from his bow string and lowered his aim, still gazing in disbelief upon the jaguar's attempts to comfort the crying child. It appeared the animal knew that these people were natives of the land and friends of the creatures living on it.

Ohtli's cries turned into laughter as the coarse tongue of the great beast tickled his soft skin. Kelia and Chimalli, while still alert and weary of the jaguar's intentions, both formed smiles on their faces upon hearing Ohtli giggling and cackling. The baby turned to face the jaguar and wrapped his tiny arms around the cat's head, stroking his fur and playing with his ears.

This sweet moment between the baby and what seemed to be his new pet jaguar proved to come at a cost, though, as the screams Ohtli had emitted drew the ire of the most undesirable creatures that existed in the jungle.

Through the thick leaves behind him, Chimalli heard a trampling of footsteps and turned to face them, but before he could lift his spear to defend himself, a Spanish conquistador leapt through the brush and knocked the Aztec boy to the cold earth.

The impact of his head hitting the hard ground dazed Chimalli and caused him to wince in pain. As he lifted his head and regained his composure, he saw several other Spanish soldiers join the one that hit him. It was undoubtedly the same patrol that Chimalli had seen marching through the jungle earlier.

A few of the conquistadors that stormed into the clearing chuckled amongst themselves when they saw Chimalli's body crash against the ground, but their laughter soon turned to panic when they saw the large, spotted cat prowling around the campsite.

The jaguar ceased his licking of Ohtli's face and lifted his bloody nose to face the rowdy intruders. The beast sensed a difference in these humans as opposed to the Aztecs, emitting a menacing growl and turning to face the Spaniards with an intimidating gaze.

"Ready your muskets!" the startled Spanish commander ordered to his men. The few conquistadors that possessed rifles removed them from their backs and prepared to fire. The jaguar inched closer to the Spaniards in a low, prowling motion as he appeared eager to pounce on the soldiers and feast upon their flesh.

"Aim!" the commander yelled as the musketeers raised their weapons.

Chimalli, Kelia, and Ohtli looked on with horror, but they were powerless to stop the events to come.

As the jaguar leapt out of his stance and soared towards his targets, the Spanish leader gave one final command to his men, but it was the last command he would ever give on this earth.

"Fi–", his word tailed off as he never finished the order to fire, for out of the jungle and all around the Spanish soldiers, a whole pack of jaguars surged into the clearing with ferocity. The Spanish leader's neck was ripped open in an instant as even the faintest scream proved impossible for him to produce. The other soldiers had no time to squeeze the triggers of their muskets as they too were set upon with relentless force.

The pack of jaguars, likely to be the family of the one who cleaned the tears from Ohtli's face just moments earlier, tore through the screaming Spanish soldiers with ruthless intensity. As the Spanish cries for help echoed through the once-peaceful morning air, all the Aztecs could do was stare in shock at the slaughter.

While the beasts still savored their kills, Chimalli rose from the ground and raced over to check on Kelia and Ohtli, who welcomed Chimalli with long hugs and deep sighs at what they had just witnessed.

"We must go, now," Chimalli urged to the group as he was still unsure of how the jaguars would treat them, especially after the wild cats had already torn through the conquistadors with ease.

Rising to their feet to scurry away, the Aztecs stopped as the sound of tearing flesh ceased. They turned to see the entire pack of jaguars, now all possessing bloody snouts and cautious looks on their faces, staring at the Aztec trio in unison.

Chimalli motioned for Kelia to remain still as the Aztecs held their breath in anxious anticipation of the jaguars' next move. The pack continued to look at them while the jaguar that Ohtli had grown fond of stepped forward and marched towards them. When the large animal reached their position, Ohtli let out another sweet chuckle and reached his hands out to pet his new friend.

The jaguar looked back at his family and cocked his head sideways, presumably motioning for them to disperse and leave this group of humans alone. The rest of the pack obeyed his wishes and turned away, disappearing into the thick jungle and leaving what remained of the Spanish corpses to rot in the rising sun.

The jaguar sniffed and licked Ohtli's outstretched fingertips, much to the delight and relief of the Aztecs. The Spanish blood from his tongue stained the baby's fingers, but Ohtli hardly cared. The child continued to giggle at the touch of the large cat.

As Chimalli and Kelia both looked at each other in amazement, the miracle of them still being alive set into their minds. Not only had they avoided certain death at the hands of the Spaniards and the teeth of the jaguars, but they had also picked up an unlikely new pet along the way.

Alongside their feline companion, the Aztec children gathered their belongings and set out in the direction of the Inca Empire. Although they still had a great distance to travel, Acalan's words about this vast, foreign empire still resonated in Chimalli's mind, and he was willing to give his life, if it came to it, to get his family to the safety of the Inca lands.

Codex Volume II

New World, Old Habits

Volume II, Part I
End of an Endless War

A severed head on a jagged pike.

Mangled remnants of the dead hanging from a nearby tree limb.

An endless sea of corpses. Many of the bodies disemboweled from deep cuts formed in the shape of an X across the torso, no doubt meant as an ominous warning to any would-be dissenters.

Such was the horror of war in the lands of the Inca.

Such was the reality of life for those who would not suffer the rule of the false emperor, Huascar.

The road from Quito to Cuzco was lined with death.

"I knew these men," Chasca, daughter of the true emperor, Atahualpa, remarked in the Quechua language with a stoic and unmoved tone. The young warrior's beauty was matched only by her skill with a blade, which gained her the respect of the most hardened warriors in the whole of the empire. Chasca's reputation amongst Atahualpa's followers was legendary, despite her youth of only twenty-four years. Many within the empire scarcely believed she existed at all due to the embellished stories of her countless victories over Huascar the Cruel, usurper of the Inca throne.

Chasca stood at her father's side at the head of the large war party consisting of five thousand Inca warriors, all fiercely loyal to Atahualpa. Upon seeing the field of bodies that littered the mountainous pathway on the road to Cuzco, the largest city in the empire and seat of Huascar's power, Atahualpa stopped and raised his fist into the air, signaling to his commanders to halt their regiments.

"As did I," the tall and broad Atahualpa replied to his daughter in a deep, distinguishable tone. "These were the men of Cuzco that rose up against Huascar. This is only a taste of what my brother can unleash."

Chasca shuffled anxiously as she continued to glance at the dismembered corpses of her father's followers dangling from the trees. "My uncle rules through fear, but he is no leader. I have broken his battle lines time and again, and I know you have too, father. The man possesses cruelty but lacks anything resembling strategy."

"We will use that to our advantage today," Atahualpa remarked quietly as he leaned in closer to Chasca's ear. "Is your man reliable? Or am I marching these warriors to their deaths?"

Chasca thought hard about her father's question. He was right to be cautious. The fate of the empire rested on her answer. She turned her head slightly and responded with "Huascar's reign of terror ends today."

This answer apparently satisfied her father. Atahualpa pondered her response for a moment before nodding his head and giving the order to his generals to continue their march. The war party made their way through the ominous abyss of the forest as the evening sun began its descent behind the towering Andes mountains, shrouding the land in semi-darkness.

Chasca, adorned with quilted, brightly colored armor made from animal hides, grasped the hilt of her copper-headed battle axe that had been nicknamed Huascar's Bane by her men. The weapon had personally claimed the lives of many warriors loyal to Huascar, and Chasca's skills as a fighter now trumped even the bravest of Inca warriors.

Atahualpa, a man of only forty-two years and still in capable fighting shape, marched beside Chasca with a much more relaxed demeanor than his daughter. "Remove your hand from your weapon, child," he commanded in a low tone. "They must believe we know nothing about the ambush."

"Yes, father," Chasca obeyed, respecting his authority without question. He had taught her everything she knew about warfare and strategy, which were rare traits for an Inca woman to possess, especially one of royal lineage.

"Only draw your weapon once Huascar springs his trap," Atahualpa ordered to her once more.

Chasca nodded in acknowledgment of her father. "They will attack when you and I pass the large gods' tree on the left-hand side of the road. Huascar will approach from the west, and Rumi will feign his attack from the east and join us against Huascar."

"Do you trust Rumi to honor his word?" Atahualpa questioned while still maintaining his low tone of voice. "If he does not, we will all perish on this day and Huascar will have his slaughter...and my throne."

Chasca glanced at the small piece of parchment that she had received from one of Rumi's messengers just hours before that stated his intentions along with Huascar's plans to ambush the approaching column.

"Rumi is finished with Huascar's lies, as is most of the empire," she replied. "I know he's fought against us in the past, but I trust him. He's a man of honor and he always has been. He wishes to follow you now, father, just as he followed *your* father for many years."

"Yes, he did. I was devastated when he took up arms against me, but perhaps he will redeem himself today. I believe he's also in love with you, so that doesn't hurt our cause."

Chasca rolled her eyes as her father grinned and chuckled softly.

The war party continued its march through the mountain pass as the high peaks of the Andes ascended above them, stretching to the clouds and connecting the mortal realm with the godly one, or so the stories told. The warriors of Atahualpa would need the gods on their side if they had any chance of besting Huascar and removing his claim to the Inca throne.

As Chasca and Atahualpa rounded a bend in the pathway, their vision cleared to reveal a large gods' tree resting on the left side of the road. Its branches, like many they had passed already, hung several mangled corpses of Cuzco rebels loyal to Atahualpa.

The emperor and his daughter glanced at each other in acknowledgment of the sacred tree, and Atahualpa gestured a subtle nod to his commanders to prepare the men for combat.

Chasca maintained her composure and continued pacing forward as the gods' tree loomed larger with each step. Her steady hand rested just outside the reach of her axe's hilt, and the sweltering heat induced a bead of sweat that trickled down her temple. She veered into the surrounding woods to scan the trees for any signs of Huascar and Rumi's ambushing warriors, but the height of the Andes mountains blocked out almost all assistance that the sun's rays could have provided.

If the enemy was truly lying in wait, there was no trace of them. No snapping of twigs. No rustling of leaves. The footsteps of Atahualpa's men resonated at their backs, but Chasca could barely hear them. She focused on the trees, and the trees focused on her with an ominous silence. It felt as though the forest had sensed death approaching, and the gods atop the peaks of the Andes remained calm in the face of an impending slaughter. The only question now was which side the gods would choose to join them on that fateful morning...Huascar's or Atahualpa's? The arena was set and the warriors of the greatest empire to ever exist in this land would now decide its fate. The civil war between two brothers, the conflict that had lasted for five long years after the death of their father, would be settled before the sun could make its ascent back across the mortal plane.

Chasca felt a rush of intense anxiety course through her veins as she and her father passed the beauty and horror of the large, corpse-littered gods' tree. This was the moment that Rumi said the trap would be sprung, but silence still engulfed the air. Chasca held her breath and glanced at her father, who also appeared anxious and confused at the continued stillness of the dark morning.

Just as the emperor opened his mouth to question Chasca's information, a deafening barrage of Inca war cries echoed through the air around the mountain pass. The shouts of the enemy warriors resonated even louder than expected, and Atahualpa prepared his men for combat.

"Warriors! Battle formations!" the emperor ordered.

While his men had been marching as though they were unaware of the ambush, they formed up tightly and presented themselves with great composure and discipline.

"We must defend the western side of the pathway!" Chasca ordered with haste. "Battle lines focus to the west!"

The men of Atahualpa turned in unison to lock their shields together as one formidable unit, but they left their backs exposed to the east upon Chasca's orders. Rumi was to feign his attack from the east, and the fate of Atahualpa's men rested on Rumi keeping his word to betray Huascar.

The battle cries of Huascar's men on the west side of the path grew louder as his men scrambled through the darkness of the forest and into eyesight. Rumi's men on the other side also screamed and chanted as if they meant to engage Atahualpa and Chasca.

"If Rumi attacks us, we will all be slaughtered!" Atahualpa shouted to Chasca as their flanks were completely exposed to Rumi's mercy.

"He will join us, father! You will see! He will not forsake his word to me!"

"I hope you're right, my child! If he doesn't fight with us, we will surely feast with our ancestors tonight!"

Huascar's archers unleashed a barrage upon the waiting warriors of Atahualpa, felling many to the ground. Huascar's infantry drew within a few paces of the defenders, and the decisive battle of the Inca Civil War commenced at the feet of the gods on the mountain pass near Cuzco.

The warriors of Huascar slammed into Atahualpa's formations with a thunderous clash and pushed them backwards with their charge. Chasca and Atahualpa, both positioned to lead from the front of the column, repelled Huascar's charge and struck back with their copper and obsidian weapons.

"Hold the line, men! Hold the line!" Chasca shouted as she caught a glimpse of her treacherous uncle Huascar, who commanded from just beyond the front line. The false emperor, dressed in lavish imperial battle robes, cursed wildly at his men to persist with the attack as he shoved them aimlessly into the fray.

"Rumi! Slaughter them!" Huascar shouted with bloodlust as his second-in-command presented himself and his men behind Atahualpa's line.

Rumi's men charged down the hill towards Atahualpa's warriors, and Huascar emitted an ominous grin at the impending defeat of his brother. All Rumi had to do was thrust his fighters into Atahualpa's back line and the war would be over. Huascar would prevail, and he would undoubtedly place Atahualpa's head on a pike outside the walls of Cuzco.

Huascar the Cruel's grin turned to confusion, though, when Rumi ordered his men to pull back at the last moment before the impact. Rumi separated his warriors into two columns and proceeded to flank around the sides of Atahualpa's men.

"Rumi! What are you doing? Kill them now!" Huascar shouted in a desperate attempt to get his commander back in line. This was not meant to be, though, and Huascar quickly realized the extent of Rumi's treachery. Rumi and his subordinates raced their men around Huascar's lines and prepared to strike them in the rear.

Chasca and Atahualpa, along with the rest of their men who were still fighting valiantly on the front line, witnessed Rumi's men positioning themselves to assist in the destruction of Huascar's army.

"The gods are with us, men!" Atahualpa shouted with a commanding fervor in his voice. Push forward and break their spirits!"

This emboldened the battered lines of Atahualpa's warriors, who roared a glorious battle cry as they powered their way into Huascar's men. At the same time, Rumi charged his warriors into Huascar's flank and choked out any chance the usurper had of escaping.

As Chasca slashed her axe across the face of a Huascarian warrior and sprayed his blood across her armor, she pulled back and observed the battlefield. Time seemed to slow and her senses became heightened at the sight of such a brutal slaughter of her foes. As misguided as their actions had been by the false claims of her uncle, they were still Incas. Still children of Tawantinsuyu, the land of the four quarters. The gods wept for their sacrifice.

The warriors of Huascar fell one by one as his men became encircled on all sides. The false emperor felt the noose tightening around his neck, and so did his men. While Huascar himself remained defiant even after the battle was all but decided, his remaining warriors recognized defeat and refused to die for a tyrant's greed. They laid down their weapons and surrendered to the will of Atahualpa.

"Pick up your blades, you cowards!" Huascar ordered to his men. "Fight for me! Fight for my throne!" The reality of the situation finally sunk into Huascar's heart when he saw his men abandon all obedience to him.

"So this is what it's come to, then?!" Huascar shouted with a fake smile plastered on his face. He spoke to every soul who was close enough to hear as the bloodied faces of Atahualpa and Chasca came into his view. "This is what it means to be Inca, now?! You would place an incompetent usurper on the throne rather than the one true emperor, ordained by the gods?!"

All warriors from both sides of the conflict remained still and silent as Huascar continued to spout curses and obscenities at the onlookers. Atahualpa grew tired of his brother's incessant whining and stepped forward to interrupt his squabbling.

"Enough, Huascar! It's over! Let this be the end of this senseless war! No more Incas need to die because of our feud! Father chose me to be emperor! Not you! You dishonor his memory every time you lead men into combat against me! You spit on his grave every time you claim yourself to be the true successor to our father's throne!"

Huascar veered his eyes away and chuckled softly upon hearing the words of his younger brother. "Father was a fool, Atahualpa. I am the elder! It is my divine right to rule! Who are we to challenge the will of the gods?!"

Rumi, whose garbs were stained with the blood of his fellow Incas, stepped through the dense crowd of warriors that had encircled the quarreling brothers. His face, chest, and arms were covered in elaborate tattoos honoring the Inca gods. "The people have suffered enough under your tyranny, Huascar," declared the tall, imposing Inca commander who had just betrayed his emperor. "*I* have suffered enough. Your right to rule ends today."

Huascar scowled at his former second-in-command who had just betrayed him. "Uku Pacha awaits traitors and cowards like you, Rumi. An eternity in the house of the devil is still not punishment enough for what you have unleashed on this day. You have cursed us all. And for what? To bed my brother's whore of a daughter?"

Rumi flew into a rage upon hearing Huascar's insults towards Chasca. He lashed out and struck the embattled emperor in the face, sending him crashing into the muddy earth. Rumi mounted Huascar and continued to inflict a flurry of punches upon him. "You will not speak about her! Ever again!"

There were none who intervened in the beating. At least not for several seconds. There was no love or respect for the eldest son of the former emperor, Huayna Capac. The warriors who followed Huascar had done so out of fear or respect for traditional succession, but certainly not love.

Chasca finally stepped in and calmed Rumi's rage. "Stop, Rumi, stop," she said as she pulled him away and placed her hand on his own. Upon feeling the contact of Chasca's smooth skin, Rumi's demeanor lightened and he returned to his senses. The two Incas looked into each other's eyes while Huascar formed his bloodied, battered face into a smile.

"Let's have his head and be done with it, father," Chasca pleaded to Atahualpa. A collective acknowledgment from the surrounding warriors, even by some who had fought for Huascar, indicated they were not opposed to this.

Atahualpa pondered his daughter's words, but now that he saw his brother, the son of a great emperor, lying beaten and helpless on the ground, a sense of mercy entered his heart. Atahualpa approached Huascar and offered his hand out to help him to his feet. Huascar saw the outstretched palm of his brother and scoffed at it. With a heavy wince of pain, he lifted himself off the ground on his own volition.

Atahualpa ignored this slight and spoke to Huascar in a calm, passive manner. "We are brothers," he said with sadness in his voice. "We shame our father. We shame this land. Let us put all this behind us, now. Swear fealty to me and you shall receive a place on the Council of the Realm."

Huascar, along with Chasca, Rumi, and all the other warriors that had gathered on the mountain pass, were surprised at Atahualpa's lenience. Huascar took a deep breath and thought about his answer for what felt like an eternity.

"My tongue will never swear fealty to a usurper," Huascar finally replied with a smirk, breaking the prolonged silence. "Kill me and be cursed by the gods."

Atahualpa frowned in disappointment at his brother's response.

"I will not kill you, Huascar. But if your tongue will not swear allegiance to me, then I shall rip it from your mouth."

Huascar's eyes widened as Atahualpa gave the order to one of his subordinates to remove the former emperor's tongue. The warrior brandished his obsidian blade and stepped forward as several other warriors held down the wriggling and defiant Huascar. The blade flowed swiftly through his tongue as he let out an agonizing cry of pain.

With the loss of Huascar's tongue and ability to speak also came the loss of his claim to the throne. Atahualpa marched away from his screaming brother as the new ruler of Tawantinsuyu, the land of the Incas. He was the first unchallenged emperor of the realm in over five years.

The Inca Civil War was over.

The empire was made whole again.

As tales of Atahualpa and Chasca's conquest spread through the land, a storm began to rise on the shores just north of the Inca borders. The same storm that swept away the heart of the Aztec Empire was now heading south while the exhausted Inca warriors finally settled down from the brutal five-year war that had just concluded.

Whether by the will of God or the gods, a storm was coming.

Volume II, Part II
A Port in the Storm

"Chimalli, listen," Kelia pleaded as she placed her hand on the young Aztec's shoulder to stop his movement through the brush. Chimalli halted his feet with an audible squish into the muddy surface of the ground and held his breath. The sound of voices echoed in the distance.

Ohtli faced outward in Chimalli's harness that attached to his chest, and the baby stopped babbling and playing with his fingers just long enough to glance up and see why Chimalli and Kelia had stopped moving.

"Khuno...K-Khuno," the baby continued to babble after a moment's pause, reaching for the jaguar that picked at the bushes beside them. The large cat, which Ohtli named Khuno, had marched beside the trio of Aztecs since he and the other jaguars saved them from the Spaniards in the forest a few weeks prior. Khuno also slowed his pace before turning to wait for his human counterparts to make a move.

"Quiet, child," Chimalli pleaded with his nephew as he cupped his hand around the baby's mouth.

Chimalli inched his way cautiously through the thick brush that surrounded them, allowing the voices to come clearly into focus. As the Aztecs approached the clearing ahead, a small native village emerged into their view on the side of a riverbank.

"At least they're not Spaniards," Kelia commented with a sigh of relief. The sight of water and the sound of native tongues instilled hope inside the young Aztec girl, a hope that constantly waned and hung by a thread. Although the inhabitants of the village were clearly native to the land, their language was still much different from Nahuatl and indecipherable to the Aztecs.

"Are they Maya?" Kelia asked Chimalli in a muted tone.

"I think so, but it's hard to tell. I don't know any of the Maya languages."

"We should ask them for help."

"Are you crazy, girl?" Chimalli snapped. "What if they're friends with the Spanish? What if they turn us in to the next patrol that comes along? The number of white men in this land grows more and more by the day."

"No, I'm not crazy, Chimalli, and I don't appreciate you calling me that," Kelia replied with a scowl.

The two young Aztecs stared at each other briefly, both with annoyed expressions, before Chimalli broke his demeanor. "I'm sorry," he conceded with a lighter disposition this time. "It's still too risky, though."

"Look at us, Chimalli. It's been months since Ohtli has eaten the proper food of a one-year-old child. You give us most of the food that we're fortunate enough to find and barely keep any for yourself. We're tired, hungry, and we've been on the run for too long."

Chimalli looked away in contemplation, knowing that Kelia's words were true. It had been many long months since they escaped the sack of Tenochtitlan. It would be an even longer journey to reach the safety of the Incas. They would not survive unless they found some help, even if that meant trusting complete strangers.

After another inaudible babble from Ohtli, followed by a grunt/sniffle from Khuno, Chimalli nodded his head in agreement with Kelia.

"Alright, I'll go find someone to speak with in the village. You stay here."

"No, Chimalli." Kelia responded with conviction. "We do this together. The fate of one of us is the fate of all of us. If something happened to you, we wouldn't survive out here anyways."

Once more, Chimalli reluctantly agreed with Kelia, this time with a slight grin. He plucked an arrow from his quiver and prepared it along the thin strings of his bow, which was now old and unreliable from months of use and exposure to the elements.

The battered crew of young Aztecs trotted their way into the clearing and came upon the outskirts of the village. Though they moved with caution, there were few places to hide, seeing as though there was no cover between the tree line and the closest hut. Chimalli abandoned his initial attempts to walk slowly and low to the ground since they were exposed in the bright light of the midday sun.

Suddenly, a woman carrying a basket emerged from the other side of the nearby hut and locked eyes with Chimalli before gazing upon the weapon in his hand. She stopped abruptly at first, but quickly shifted her caution to confusion when she realized they were just children. The Aztecs, along with their ferociously friendly pet, also stopped and looked at the woman, unsure of how things would play out from here.

"Hello," the woman said amicably in an unidentifiable language. "Are you lost, children?"

The Aztecs couldn't understand the woman's words, but Chimalli attempted to bridge the language barrier between them. "Please," he pleaded, "we need food and water and shelter from the rain. Can you help us?"

The woman's confusion only grew as it was evident she didn't speak Nahuatl.

"Mexica," Kelia added slowly and pointed at herself and Chimalli. "We are Mexica...Aztec."

This sparked the woman's comprehension, and her eyes widened in apparent shock. She placed the basket of fish she was carrying on the ground.

"Aztec? Oh my," she pondered with hesitation as she ushered them along with her. "Come with me, children. Quickly."

The woman's hand gestures and heightened sense of urgency signaled to the Aztecs her desire for them to follow, and with no other choice, follow her they did.

"Leave your cat here, though," the woman said as she looked upon Khuno nervously and motioned to the Aztecs that Khuno couldn't join them. "He will frighten the others."

Chimalli reluctantly signaled to Khuno to stay put and had to do so a few different times before the beast finally understood Chimalli's command. Khuno whimpered and plopped his large frame into the mud outside the village where he waited anxiously for the children's return.

Kelia and Chimalli, who still had Ohtli fastened into his makeshift harness, marched into the interior of the village, and the young children drew the gazes of several more townspeople, most of whom stopped and stared at the new arrivals. Two children and a baby traveling alone was enough to raise a few suspicious eyebrows. There didn't seem to be any warriors amongst the villagers, though. Only fishermen, farmers, and craftsmen walked the town's muddy pathways.

"Come inside," the woman said with haste as she led the children into a small, oval shaped hut with mud walls and a steep, grassy roof.

Upon entering, the fresh aroma of copal incense filled the children's nostrils and gave them a sense of calm that they hadn't felt in quite some time. Seated at the table across the single-room hut was a man of modest height and a burly frame. He wore the tattered robes of a fishermen, and the incense surely clouded the smell of fish guts that plastered across his tunic.

The man spoke out in his native language with a curious and alarmed manner when he saw his wife (presumably) leading three strange children into his house. The two villagers bantered back and forth for a moment before Kelia caught the sound of the word "Aztec" emit from the woman's mouth.

Upon hearing this word, the man stopped his pestering and turned anxiously to face the children.

"You children are Aztec?" the man questioned in the Nahuatl tongue, much to the surprise of the children. They hadn't heard a Nahuatl word come out of someone else's mouth since Acalan had commanded them to leave without him...just before he was felled by Spanish blades on the ash-covered shores of Tenochtitlan.

"Y-yes," the startled Kelia answered.

"You'll have to forgive my words if they are incorrect," the man replied. "I have not spoken the Nahuatl language in some time."

The children stood in silent anticipation as Ohtli let out a babbling grunt.

"How do you speak our language? Where are we?" Kelia finally asked, breaking the long pause.

The man chuckled. "I am Aztec, my child, just like you... or at least I used to be. I was sent as a hostage to these lands when I was a boy to ensure peace between our peoples. My father was a shaman. My mother, a seer. I heard they were both killed in a Tlaxcalan attack a few years after my departure from Tenochtitlan. After their death, I just assumed I was forgotten by the Aztecs. That's when I found my new home here...in this village of Chinquila amongst the Maya people."

"Mayans," Kelia repeated. "I knew it."

"I am Ichtaca," the man said. "This is my wife, Itzel. She does not speak your language, so I assume you have not been properly introduced yet."

"I am Kelia, and this is Chimalli and Ohtli."

"How have you come to be he-"

"Have you seen any white men? Uhh Spaniards?" Chimalli interrupted Ichtaca and changed the subject abruptly as his young mind strayed from pleasantries and small talk.

Ichtaca paused and sensed the hesitation in Chimalli's voice and demeanor.

"No, boy, not yet, but these lands are not safe anymore," he replied. "We've heard stories of a Spaniard in these parts, a man they call El Carnicero, The Butcher. He roams from village to village with his soldiers, slaughtering anyone in his path."

"The Butcher?" asked Kelia.

"No one knows his real name," responded Ichtaca, "but from what I've heard about the way he carves up his victims, hell itself would spit him back out."

Kelia shuffled with concern. "If this is true, then why are you still here? Why don't you leave?"

"And go where, child? This is our home. Itzel and I have lived in this village for forty cycles of the sun. Our son is buried here, next to the small tree behind the house. He was taken from us a few months ago from the sickness. The gods watch over his final resting place, and we will remain here to pray for his soul."

"I have seen what these men are capable of doing, if you can even call them men," Kelia said with a sinister look on her face. "They are more like beasts...savages, preying on the weak and shedding the blood of the innocent. All in the name of their god. Pray all you want, but that won't stop the Spanish from destroying everything you love."

Kelia turned away in anguish as she recalled the sacking of her home. Thoughts of her mother being raped, tortured, and left to suffer an inglorious death at the hands of the Spanish once again entered her fragile mind, as they often did. Such was the fate of so many inside Tenochtitlan when it fell, and it left a scar across the hearts of both Chimalli and Kelia.

"What happened to you?" Ichtaca said as he looked upon their beleaguered, childish faces. "Were you there when it fell? Tenochtitlan?"

"Come now, children," Itzel interrupted in the Mayan language before they could respond as she sensed the children's sorrow. "That's enough for today. Let's get you some fresh clothes. You can join us at the festival this evening and sleep in our son's bed tonight."

Itzel's unknown Mayan words provided a comfort to the Aztec children. Between caring for an infant and running for their lives over the last several months, Chimalli and Kelia often forgot that they were only kids, and they too needed to be comforted and treated like normal children.

Later that evening, after they retrieved Khuno and put him in a relatively luxurious cage nearby Ichtaca and Itzel's home, the Aztecs feasted and met with some of the other townsfolk, most of whom proved to be kind and welcoming to the foreigners. Although no one could really understand the other's language other than Ichtaca, there was a bond the children felt with these Mayans that they had not experienced with other humans in many moons. Chimalli and Kelia sang and laughed with one another, and Ohtli giggled at the sight of the elaborate costumes the dancers and fire breathers wore as they chanted around the flames. These moments of joy were precious and rare to the battered children. Since their lives were torn apart by Cortes and his conquistadors, Chimalli and Kelia had experienced very few occasions like this, especially ones with such good food and company.

As Ohtli rested his little feet in the dirt beside Kelia's, they watched in admiration as Chimalli played a Mayan game known as Jai Alai with the other villagers, where two opposing players hurled large rubber balls against a granite wall and tried to make it land in a marked zone. If the other player caught the ball and threw it back into his target zone, then that player scored a point. The Mayans quickly became impressed with Chimalli's fast reflexes and skills in a game he had never played before. After defeating many opponents, the boy beamed with excitement at the praise heaped on him by the Mayan villagers. He experienced pride within himself and began to feel like a child once again, young and naïve, but also strong-willed.

When the festivities of the evening concluded, the Mayans wound down for the night and extinguished the flames of the large fire they had built in the center of the town. The Aztecs retired back to Ichtaca and Itzel's home, where their bed for the night was already prepared. It was the first time they slept on a soft surface in many months.

"Come up here, Chimalli," Kelia whispered in the middle of the night so as not to awaken Ohtli or their Mayan hosts. "You don't have to sleep on the floor. There's plenty of room."

Chimalli's heart raced as he remained frozen at Kelia's words, attempting to fake like he was asleep.

"I know you're awake, stupid. You're a terrible liar."

Chimalli took a deep breath and turned to face Kelia from his position on the pile of quilts laid out on the floor. Being the gentleman that he was, Chimalli had chosen to let Kelia have the bed.

"There's not enough room," Chimalli whispered back. He had slept on the ground beside Kelia for months, but the thought of sleeping in the same bed as her caused his anxiety to peak.

"Yes, there is, now get your scrawny ass up here."

"Scrawny?" Chimalli grinned as he used this lighthearted opportunity to pick himself off the floor and nestle into the bed in the least awkward way possible, though he failed miserably at this. "See, I told you. There's not enough room. I'm hanging off the bed."

"Well not if you're laying way over there," Kelia said with a muted chuckle as she pulled him in closer and their legs contacted each other. "Plenty of room now."

Chimalli tried to mask his overwhelming nervousness with little success. As he had grown older and his boyish innocence progressed into adolescent desires, he often shuddered at the moments when Kelia would touch his hand or stare into his eyes. Now, he found himself in the most provocative spot of his young life, face to face with a girl, but not just any girl. His bond with Kelia had strengthened over the last several months into something he considered to be love, although he would never admit it to anyone but himself.

"What will become of us?" Kelia whispered, breaking the silence and calming Chimalli's racing heart.

"What do you mean?"

"I mean, how do we know these Incas even exist? Why are we marching half-way across the world to reach a land that we've only heard stories about?"

"Acalan said it's the only place that we can be safe–,"

"Acalan is gone," Kelia interrupted. "We are here. This village is here. Running through the jungle, not knowing where our next meal will come from, it's no place for Ohtli, or for us."

Chimalli pondered Kelia's gentle words and knew them to be true. She was right. Ohtli needed stability. He needed a place to grow up and be a normal child, and so did they.

"What if they don't accept us?" Chimalli asked, maintaining his whisper so that Ohtli wouldn't wake from his slumber in the makeshift crib at the foot of their bed. "We're Aztec, not Mayan."

"Look around you, Chimalli. Everyone who looks like us is now the same. It doesn't matter what language we speak or what names we call our gods. We are all sons and daughters of this land, united by a common enemy."

Chimalli chewed on his response for a moment. "Perhaps you're right. Ohtli did look happier tonight than I've seen him in a while. And I'm probably the best Aztec to ever play Jai Alai."

The two children chuckled aloud at Chimalli's comment, which caused Ichtaca to groan and shuffle in his sleep from across the room.

"Shh..." Kelia said to Chimalli with a smile as she placed her hand over his mouth to mute his giggles. The warmth of Kelia's touch brought back his nervous thoughts. Chimalli cleared his throat and struggled to find the right words to say.

"Alright," Chimalli said after a pause, "as long as they'll have us, we'll stay."

Kelia grinned from cheek to cheek. "And we'll forget this silly notion of a distant empire of Incas?"

"Yes," confirmed Chimalli, though his heart was so full he would have likely said anything in that moment.

Kelia leaned over and gave Chimalli a single kiss on the cheek, turning his face strawberry-red. He froze like a statue at the contact of her soft lips against his skin.

Kelia smiled and chuckled at Chimalli's not-so-subtle anxiety before rolling over and resting her head on the pillow.

"Goodnight, Chimalli," her soft voice rang out for the last time that evening as she reached over to grasp Chimalli's hand with her own.

Chimalli swallowed the biggest lump in his throat that he'd ever felt while staring at the ceiling and struggling to muster a response.

"Goodnight...Kelia."

Volume II, Part III

Death in the Streets of Cajamarca

It all happened so fast. Atahualpa, the sun god's mortal embodiment on earth, who had just wrestled control of the Inca empire away from his brother, lost that control much quicker than he had gained it.

The evening was dark, gloomy, and devoid of all hope, in every sense of its meaning.

Atahualpa rested on his knees with his hands tied behind his back. Blood seeped from an open wound in his head. The embattled emperor wept, but not from the physical pain of his injuries. He wept for his people. He wept for the souls of his warriors who lay dead and scattered amongst the ruins of Cajamarca in the Peruvian highlands.

Beside Atahualpa knelt Rumi and Chasca, both of whom were exhausted from battle and possessed several wounds of their own. A Spanish swordsman had knocked Chasca's axe, Huascar's Bane, from her hands before slicing through her leg with the steel of his weapon. He would have killed her if Rumi had not thrust his blade through the Spaniard's neck before his sword could strike again.

A blood-stained Spanish face leaned in close enough so that Chasca could smell the man's stinking breath infesting her nostrils like poison. This invader of their lands clearly knew Chasca's fame and status within the empire, as he chose to speak to her over her father.

"I imagine you didn't think it would go like that, did you?" teased the Spaniard, Francisco Pizarro. His breath was even worse when he spoke.

A captured native woman from a different tribe stood scared and timid beside Pizarro and was forced to convert his words into the Quechua language so the Incas could understand.

Chasca gave no reply to the Spanish leader, and she kept her head held high in the face of defeat. As Pizarro continued to insult her and bask in his victory, Chasca's mind raced.

How did this happen? she thought. *How did we underestimate them?*

Chasca was right to have such confusing thoughts. Fresh off the victory over Huascar and his tens of thousands of warriors just a few weeks earlier, the powerful Incas saw little threat in a small band of foreigners that had been raiding the northern parts of the empire like petty bandits.

Several thousand Incas against a few hundred Spaniards. The conflict was supposed to be short lived. Atahualpa and Chasca had only come along to parlay with the strange white men and get a glimpse at these new weapons they had heard about. When the negotiations broke down, they got much more than a glimpse. Pizarro had used the narrow pathways of Cajamarca to funnel the Incas into his trap, where he then unleashed his cannons and firearms on the unsuspecting natives.

Even when the Incas got close enough, the Spanish, who were clad in thick, steel armor, overwhelmed the Incas and their primitive weapons. The Spanish muskets and cannons produced what sounded like thunder to the Incas and ripped through their formations. The steel of the Spanish armor was matched by that of their swords, which cut through the thin layers of animal hide that provided very little protection for the Inca warriors. The Spanish horse riders then cut down the last lines of resistance that the Incas could offer.

Like a flash of lightning through the night sky, forged by Illapa, the Inca god of thunder, it was over. It was all over. Not just the battle. The spirit of the Incas bled dry that day. Atahualpa had tasted defeat before, but this was different. This was a show of force and dominance never witnessed by the Incas to that point. Years of civil war and struggling for the throne of Cuzco were all deemed irrelevant in a matter of hours.

Before Atahualpa could rally his men and retreat, death had scorched its way through the streets of Cajamarca. Few Incas were left standing by the end of the fight, and a crushing, demoralizing defeat hung over the heads of the survivors, including Atahualpa and Chasca.

"Speak, savage!" Pizarro shouted as he yanked up the defiant Chasca by the back of her head and forced her to look at him. "Your new god demands it!"

"Stop!" Atahualpa yelled in a desperate attempt to save his daughter from the Spaniard's unhinged wrath. "Leave her alone! It's me you want! Let these people go and take me!"

Atahualpa regretted his decision to meet with Pizarro the previous day under the guise of peace. Pizarro had discovered that Chasca was the emperor's daughter, and he clearly intended to use this against him.

Pizarro chuckled. "Oh, I plan on taking you…your majesty. Your life is of great value to me. But before we go, you get to watch your child die at my hands."

The translator reluctantly relayed Pizarro's message to the Incas, and the Spanish leader, grinning and laughing ominously, produced a steel dagger from its sheath.

"Stop this, please!" Atahualpa continued to plead for his daughter's life.

Rumi, surprisingly, had no response to the Spaniard's threats against the woman he loved. The bloodied Inca commander stayed quiet and bound with a blank expression on his face.

Chasca, too, remained silent and defiant even as Pizarro placed the blade against her neck. Despite her father's continued efforts, Chasca prepared herself to leave this life and join her people in death. She was ready. She closed her eyes and welcomed the blade that pressed against her skin.

"I have another idea," Pizarro said abruptly as he stood and removed the blade away from Chasca's neck.

"Bring my sons up here!" the Spaniard called to his conquistadors. "It's time they learn how to deal with these savages."

A few of Pizarro's men paced down the street and away from the center of the war-torn city of Cajamarca where the Inca prisoners were gathered. A few moments later, the soldiers returned with two young Spaniards at their side.

Chasca gazed upon the boys with confusion. One of them looked identical to his father. He possessed the same smug expression, and he carried himself like an annoying brat of a child, giggling and laughing at the dead Inca warriors as he stepped over their bodies.

The other boy, though...he was different. His skin was darker than that of his brother's and father's. He appeared emotionless and held his head low to the ground. Unlike his brother, the boy was careful not to step on the dead bodies out of respect as he reluctantly joined his father's side.

"Take this dagger, Alejandro," Pizarro commanded as he unsheathed a large steel knife and presented it to his son.

A single tear ran down the frightened boy's face and he shook his head in defiance of his father.

"Take it, boy!" Pizarro yelled with fury. "Make me proud of you for once in your life and plunge that blade into her flesh!"

Pizarro forced the dagger into his son's hand and clinched his fist around the handle. When the blade was firmly within

Alejandro's grasp, Pizarro jolted him forward in the direction of Chasca. The young Spaniard stopped at the feet of the kneeling Inca commander and trembled in horror at his father's order.

Chasca sensed the boy's fear as she gazed into his eyes and never broke eye contact. Alejandro stared back at Chasca, and for a short moment, he felt a sense of calm and tranquility. Her face was bloodied and bruised, but her resolve was unwavering. The Spaniard had never seen such bravery in the face of impending death.

"Alejandro," Chasca repeated the boy's name in a gentle tone as she raised her chin to give him a better target at her neck. "You have a great spirit surrounding you. I am honored to die at your hand."

Although Alejandro couldn't understand her, he stood in shock at how she welcomed death with such bravery and composure.

The translator began to interpret Chasca's words into Spanish, but Pizarro interrupted her before she could do so.

"Enough!" the Spanish leader shouted as he grew increasingly agitated at the banter. "Kill her now, Alejandro!"

Fear once again returned to the boy's face. He pondered his father's words for another moment before turning and gesturing the dagger back to Pizarro.

"I won't do it, father. This is wrong."

Chasca cocked her head in surprise and emitted a slight grin at the boy's courage to stand up to his father. The energy she felt inside the boy's soul radiated even more now, and despite his youth, Alejandro possessed a powerful spirit within him.

Pizarro, however, looked on in disgust at his son's continued disobedience, but before he could berate Alejandro, Pizarro's other son broke his silence and pushed himself past the Spanish guards in front of him.

"I'll do it, father," he said in a sniveling tone. "I'll make you proud."

The young weasel of a Spaniard caught his brother off guard, and before Alejandro could react, the boy wrestled the dagger away from him and shoved him to the ground.

"Valentino! Stop!" Alejandro shouted as he tumbled into the dirt.

Without hesitation and with great evil in his eyes, Valentino thrust the blade towards Chasca to cut her throat.

As Atahualpa shouted in terror, Rumi suddenly rose from his knees and revealed a dagger that he had concealed in his wasteband. The Inca warrior had worked his hands free of the bonds around his wrists while the others were talking, and he leapt forward towards Valentino. Just before the Spanish boy's strike could land upon Chasca, Rumi slashed his blade through Valentino's right hand, cutting straight through two of his fingers and spraying his blood across the boy's own face.

Valentino let out a deafening shriek and fell backwards onto the ground. The young boy writhed in pain as Rumi dropped his dagger and awaited his fate.

Pizarro reacted in horror as he watched his favorite son's blood gush onto his tunic. "Seize him!" the Spanish leader shouted to his men.

The brave Rumi, half-naked with his tattooed face raised to the heavens and gleaming in the light of the setting sun, stood tall and resolute to face his punishment. A Spanish guard stepped forward and thrust the hilt of his sword into Rumi's face, breaking the Inca commander's nose and sending him careening backwards.

"Rumi!" Chasca shouted as the man she loved landed at her feet. Rumi winced in pain, and Chasca nestled closer to try and comfort him, although her hands were still bound.

Most of the other onlookers stood by in shock at what they had witnessed. Atahualpa still rested on his knees with a concerned glance at his daughter and the man who had just saved her life. The emperor felt relief at Rumi's act of courage, but he also worried about Pizarro's reaction to this act of defiance.

Still lying on the ground from his brother's shove, Alejandro struggled to form a proper reaction to what had occurred. He looked down and spotted Valentino's bloody fingers lying in the dirt beside him. It appeared to be the two fingers furthest from his thumb on his right hand that had been severed, and Alejandro couldn't help but chuckle as he watched his hated brother scream in agony.

More Spanish guards rushed over to help Pizarro and Valentino, while others pulled Rumi off the ground and began slamming their fists into his face and stomach. The embattled

Rumi buckled but withstood the attack with great courage, even as his face transformed into a mangled, bloody mess.

"Stop! You're going to kill him!" Chasca shouted to the Spanish conquistadors while Rumi's body crashed into the ground once more and his attackers kicked him with violent force. The Spaniards were in no mood for mercy.

"Get him up!" the seething Pizarro ordered to his men as he rose from his son's side. "Bring that savage to me!"

With one soldier on each arm, the Spaniards lifted Rumi's limp body and dragged him to their leader as his feet dangled helplessly against the dirt. Pizarro cracked his knuckles and gritted his teeth while contemplating what to do with the man who had just mangled his son's hand.

Pizarro gave Rumi another blow to the face, as if he hadn't received enough of those already, before grabbing the Inca's head and forcing him to look at Valentino.

"Look what you've done to my son!" Pizarro shouted and fumed.

"Kill him, father!" Valentino paused to gasp for air. "Kill him now!"

Rumi fought through the pain and formed his bloody lips into a grin at seeing what he had done to the sniveling little boy.

"No, my son," Pizarro responded while glancing upon Rumi's smirk. "These three will watch as their people suffer in their stead."

Pizarro then stood to address his soldiers. "Go to each house in the city! Burn the women! Impale the men! Throw the babies from the highest windows you can find! I want every last barbarian in this God-forsaken place dead by nightfall! These people will know that to defy Francisco Pizarro means you will forfeit your life!"

Although the Incas couldn't understand Pizarro's Spanish words, they sensed the horror that was about to unfold. Even the Spanish soldiers shuddered and hesitated at their leader's orders. In all the years of terror that Huascar had imposed on his people during his reign as emperor, never before had the Incas been exposed to this level of brutality.

The Spanish conquistadors forced the civilians of Cajamarca from their homes and ordered them to assemble a large pyre out of wood from the town's lumber reserves. They held knives to the throats of the city's children as a warning to anyone who refused to help. The civilians were also made to construct a pit with sharpened stakes protruding from the bottom.

Pizarro wrath was unhinged, evil, and absent of any moral limitations. The sight of his son losing his fingers sent him into a violent rage where the unwritten rules of war no longer existed. He outwardly blamed Alejandro for what happened to Valentino, constantly shouting at him to watch the massacre as it occurred.

Over the next two hours, the trembling but brave women of Cajamarca were herded together and shoved onto the pyre as flames engulfed their bodies. Their screams echoed throughout the entire town...perhaps the entire empire. Pizarro also kept his promise to execute the smallest of children and babies, and he made the Inca men watch as the soldiers carried out this monstrous act.

After the women and children had been slaughtered, the remaining Inca warriors, except for Chasca, Atahualpa, and Rumi, were driven into the pit and impaled upon the stakes. Many tried to escape or fight back, but they were quickly met with Spanish steel that the guards drove into their bellies before throwing their lifeless bodies into the pit.

Tears of great sorrow flowed down Chasca's face as she, Rumi, Atahualpa, and Alejandro rested helplessly on the ground near the killing pits while the massacre ensued around them. The three Inca warriors had their hands bound together and were made to watch the brutal deaths of their people, and Alejandro curled into a nearby corner with his eyes directed at his feet.

No words were spoken.

There was nothing to say.

The cries of dying Incas provided all the noise they could take.

The savagery of the Spanish rendered the four onlookers speechless, unable to wrap their minds around what their eyes were witnessing.

"Ch-Chasca," Rumi finally said as he struggled through immense pain to get his words out. "I'm s-sorry, my love. For everything. This is all my fault."

"No, Rumi," Chasca replied sternly. "Don't you dare do that. Don't you dare blame yourself for this. You saved me... twice."

The thought of hundreds of people meeting their gruesome end all because Rumi had rescued the woman he loved from death made Chasca's stomach turn. She keeled over and vomited on the ground, retching at the smell of burning flesh and the continued screams of her people.

After regaining her composure and spitting the remainder of the blood and vomit from her mouth, Chasca lifted herself back up and glanced at Alejandro, who possessed a look of defeat while resting against a nearby building.

"Hey, you," she called to the boy in Quechua.

No response. Alejandro continued to plant his head between his knees.

"Hey, you!" she said a little louder, this time drawing the gazes of Atahualpa and Rumi.

Still no response from the boy.

Chasca then spotted something on the ground beside her that piqued her interest. With her hands still bound behind her back, she twisted her body and picked it up before letting out a gentle whisper in Alejandro's direction, much like the call of a bird on a peaceful spring morning.

This time, Alejandro perked up ever so slightly at the sound of Chasca's voice and glanced at the Inca warrior princess with a blank stare. Chasca wiggled her clinched fist and motioned for him to come over, indicating she had something to give him. Alejandro paused for a moment until Chasca once again gestured the object to him.

The timid, dark-skinned Spaniard, who had seen far more than a boy of his age ever should, glanced around to make sure his father wasn't around at the moment. When he deemed himself to be clear of prying eyes, he crawled over towards the kneeling Incas.

Alejandro felt a slight apprehension as he approached the foreigners. He thought that maybe she was trying to trick him and cut him with the object in her hand, but death no longer frightened the boy after the mass genocide he had witnessed that day. In fact, death would offer a sweet release from the pain he felt in his heart, so any hesitation he had about being near the Incas faded.

When Alejandro reached her side, Chasca continued to watch the boy intently with an empty stare while Atahualpa and Rumi turned to face him as well. Chasca opened her fist to reveal its contents, and much to Alejandro's surprise, the Inca warrior presented a small yellow flower with pedals blowing gently in the evening wind.

Chasca held the stem of the flower out towards Alejandro, who accepted the gift timidly and with no emotion. Chasca formed her lips into a grin, and Alejandro did the same after seeing her expression. Alejandro then glanced at Atahualpa and Rumi, and even through their bruised and swollen faces, the two male Incas emitted smiles of their own.

Alejandro knew from that day forward where his heart belonged. This was an unthinkable act of kindness. Here he was, an intruder on their lands. His father had just executed their people in mass numbers and made them witness every horrific death. Yet, even with all the terrible events that had just occurred, the three Inca leaders still found the strength to smile and give a piece of their land to a Spanish boy who they had deemed worthy to receive it. The Incas saw something in Alejandro that day, a great fire and spirit that no other Spaniard possessed, even if he couldn't see it himself.

With the unspeakable atrocities committed at Cajamarca blossomed a small ray of hope amongst the flames of wickedness. A bond was formed that day between a Spaniard and three Incas, a bond that would have far greater influence than any Spanish sword ever could. The battle for the heart of the Inca lands began at Cajamarca, but it was far from over. Alejandro, a boy of Spanish and native descent, was forced to choose a side in the internal conflict that flickered within him...and choose he did.

Volume II, Part IV
The Butcher of Chinquila

A heavy boot splashed into a small puddle of rainwater with aggressive force, followed by another.

Several more leather boots impacted the beleaguered puddle as a group of Spanish conquistadors and native scouts trampled through the muddy terrain outside the small Mayan fishing village of Chinquila. The violent rains of the Yucatan battered the Spaniards and clouded their vision, but the huts of Chinquila loomed ahead in the darkness of the night.

"Sir, the local village is just ahead!" yelled a native scout at the front of the column to his Spanish commander, the sound of the rain drowning out their voices. "These people are harboring the children you seek."

"Surround them," the commander ordered to his men. "Kill anyone who tries to escape but leave the Aztecs alive and unspoiled. One of them is of great value to me."

The conquistadors nodded in acknowledgment and took their positions around the village, blocking off all exits and trapping the inhabitants inside.

The Spanish commander's face was covered with a piece of cloth that shielded him from the rain, but his eyes possessed a look of hatred...of evil. He cracked his knuckles and gazed up to the night sky as the rainwater splashed against his steel-plated armor. Through his mask the commander's smile radiated from one end of his face to another like a child receiving his favorite toy on Christmas morning.

El Carnicero, the Butcher, had come to Chinquila.

As the twenty or so steel-clad Spanish conquistadors approached, the village was eerily quiet. The violence of the rain was overshadowed only by the stillness of the night. Like all towns and villages the Butcher and his men came across, that stillness and peace transformed into chaos the moment the Spanish boots hit the soil. They worked swiftly, like a plague of violence and aggression, turning the ground red with the blood of anyone who resisted them...and often even with those who cooperated.

Chinquila would be no different, perhaps even worse, since the Butcher knew who else was hiding amongst the townspeople.

"Where are they?!" a Spanish conquistador shouted at an old fisherman who he had just pulled from his own bed and cast outside into the mud.

The fisherman's son, an adolescent of modest build name Taavi, who Chimalli had defeated in Jai Alai a few weeks prior, pulled his club and attempted to protect his father. The young Maya fought bravely and even managed to land a strike against the breastplate of his father's attacker, but the conquistador regained his balance and plunged his sword into Taavi's belly. The fisherman's son dipped his head and lost his life as the Spaniard thrust his boot into the Mayan's body to remove his sword from it.

"Taavi! No!" his mother shrieked and shouted in horror at seeing her son's body fall to the ground just outside their hut.

Upon hearing the wails of the distraught mother, the rest of the villagers awoke from their sleep, only to find the invaders kicking down *their* doors as well.

The Butcher paced slowly and silently into the village as carnage ensued all around him. The conquistadors pulled every man, woman, and child from their homes and thrust them into the cold, wet mud.

"Talk, salvaje!"

"Where are the Aztec children?!"

"Start talking, pendejo!"

"I'll kill your whore mother right here! Madre hijo de puta!"

The Spaniards were ruthless and unforgiving. Their commands echoed in the Spanish language; thus, their words were unknown to the terrified Mayans. The screams of the villagers only served to fuel the Spaniards' barbarism.

A conquistador drove his fist into the face of Ichtaca, the Aztec-turned-Maya who welcomed the Aztec children into his home, while Itzel pleaded for her husband's life.

Ichtaca had learned a few Spanish words since their arrival to these lands, just enough to know why the invaders were here. "Not here," Ichtaca said wearily as he wiped the blood from his nose. "Aztecs...not here."

Ichtaca's attempt to plead with them made no difference. He quickly realized that even if the Spanish believed the Aztecs to be gone, they would still torture and murder the villagers out of spite. There was no logic or reason for their madness. Only death. Only chaos.

The masked Butcher planted his foot in the mud next to Ichtaca. While his men continued their assault on the hapless Mayans, the Spanish leader remained calm and allowed the rain to polish his armor. He scanned his surroundings and set his eyes upon a grave by a small tree next to Ichtaca and Itzel's home.

"We know they're here," the Butcher's muffled voice rang out as he bent down to speak face to face with the kneeling Ichtaca. "If you don't tell me where they're hiding, I'll dig up that grave behind your home and throw what's left of the corpse out into the mud for the vultures to feast on. Then I'll cut off your wife's head and put it on a pike in the middle of the village."

Ichtaca vaguely understood the Butcher's threats as tears streamed down his face. The dilemma he faced was unenviable and impossible to avoid. Regardless of the moral implications surrounding his decision, Ichtaca chose to save his wife and the sanctity of his son's grave, and no one could have faulted him. He reluctantly motioned his head in the direction of his home.

"In there? In your house?" the Butcher questioned.

Ichtaca nodded in confirmation before lowering his head in shame.

The Butcher rose up into an upright stance, pulled a dagger from its sheath, and sliced Ichtaca's throat, spraying his blood across the ground. Itzel screamed and charged forward to her husband's side, but a nearby conquistador shoved his sword through her back, causing her to widen her eyes and gasp for air. Itzel's body then crashed to the ground next to Ichtaca. The two people who had shown the Aztec children the most kindness on their journey now joined each other in death, and perhaps they were reunited with their son in the afterlife.

Like a predator in the night prowling for his next kill, the Butcher maintained his slow, deliberate pace towards Ichtaca and Itzel's hut and trampled his boots in the thick mud that obstructed his path. Upon reaching the entrance, the wooden boards overhead sheltered him from the rain that had already washed most of the blood from his hands. With violent force, the Butcher thrust his boot through the door and swung it open, nearly breaking it from its hinges.

The sound of the rain dissipated, and the silence of the empty hut rang like a bell inside the Spaniard's ears. The Butcher placed his muddy boots upon the creaky wooden floor and glanced around the room.

An incense candle, smelling of citrus with hints of balsamic and camphor, burned with waning conviction on a small table in the corner of the room. The single-room house appeared neat but well-lived in. A baby's crib rested at the foot of two makeshift beds that appeared to be used recently.

The beds were smaller...small enough for a child...and the sheets were sprawled chaotically across them. It appeared as though whomever rested in these beds rose from their sleep in a hurry, possibly to hide from a sudden threat, leading the Butcher to believe they were still here.

As the Spaniard creaked eerily across the old floors of the hut, the scent of the incense was replaced by that of an animal...a cat perhaps. The smell of fur filled the Butcher's nose, and his boot contacted a floor beam that emanated a creak that sounded different from the other wooden boards.

The Butcher stopped abruptly.

Silence filled the room once more.

The few seconds that passed might as well have been a lifetime until the Butcher finally took another step, this time in the direction of the doorway.

The Butcher's pace quickened, his stride hastened, and he exited the house much quicker than he entered. The Spanish leader shouted a command to his men, and mere seconds later, the hut was swarmed by five more conquistadors.

"Line up, here!" the Butcher ordered to his men as they took up formation with muskets in hand. "Prepare to fire on my command!"

A fleeting moment of pause resonated around the room before the Butcher gave his next command, this time to the inhabitants beneath the floorboards. His voice was still muffled from the tightly worn cloth on his face.

"I know you're in there, boy! Come out now and I'll give you and your friend a quick, merciful death! I'll even do the same for that unholy spawn you carry! Make me wait and I'll see to it that you leave this world in pain!"

Silence.

Apart from the sound of the rain and the screams of the villagers outside, the tension in the room could be cut through like butter.

The Butcher rolled his neck and sighed.

"As you wish."

"Julio," he said as he turned to one of his men, "get in there."

"Yes, sir!" the young Spaniard replied in eager acknowledgment of his commander.

Julio took his musket in one hand, freeing up the other to lift the wooden beams. As the conquistador bent down to place his fingers along the ridges of the floor, a deep ominous growl echoed from beneath the floor, causing Julio and the rest of the conquistadors to pause in fear.

"What the..."

Julio never finished his sentence.

The wooden boards burst upwards and shattered as the largest cat the Spaniards had ever seen exploded through the opening and tore the flesh from Julio's face before he could react.

The other Spaniards, including the Butcher, winced backwards in shock as Khuno, the jaguar who accompanied the Aztec children, ripped through the helpless conquistador.

"Fire!" the Butcher shouted in panic and desperation.

The Spaniards managed to get a couple shots off, striking Khuno in the side with a musket ball, but the cat was largely undeterred. He leapt forward with incredible closing speed and pounced on another Spaniard. Chaos erupted inside Ichtaca and Itzel's home. Khuno proceeded to rampage through the house, breaking items and attacking the rest of the Spaniards with relentless force.

The Butcher called for help from the rest of his men outside before ducking behind an overturned bed. He hid in fear from the massive creature that was currently tearing the skin from one of his men in the opposite corner of the room.

With Khuno preoccupied with the others, the terrified Spanish leader rested his eyes upon the opening in the floor that the jaguar had emerged from. The Butcher saw his opportunity to avoid being devoured and took it. He sprinted across the room and jumped into the opening where the floorboards had broken apart, his feet connecting with a dimly lit dirt path.

The sound of his boots hitting the ground inside the tunnel clearly caused a ruckus further down the path as two figures darted in the opposite direction.

"Go, Kelia! Run!" Chimalli shouted in Nahuatl from the narrow corridor.

"I have you now!" the Butcher yelled at the Aztec children. "Come back and I'll kill you first, Chimalli! I won't even make you watch what I do to the others!"

While Khuno still ravaged the house above, the Butcher raced forward through the tunnel towards the Aztecs, although a slight limp prohibited him from going as fast as the children.

Up ahead, Chimalli and Kelia bolted through the passageway, Ohtli's head bobbing as he clung to the wrap around Chimalli's neck.

"Don't stop, Kelia! Keep going! We're almost to the other side!"

"Chimalli, I'm scared! He's going to kill us!"

The three children sprinted for their lives towards the end of the tunnel as the Butcher shouted obscenities at them in the Spanish language. Although his words were muffled, Chimalli noticed a familiarity in the Spaniard's voice, like he had heard it before.

Despite the Butcher's limp, Chimalli and Kelia could feel him drawing closer. It seemed like he had a personal vendetta against the children as he spurred himself on at a rapid pace. The seething Spaniard, who had abandoned his calm, mysterious aura that he possessed when he entered the village, appeared much more invested in catching the Aztecs than he was in dealing with the Mayan villagers.

"There it is! Up the ladder, Kelia!" Chimalli shouted as the children reached the end of the narrow passage where a small wooden ladder led to a hidden hatch on the outskirts of Chinquila. Kelia swiftly ascended the rickety steps and out the hatch, and Chimalli followed close behind with Ohtli still strapped to his chest.

The events that followed the Aztecs' ascension out of the tunnel and into the woods haunted young Chimalli for many moons, as he blamed himself for what happened next. Alas, whether it was the will of the Christian god, Aztec gods, or some other force of nature, it mattered not.

"Hurry, Chimalli!" Kelia shouted as she helped Chimalli get to his feet when they exited the tunnel. Chimalli planted his bare, bloody feet on the ground at the top of the steps, but just as Kelia let go of his arm to clear away the nearby brush and make their escape, Chimalli tripped on a nearby branch and lost his balance.

With the sound of the Butcher climbing the ladder behind them, every second that wasn't spent running felt like a lifetime, and Chimalli's untimely plunge to the ground only served to add to the children's horror. To make matters worse, a loose stick protruding from a tree branch caught hold of Ohtli's wrap during the course of the tumble and ripped it clean from Chimalli's neck. The terrified Ohtli detached from his uncle's grasp and impacted the earth with force. The child's hard fall caused him to bellow in pain as Chimalli and Kelia's eyes widened with unimaginable dread.

Without hesitation, Chimalli scrambled to his feet and Kelia returned to retrieve Ohtli from the ground. As she bent down to grab the child and lock him in her arms, she stopped when she heard the clicking sound of a Spanish musket being cocked and readied to fire.

"Touch him and he dies," the Butcher's muffled voice calmly resonated in the sudden stillness of the night. His body extended half-way out of the tunnel, and he aimed his musket directly at Ohtli. The shriek of the small child was now the only sound that could be heard as Chimalli and Kelia both froze in their stance.

"Back up! On your knees!" the Butcher once again shouted, abandoning his momentary calm. The Spaniard then pulled the rest of his body out of the tunnel, and Chimalli and Kelia reluctantly followed his orders with tears filling both their eyes.

The Butcher panted from exhaustion and emitted an ominous laugh as he writhed in pain and reached down to clutch the back of his leg.

"That traitor got me good. I'll give him that much. Even after all this time, the dagger he threw into my leg still gives me trouble."

The Butcher's voice finally became clear to Chimalli.

"And you killed my uncle, boy," the Spaniard continued with a slight chuckle. "But I suppose I should be thanking you. I never really liked the man. I must admit, I felt nothing when you pierced his heart with your spear."

Chimalli had learned a bit of the Spanish language during his time with Rodrigo, and he deciphered enough of the Spaniard's words to understand. Although Chimalli had likely already discovered the Butcher's identity, his suspicions were confirmed when the Spaniard removed his face covering.

Francisco Pizarro, nephew to Hernan Cortes, stood before Chimalli once again. The last time the Aztec boy had seen him was nearly a year earlier during the sack of Tenochtitlan, where Chimalli's (and Kelia's) entire world had burned to the ground.

Although Chimalli and Rodrigo had gotten the better of Cortes and Pizarro during their encounter in the central square of the city, Chimalli now hung his head in fear and sadness.

"Ahh, don't worry, children," Pizarro said as he saw the anguish plastered across Chimalli and Kelia's faces. "You're not going to die tonight, and neither is this little guy."

With his musket now fixed upon the older Aztec children, Pizarro bent down to pick up Ohtli, who still cried at the pain of the fall he had just taken. Chimalli and Kelia both gasped at the touch of Pizarro's coarse hands against the child's skin.

"Don't hurt him!" Kelia shouted in Nahuatl as more tears streamed down her young face. "Please, kill me instead. Just leave the child alone."

Pizarro glimmered with wicked satisfaction when he locked eyes with Ohtli. The Aztec child, almost two years of age, stopped crying but glanced back at the madman in terror and confusion.

"No, no," Pizarro said, now addressing Ohtli, "I have big plans for you. My son back in Spain, Valentino, he's about the same age as you. He's going to love having a little savage brother."

The evil in Pizarro's voice grew deeper with each word he spoke.

"And what shall we call you, hmm? Your savage name will no longer be appropriate for the son of a Spanish nobleman.

Pizarro paused in contemplation before continuing.

"I know, how about...Alejandro? Yes...Alejandro. That will do."

Chimalli and Kelia could do nothing but sit and watch the psychotic Spaniard as he continued speaking softly to Ohtli, much like one would do with their own child.

"And as for you two," Pizarro said as he turned his attention back to the kneeling Aztecs. "You will make fine slaves for a Spanish nobleman, slowly withering away and knowing that this child is now in civilized hands. Alejandro will have a better life with me than he ever would running through the jungles like an animal. Consider this a courtesy."

As the caw of a nearby eagle sounded through the night, Pizarro emitted one final chuckle before thrusting the butt of his musket into Chimalli's face.

Codex Volume III
❀❀❀
Blood and Ink

Volume III, Part I
Blood on the Mountain

Chasca, wake up.

The gentle, familiar voice of a woman echoed through Chasca's mind while she faded in and out of consciousness.

It's time, my child. I must go now, and you must wake.

The voice grew louder and more aggressive.

Get up, Chasca, get up!

Chasca! Chasca!

"Mother, no!" Chasca screamed as she jolted herself off the ground and out of her slumber. A bead of sweat trickled down her forehead that was brought on by the warmth of the morning sun's rays, but she wiped it away before it could reach the safety of her eyebrow.

Chasca sat still for a moment, and as the thoughts of her mother faded, she began to relive the events that led her to this place at the foothills of the Andes Mountains. She pondered her father's last words to her while they had marched through the Sacred Valley on the way to Cuzco after the massacre at Cajamarca.

"Get to the mountain fortress of Machu Picchu! Find the hooded ones!" Atahualpa had pleaded as he helped her atop a Spanish horse where Rumi already slumped in silent agony over the steed's mane. Sounds of gunfire and clanging swords echoed all around them. The Spanish column had been ambushed by a horde of Inca warriors before they could reach the capital, and the chaos provided Chasca and Rumi with a chance to escape.

"Come with us, father!"

"No, child, I must stay with my people and fight!"

"Then we stay with you!"

"Chasca, no, you must go! Rumi won't survive if you don't get him some help, and if all three of us fall, Huascar will take the throne again and rip the empire apart! You must live, child! *You* are the beating heart of this empire!"

"But I don't know how to ride this beast!" Chasca shouted as the Spanish horse bucked wildly, causing Rumi to hold tight and groan in pain.

"Figure it out!" Atahualpa replied with understandably little empathy based on the situation. "You must get to Machu Picchu now! That is your destiny! Make your mother proud!" The emperor pounded the rear of the horse with his hand in the direction of the nearby mountain ranges, and with a burst of acceleration, the Spanish mare spurred forward and nearly threw the Incas from her back.

As Chasca glanced back at Atahualpa, he cupped his hands around his mouth and uttered one final phrase to his daughter.

"I am the blood, and the blood is me!"

Chasca, confused at why her father would choose those words to potentially be the last ones he might ever say to her, then watched from a waning distance as her father picked up a spear from the ground and helped his men fight the Spaniards. Chasca's new mount picked up speed while the chaos of the Sacred Valley, including Pizarro's commanding voice, faded from her eyes and ears.

Chasca's mind then returned to the present as she rested at the makeshift campsite she had hastily constructed the night before. A cool breeze swept in from the mountains that loomed overhead and provided a relief from the otherwise sweltering heat.

The Andes Mountain range was a truly impressive site to behold. Its high peaks and lavish scenery covered the landscape as far as the eyes could see, convincing the natives how creative and artistic their gods were. Unfortunately for Chasca and Rumi, they were distracted from the visual effects that sprawled before them as the haste of reaching the fortress of Machu Picchu took precedence over anything else.

"Rumi, get up. We must keep moving. There's no time to spare."

The embattled Inca commander, who still clung to life by the will of Viracocha, groaned and quivered on the ground. Chasca helped him to his feet as he struggled to gain his balance.

"Just l-leave me, Chasca. I'm not going to make it."

"Shut up. You'll speak no more of that nonsense. Now mount this beast and hold your tongue."

Rumi moaned in pain even louder now as Chasca helped him atop the Spanish mare. He slumped over and used the horse's mane as a cushion for his head.

Chasca prepared to mount the animal alongside Rumi, but before she could do so, the neigh of a separate nearby horse rang out and startled the unarmed Inca princess. Chasca assumed a defensive position but quickly abandoned it when she realized the peaceful demeanor of the horse.

The mare, slightly larger than the one Rumi rested atop, patted its hooves against the ground and neighed with excitement upon seeing the other horse. The two beasts then came together and nestled their muzzles against one another, finding comfort in the embrace of the other.

Chasca smiled at the strange bond the two horses shared with each other. She found it even more peculiar that both had solid white fur, as all the other Spanish steeds she had seen were brown, black, grey, or spotted in different places. Not these two though. Their fur was as bright as the sun, and they trotted with graceful elegance.

Still weary of approaching the beasts too quickly, Chasca used caution while stepping towards them. Much to her delight, though, the horses accepted the touch of her hands as she gently brushed the fur around both their muzzles.

"Looks like you've made some new f-friends," Rumi said, still slouched over the smaller one's mane and struggling through his words.

Chasca grinned at Rumi's comment as her eyes remained fixed on the two white mares. "They're beautiful, are they not?" she replied. "Animals this pretty should have names. They look like they could be sisters."

"I'm sure they already have n-names, Chasca...Spanish names."

"I'm not talking about those barbaric sounds the white men use to refer to themselves and their animals. No, no, they need to be called something fitting of a queen or goddess."

Chasca pondered for a moment, veering off in thought as Rumi lost the energy to continue humoring the woman he loved.

"Lilly," she said while looking at the larger horse. She then turned to the smaller one. "And...Lyla."

The two horses neighed and almost seemed to nod in approval of their new names.

"It's settled, then. Lilly and Lyla...twin goddesses and rulers of the mortal realm of beasts and men."

"How poetic," Rumi said, "but I'm losing a lot of b-blood here, so if you're finished, I'd like to be off now."

"Of course, my love. My apologies. I wouldn't want you bleeding too much all over this beautiful animal."

Rumi chuckled softly through his agony at Chasca's joke, but he felt the sting of his wounds infecting him beneath the surface of his skin and down to his bones. Rumi tried not to alert Chasca and worry her, but something didn't feel right inside him, like he was bleeding from more than just his external wounds. He also had too much pride to constantly complain about the pain.

Chasca then positioned herself around Lilly's side and placed her foot in the strap that hung down from the saddle. She thrust herself atop the majestic beast, which felt slightly harder to mount than Lyla due to her size.

With Rumi atop Lyla and Chasca atop Lilly, the four beings of different worlds set off up the mountain pass that ascended to the heavens. Chasca's riding skills had improved over the last couple days since she mounted Lyla during the ambush at the Sacred Valley, though she still had much to learn. Rumi, on the other hand, looked like a child trying to steer his horse, but this likely had much to do with his condition, which was slowly deteriorating.

"My mother always said that Machu Picchu was at the very top of the highest peak that looked down on Cuzco," Chasca remarked after several hours of riding up the pathway. "She said it was the birthplace of the gods, and they use it to watch over the Inca people."

While it wasn't snowing on top of the mountain, which she had witnessed before from the balcony at the royal palace in Cuzco, the air still felt thin and cold, much colder than the heat of the valley below. This was a new, unwelcome feeling for Chasca and Rumi, who were lightly clothed with exposed arms, legs, and abdomens. The quilted breastplate of a warrior was no longer useful in the fight against this new foe.

Rumi didn't respond, but instead shivered from the cold and kept his focus on steering Lyla in the right direction. His eyes were heavy, and the bruises he had received from the beating at Cajamarca lingered on his face.

"Are we a-almost there, Chasca?"

"I wish I knew. I only know it's supposed to be located somewhere on this mountain, close to Cuzco. Beyond that, I'm lost."

"I need–" Rumi's words trailed off as his body slumped and his eyes began to shut.

"Rumi, what's wrong?" Chasca questioned, quickly realizing that his condition was much worse than she thought. Blood formed on the edges of Rumi's lips, and he lost control of Lyla's reins. "Rumi?!"

Chasca positioned Lilly closer to Rumi and caught his body just before he could tumble to the ground. She propped him up and used all her might to sling his solid frame atop her horse with her.

"With haste, girls, there's no time to spare!" she commanded the horses, grabbing both of their reins and spurring them faster up the pass.

Lilly galloped hard at Chasca's behest while Lyla matched her speed and followed closely behind. After what seemed like an eternity of riding fast into the wind, which seemed to get colder the higher they went, Chasca's heart began to sink as the pathway faded off into a wooded area of dense trees. The vastness of the mountain was overwhelming, and with nighttime approaching, the desperation on Chasca's face became evident.

The sun slowly crept behind the distant mountain next to the one they were on, and any warmth it had provided perished with its fading rays of light. A deep cold set into the

Inca warriors' bones, and a feeling of hopelessness came with it. At least Rumi had the relative fortune of being unconscious now, which was useful when nature decided to pierce their flesh with a much more deadly weapon than steel or obsidian.

Chasca, on the other hand, felt every sting and bite of the cold's wrath. She could see the air from her breath with each exhalation of her lungs. Alone with inadequate clothing, no way to build a fire, and a waning food supply (only a few berries she had picked at the bottom of the mountain), Chasca felt the noose tightening around them as she stopped to contemplate their next move. She knew they wouldn't survive the night if they couldn't find help.

"Apu, Lord of the Mountain, w-watch over us and hear my c-call for aid," Chasca said as her voice cracked and she looked towards the peak of the mountain. She then unsheathed her dagger and cut the skin from her hand, allowing her blood to drip onto the cold earth. "Receive my b-blood as a sign of my submission to you. Please...send me a sign and s-save us from this misery."

Suddenly, before Chasca could even close her fist, a sign appeared in the most unexpected of forms. The largest and most magnificent eagle that Chasca had ever laid her eyes on soared around the mountain's peak and shrieked overhead. The creature, whom Chasca figured must have been sent by the god of the mountain, or perhaps was the earthly form of the Apu himself, descended and landed gently on Lyla's saddle.

Stunned, entranced, and slightly fearful all at the same time, Chasca locked eyes with the eagle, whose stare never wavered. The bird's glare seeped into Chasca's soul and injected its energy into her life force. She felt a sense of calm and safety in the eagle's presence as the cold became less daunting against her skin.

Chasca emitted a grin and maintained eye contact with the godlike creature. Out of the corner of her eye and almost directly behind the large bird, Chasca caught a glimpse of something that should have appeared ominous, but it wasn't. A bloody handprint plastered against the bark of a nearby tree. As Chasca directed her gaze around the woods, she noticed another handprint, and another. Every tree in sight had this bloody sign on it, and it took the eagle's bestowment of clarity for her to see it.

While Chasca still marveled in relative delight at being close to their destination, an arrow whizzed through the air right in front of her face and struck a nearby tree, sticking directly into the center of a handprint. The eagle appeared undeterred and held his position on top of Lyla's back, but Chasca perked up into a defensive posture.

"Who's there?!" she shouted. "Show yourself!"

Silence. The wind of the mountain was the only sound that filled the air.

"This man needs help!" she called out once more in reference to Rumi. "He was attacked by the foreign invaders! Please help us!"

Once again, silence.

Chasca scanned the trees through the darkness, which now covered most of the mountain. Afraid and on the verge of abandoning hope, Chasca finally spotted a figure emerge from behind a tree from the direction the arrow was fired. The hooded man stood still, erect in his stance with no slouch, with his hands grasping what appeared to be a bow.

Then, from behind several other trees surrounding Chasca and Rumi, more figures began to emerge. Each one appeared to be hooded and cloaked in long, black robes, although the darkness prevented Chasca from making out any of their facial features.

"I search for the hooded ones," Chasca continued, trying to mask her fear and not speaking to anyone directly, but to all the silhouetted figures that gathered around her. "The ones that call themselves Yawarchasqakuna...The Blooded."

Upon hearing Chasca's words, one of the hooded ones stepped forward to address her and planted his feet into the ground about ten feet from where Lilly and Lyla's hooves rested.

"You have come to the right place," the man, whom Chasca deemed to be the leader, spoke in a deep tone, "but this mountain is forbidden to outsiders. You must return to where you came from, warma."

"There is nothing to return to!" Chasca shouted back in frustration, eclipsing the hooded one's calm tone. "The white men burn our homes to the ground! They kill our people and march on Cuzco as we speak!"

"That may be true," the hooded leader replied, "but the affairs of the valley do not concern us at this time. We must look to our own defenses here...to protect the realm of the gods on this mountain."

"Do not concern you?" Chasca repeated as she dismounted her horse and approached the man. While he stood resolute and unaffected by her aggressive demeanor, the rest of the hooded ones met her approach with hostility. They unsheathed their weapons in unison and drew closer, only standing down once their leader put his hand up to stop them. "What about the stories I've heard of the Blooded? The ones who live and die for the people of this land? Are these stories all lies?!"

The Blooded leader, whose face Chasca could see more clearly now that she was closer, pondered his words for a moment before reciprocating with his own. "Those are just stories, warma. We are too few in number to make a difference in the world below. And we have many enemies. How do we know you aren't spies? The risk is too great. I'm sorry, child, but you must return...now."

"We are no spies," Chasca replied firmly. "I am Chasca, daughter of Emperor Atahualpa and Cusi Ocllo. I am commander of the royal guard of Quito and heir to the throne of Cuzco. That man dying on the horse is Rumi, former second-in-command to Huascar and now loyal servant to my father."

Chasca's claims caused the hooded man's eyes to widen, and his followers shuffled in their stances and whispered to each other.

"*You* are the daughter of Cusi Ocllo and Atahualpa?"

Chasca nodded her head as the leader paced in deep thought.

"Come, warma," he finally said after a long pause, "we must get to Machu Picchu. We will know very soon if your words are genuine. The Blood Council sees all."

"Blood Coun–" Chasca couldn't finish her question before a hood was suddenly pulled over her head, clouding her vision in darkness.

"What is this?!" Chasca shouted.

"It is necessary, child, I assure you."

The hooded ones did the same to Rumi, who still laid unconscious on Lilly's back. They also provided insulated cloaks to drape around their new guests…or hostages. Chasca couldn't quite figure out which one it was.

The next half hour for Chasca was spent riding atop Lilly in darkness and relative silence aside from her occasional outburst that it was taking too long and that Rumi would die if they didn't get him help soon.

The answer was always, "We will arrive shortly," or, "He's in the hands of the gods now," much to Chasca's chagrin.

The procession of Incas (at least Chasca assumed the members of The Blooded to be Incas) marched further up the mountain until finally they halted by command of their leader. Chasca's hood still covered her eyes, but she could hear the shuffling of footsteps up ahead.

"I am the blood, and the blood is me," the leader declared in an elevated manner. Upon his statement, Chasca heard the creaking of a large gate opening in front of them.

So that's why father called that out to me, she thought to herself. *I should have just said that from the beginning.*

When the gate finally finished opening, the hooded ones ushered Chasca and Rumi inside before helping her down from Lilly. Rumi still laid motionless atop Lyla.

"Please, you must help him now," Chasca pleaded to her captors when her feet touched the dirt. "He's going to d—"

Chasca's voice trailed off as a Blooded removed her hood, revealing to her eyes the most majestic and awe-inspiring sight.

She and Rumi had finally made it.

Machu Picchu stood before them in all its splendor.

The clouds hung just overhead, closer than Chasca had ever been to them, and they appeared to lean down and welcome the new arrivals to their lair. The structures weren't as large as the ones in Quito or Cuzco, but the way they nestled into the landscape of the mountain was breathtaking, even in the darkness of the night. The bulk of the citadel extended higher up the mountain and looked down upon the gatehouse. Torches lined the stone walls of each ascending level with such symmetry, and the pathways and staircases wove throughout the fortress with graceful elegance. Chasca could see why her parents had always talked about its beauty. Machu Picchu was truly fit for the gods.

"—die," Chasca continued calmly, finishing her sentence.

"We will do what we can for this man," the Blooded leader replied, removing the hood from around his head. Appearing to be around his mid-forties in age, the man possessed various tattoos on his face with symbols that honored the gods, much like Rumi's. "We have the best healers in all of Tawantinsuyu."

Chasca watched as a host of holy men, who she assumed to be the healers due to their lavish religious robes that were typically worn by priests and medicine men, gently removed Rumi from his horse and placed him on a moveable bed of woven straw and thick leaves. The healers then carried Rumi further up the mountain with four of them on each corner of the cot.

"I am Tullu," the Blooded leader continued, ushering Chasca to follow him along the trail behind the healers. "Welcome to Machu Picchu. I'm sorry about relieving you of your vision. As I said before, it was necessary."

"I understand," Chasca responded as she paced up the mountain alongside Tullu. "And I apologize if I seemed disrespectful before. This man's life is very important to me. He and I are to be bonded in matrimony. I could not bear the thought of losing him."

"Ahh, to be young and in love again," Tullu stated with a chuckle, surprising Chasca with his lighthearted dialogue. "Don't worry, warma, if his destiny is to live, the gods will not allow him to succumb to his wounds. We will take good care of him, and you, and your foreign beasts too...provided you haven't lied about your identity."

"And how will you test my identity, might I ask? Interrogate me with questions about the royal family and pass judgment for yourself? You are the leader here, yes?"

"In a sense, I suppose, but we Blooded are all equal in the eyes of the gods. If by 'leader' you're referring to the Blood Council, then yes, I am one of three Grandmasters amongst ten other masters."

"Three? Chasca questioned. "And who are the other two?"

Tullu raised his head and laughed. "Oh, child, if you have to ask that question, you're in for quite a night." His words confused Chasca, but she chose not to pry further.

The group of warriors and healers marched up the winding pathways of the fortress, and Chasca kissed Rumi's forehead before the priests carried him into a nearby temple complex. Lilly and Lyla were also led off the trail to be fed and watered, just as Tullu had promised.

Chasca and Tullu made their way even further up the mountain, sharing stories of their past and how they came to be in this place. Tullu informed her that he had been born in Collasuyu, the southernmost region of the Inca empire before his parents moved him and his siblings to Cuzco. Years later, he met the other two members of the Council during his time in the capital, and together they formed The Order of Blooded Natives, or simply The Blooded, just before the onset of the civil war between Atahualpa and Huascar. Despite Tullu's transparency about his own life, he still remained tight-lipped about the other Council members.

"Here we are," Tullu said as they reached a large building at the highest level of the fortress. It was constructed deep into the heart of the mountain, with the land forming up and around its stones, encapsulating it like a gateway to the spiritual realm. "This is the Great Hall of Machu Picchu, sanctuary of the gods and meeting grounds for the Blood Council."

"Alright, I'm ready," Chasca replied as she took a deep breath, brimming with nervous anticipation.

"I must warn you, warma, the other Council members do not typically take well to outsiders. Huascar's spies frequently tried to gain access to the riches and spiritual enlightenment of this place during the war. But, in your case, judging by what you've told me about yourself, I believe they will make an exception. Or at least one of the Grandmasters will."

Tullu placed his hands on the giant stone door of the Great Hall and swung it open before Chasca could question him further.

The entrance was dark and lined with torches as Tullu led Chasca through a winding labyrinth of dimly lit hallways. With the air becoming thinner and colder the deeper into the complex they went, it felt to Chasca like she had stepped into a portal to a different realm.

Chasca and Tullu finally reached the doorway to the inner sanctum, and upon entering, the Inca princess was presented into a room of considerable size, also dimly lit but with high ceilings and a large, open area on the bottom level. Lording over this wide space of stone flooring from above were two other ascending levels in a semi-circular fashion, one with ten seats and the other with three. The ten seats on the middle level were filled with figures in black hoods and cloaks, and two of the three seats on the upper level were occupied by individuals in red hoods and cloaks.

"Step forward," one of the figures in red, whom Chasca assumed to be one of the Grandmasters, commanded to her.

Chasca nervously moved onto the stone slab in the center of the room, which was stained with dried blood, as Tullu donned a red hood and cloak of his own that he had removed from a nearby wall. The Grandmaster then maneuvered his way up the chamber and took his seat beside the other two Grandmasters.

"Child of Tawantinsuyu," Tullu uttered to Chasca from above after all eyes were fixed upon the Inca warrior princess, "you already know who I am. Now, I present to you the Blood Council and the Grandmasters of The Order of the Blooded Natives."

Chasca's eyes widened as Tullu called out the names of the other Grandmasters.

"Cusi Ocllo of Quito and Acalan of Texcoco."

Volume III, Part II
Two Flowers, Unwithered

"Maintain your posture, Kelia. This isn't a slouching contest. Chin down. Weight back."

"Ugh, I'm trying! I'm doing exactly what you said!"

"No, you're not, try harder. And don't shout. You want the masters to come back here and see what we're doing?"

"I'm sorry, Erandi. This is just harder than I thought it would be."

Erandi, an Aztec woman in her mid-forties with a slender build and overtly attractive facial features, paced around Kelia and attempted to reconstruct the girl's combat stance, which clearly needed some alteration.

"When we get out of here one day, do you think these brutish men are going to give you a chance to figure out your stance before you strike at them? No, conetl, this is a man's world, and we are women. Our beauty is our curse. The Spaniards will beat you, rape you, and leave you to rot in the sun."

Kelia's expression turned from annoyed to determined as she wrapped her fist harder around the base of her wooden stick, which served as the closest thing to a weapon they could find.

"Now, strike, conetl, strike me down," Erandi ordered.

Kelia surged forward and used the techniques that Erandi had shown her over the last few days to attack her trainer. Thoughts of Chimalli and Ohtli being stripped away from her (hardly a month prior) flowed through her mind and forced the young girl into a frenzy of strikes, most of which lacked the control to make any real impact.

"You fight with passion, Kelia," Erandi commented while easily parrying her student's wild swings, "but without discipline. You must learn to channel your anger into something useful. Control your pain before it controls you."

Erandi caught Kelia's stick within her grasp and swept the young Aztec's feet from underneath her, sending her crashing into the ground.

"Enough!" Kelia shouted while picking herself off the ground. She then lowered her voice, remembering what Erandi had said about not alerting the masters. "I'm done with this. What's the point anyways? I'm going to die a slave."

Erandi saw the pain on Kelia's face as her eyes filled with tears. She bent down to comfort the young girl who had already been through so much at such a young age. "This place will not be your tomb. You have a great spirit, conetl. Your short thirteen years in this life will pale in comparison to what the gods have in store for you."

"But I'm so hungry all the time. I'm hungrier now than I was marching through the jungles with Chimalli and Ohtli and Khuno. Chimalli always took such great care of us..."

"Tell me about these people," Erandi replied, attempting to remove Kelia's mind from the lack of food in her belly. "They must have been very important to you."

"Yes, yes they were. Chimalli and Ohtli, they...they saved me. When the soldiers came into our home in Tenochtitlan, it was Chimalli and Ohtli and his older friend...Acalan was his name I think...they killed my attackers and nearly saved my mother, but it was not to be."

"You lived in Tenochtitlan?" Erandi asked as Kelia nodded in confirmation. "So did I, with my husband and our three children. All gone now."

"I am sorry for your loss," Kelia replied, sensing Erandi's pain. The two Aztecs, now slaves, both clearly harbored great sorrow from their experiences.

"Thank you, conetl, but please, go on. You were telling me about your friends."

Kelia's paused for a moment before continuing. "The night the Spaniards came to our village...they killed all the Mayas and took Ohtli from us. He was only a year old. As for Khuno, our...cat. They probably killed him as well."

"And your friend, Chimalli, where is he?" Erandi questioned.

"I don't know, honestly. Possibly back in that Spanish city, Veracruz, I think it was called. Or possibly dead. The last I saw him the guards were tearing our hands from each other when they loaded me onto the slave ship at the port. I watched him fade into the distance and out of my life forever..."

"You will see them again one day, conetl, your friends. The gods have a way of bringing everything back into balance."

"Perhaps," replied Kelia with sadness in her eyes. "Perhaps one day."

"Come now, we must get back to work before the masters get suspicious and wonder where we've gone. This is an important night. If the Governor likes us, he might just keep us inside the big house from now on."

Kelia wiped a tear from her cheek that had snuck down her face as she and Erandi made their way from behind the slave quarters on the side of the villa. The Governor's plantation in Havana on the island of Cuba was quite a wondrous place despite the abundance of native slaves and the beatings they frequently endured from the masters.

Kelia had learned by this point to keep her head down and do what she was told. The less attention she could draw to herself, the better. Erandi and some of the other slaves had taught her that, and she managed to steer clear of the lashings that some of her counterparts often received.

"Each setting gets a plate, a napkin, one glass for wine and one for water, and the silverware must be lined up like so," Erandi said to Kelia later that evening as she pointed at the display on the Governor's large, ornate table. "This could be a big night for us, conetl. All of the most important men on the island will be here, sitting at this table, eating the food we serve and drinking the wine we pour."

"You seem excited," Kelia pointed out with a melancholy expression.

"Look where we are. Look what we're wearing," Erandi responded. "This is the finest outfit I've worn in the entire year I've been here. I got a bath today for the first time in weeks."

Kelia adjusted the poofy bonnet atop her head that they were forced to where inside the big house. "We look like frumpy maids with little frilly hats, standing inside a palace of fake luxury built on the backs of our people."

"We *are* frumpy maids," Erandi countered before lowering her voice to a whisper. "And I don't like serving these pompous brutes any more than you do. But until we can get out of here, I would rather not spend my time wearing dirty rags and having my back carved up by a whip."

Kelia didn't reply, but she silently agreed with Erandi. She knew she wouldn't survive in the cane fields, where her calloused hands had been worked raw from the moment she arrived. Over the last several months, Kelia and the other slaves at the Governor's plantation had been forced to work long hours cultivating stalks of cane and producing a shiny, powdery substance called sugar, which was one of the most difficult and grueling tasks the young adolescent had ever undertaken. Kelia had heard that the sugar apparently made all the rich men's food even better, as if they didn't eat like kings already.

The two Aztecs, along with a few other house slaves, finished setting the table and preparing dinner for the guests. Kelia wanted to spit in the food that she was forbidden from eating, which emitted the most heavenly aroma from the kitchen. Erandi warned against it, though, saying that many of the other slaves would rat her out to gain favor for themselves. Apparently, the masters even had a way of turning the slaves against each other. It was an inhumane game orchestrated by inhumane people.

"Governor Velázquez, what do you think about this Treaty of Bruges, as they're calling it back home?" a pompous-sounding Spaniard asked from his seat towards the middle of the table after the guests had all arrived and been served. "Do you think the English are reliable?"

The Governor, an equally arrogant man with a large, wavy mustache that curled over his bushy beard, took a moment to respond while chewing his food. From Kelia's position in the corner of the room, she could see every particle of food being crunched between the man's teeth as he ravenously tore into his roasted lamb. Kelia was not one to judge others from their table manners, but there was something about this Spaniard's barbarous chewing that turned her stomach. The man's house was a palace of luxury, possessing lavish gold-trimmed paintings and flowing fountains of decorative water, yet he feasted like a hound who had not eaten a meal in days.

"Well, Agustín," the Governor responded while licking the sauce from his fingers, "I think Charles is a damn fool, and you can go back to Spain and tell him that. But he keeps my coffers flowing and my foreign interests secure. I have no love for the English, but King Henry has proven to be quite an adept ruler. He will make a most useful ally against the French, if not the most desirable one."

"And Henry beds the daughter of our late king, Ferdinand," another nobleman from across the table chimed in. "They say behind a smart man is always a smart woman."

"If he's so smart, then why isn't *he* behind *her*?!" the Governor shouted with food still in his mouth, making a sexual joke and prompting the combined laughter of the twelve other egotistical men around the table. Their love for themselves and disdain for others who were different seeped from their black hearts with a every fit of laughter they emitted. "There's no such thing as a smart woman. Only those that listen and those that don't."

Kelia, unable to understand the Spaniard's language, teemed with boredom in the corner of the room and began to tap her foot anxiously.

"More wine!" one of the guests yelled, holding his glass in the air while not being bothered to look up from his meal. Kelia perked up, holding the jug of wine in her hands, but she froze in her stance at the Spaniard's command. Erandi noticed her hesitation from the adjacent corner and moved to assist the startled girl.

As Kelia's young hands shook and her body refused to move, Erandi passed by and pulled the jug from Kelia's grip before making her way to the waiting Spaniard, who still held out his glass.

Erandi reached the side of the table as quickly as she could and filled the man's wine glass, only to receive a response of, "Took you long enough." She was used to the disrespect, though, ignoring the man's rudeness as she withdrew the jug from his glass.

Suddenly, as Erandi turned to walk away and give the jug back to Kelia, another Spaniard, a man of old age with a balding head and a shockingly unattractive face, shoved his chair back in a fit of laughter from a conversation they were having, and the leg of the chair caught Erandi's foot as she passed.

The Aztec woman's face filled with terror as the jug of wine, still mostly full, emptied out across the laughing man's arm and shoulder, coating his expensive white linen shirt in a deep red color.

"Damn you, woman!" the old man shouted as he rose from his chair in anger. "I should kill you right here!"

The other guests ceased their conversations and watched the enraged man grab a knife from the table and hold it to Erandi's throat.

"Mr. de la Vega," the Governor addressed his guest firmly, but not in some moral defense of Erandi, "if you kill my slave, you will give me ten more from your stock."

The man, apparently called de la Vega, seethed with anger but quickly altered his mood once he calmed himself. He also began to look at Erandi with lust in his eyes.

"I'm sorry, Governor," de la Vega said as he lowered his knife and sat it back down on the table. His eyes gleamed as he stared into Erandi's. The Aztec stared back at him with a defiant expression. "This one is pretty...and feisty. I should not like to soil your table with her blood."

"If you wish to bed her in compensation for her foolishness, then you have my permission," the Governor replied.

"I should like that very much!" de la Vega shouted as he took Erandi by the back of the neck and bent her down over the table in full view of his colleagues. Erandi squirmed and struggled to remove herself from the Spaniard's control, but she couldn't escape the grip of his hands, which were surprisingly strong for a man his age.

While a few of the Spaniards cheered de la Vega on and seemed to sanction his attempts to rape the poor woman right there on the table, the Governor once more intervened.

"Not here, you brute!" he barked. "You would not soil my table with her blood, but you would with your seed? I have no desire to see your tiny cock, so take her upstairs and handle your business!"

The Governor's comment about his manhood clearly perturbed de la Vega, but he shrugged it off and took out his frustration on Erandi. Kelia watched helplessly as the Spaniard yanked the Aztec woman's arm, pulling her behind him and making his way to the staircase.

Kelia had seen Erandi fight. She knew her friend could likely escape the Spaniard's grasp and subdue him, but to what end? Striking a Spanish nobleman, especially within the walls of the Governor's mansion, would only make things worse for Erandi. Kelia's closest companion accepted her fate and followed da la Vega up the stairs to receive her "punishment."

"And do not plant your offspring inside her either, you fool!" the Governor shouted while still sitting at the table. "I would have to kill her, and you would still owe me ten more to replace her!"

Kelia struggled to hold back her tears at the sight of Erandi being dragged behind the revolting Spaniard. Thoughts of what happened to her mother during the fall of Tenochtitlan raced through the young girl's mind. Kelia prayed to Quetzalcoatl she wouldn't have to set eyes on Erandi's corpse as well, violated and devoid of life like her mother's.

The Governor's stern voice resounded once more across the room. "Girl! Clean this mess! Quickly!" His tone startled Kelia, and although she couldn't comprehend his words, she understood his hand gestures as he motioned to the ground where Erandi had spilled the wine.

Kelia moved her feet at a brisk pace to retrieve a towel and clean up the wine before she too could incur the wrath of the Spaniards and end up being dragged to a bedroom by a filthy old man.

"You sure are lovely," commented the Spaniard who had been sitting next to de la Vega as Kelia knelt to clean the wine from the floor. While the others resumed their conversation about politics or whatever they had been talking about, the man (another wrinkly old pervert) ran his coarse, intrusive hands across Kelia's young face. "You remind me of my granddaughter back in Spain."

Kelia felt sick to her stomach at the touch of the Spaniard's hand, which had not ceased caressing the side of her face. Her blood boiled with anger at the barbarism shown by these supposed "men of class and high esteem" as Erandi had jokingly called them earlier that night. She wanted nothing more than to reach out and thrust a blade into the gut of this disgusting old man, who proceeded to whisper his Spanish words into her ear.

But Kelia had no blade.

She had no way to kill a table full of grown men.

Not yet at least.

The old Spaniard finally finished speaking to her and touching her face as he rejoined the conversation with his equally demented companions. Kelia turned and breathed a relative sigh of relief upon escaping his grasp.

As she stood up and walked back into the kitchen to dispose of the wine-soaked rag, Kelia's lips pursed, her heart filled with anger, and her eyes filled with more tears. She vowed right then and there that she would escape, that she would not allow herself to be subjected to this cruel existence for the rest of her life. She didn't know when, and she didn't know how she would do it…only that it would be done, or else she would die trying.

Kelia remembered a speech she had heard from Cuauhtémoc the previous year when he took over as emperor of the Aztecs after the death of his father, Montezuma. The young emperor, who was one of the most inspiring leaders she had ever seen, had said, "Every man dies. Not every man lives. Either you start living or you resign yourself to an early grave." Kelia carried those words with her and remembered them for times like these. While Cuauhtémoc was now dead, she knew he lived a life of honor and discipline...a life to be proud of.

While Kelia's inner flame had been diminished by the foreign invaders, she knew in her heart that it would never be fully extinguished as long as she had breath in her lungs.

Over the next ten years, Kelia's jaguar spirit rumbled with each passing day. Although she was frequently abused, primarily in a sexual manner by the Governor and his associates, she used her free time wisely, perfecting her fighting techniques in secret with Erandi and waiting for the right moment to leave this life behind forever. She also learned two new languages, Spanish and Quechua (the tongue of the Incas) from some of the other well-traveled slaves. Kelia frequently thought about Chimalli and Ohtli and wondered what their lives were like now. While she never gave up the hope of one day reuniting with them, it became less and less likely with each passing year.

And then it came. On the most random of days and in the most improbable of ways, that hope of escape was finally restored.

Kelia, now a grown woman of twenty-three years, who had been subjected to a decade of abuse and sexual torment, finally found the break she was searching for all those years. A sign, which she presumed was from the gods, came in the form of a large eagle with a small key clutched in its talons.

Kelia, a stout woman of unrivaled beauty, whose mind had become as strong as her hands, leaned in to view the inscription on the key that the eagle had dropped at her side.

"Armory," she read aloud with eyes wider than the great blue sea.

Volume III, Part III
Child of the Blood

"Grandmaster," a young Blooded scout whispered to Acalan, leaning in close as not to disturb the peaceful silence of the ceremony, "the Spanish have ceased Cuzco and taken Emperor Atahualpa as their hostage. He is to renounce our gods and surrender all Inca lands to the invaders."

Acalan pondered the scout's words with a grim disposition before nodding in acceptance of his message. "Thank you, son."

Chasca wiped the tears from her eyes as the Inca holy men chanted a ritual tune of death and rebirth. There was an overtly spiritual energy about this place along the highest plateau of Machu Picchu, as if the mortal souls of man and the immortal spirits of the gods combined to form one symbiotic lifeforce. The darkness of the night, illuminated only by the various torches wielded by the servants of the gods, proved to enhance the divine revelation of the ceremony.

Cusi, a woman of small stature yet enormous influence, rested idly in her bright red Grandmaster robes. She glanced at her daughter from across the sacred grounds at the top of the mountain and studied the young woman's emotions. Chasca struggled to hide her pain and closed her eyes to shield them from the inevitable realization that lay before her.

The two women stood alongside hundreds of their brothers and sisters of the Blood, all gathered around a central altar of stone. Most of the Blooded lingered atop an ascending flight of naturally formed hills that elevated around the stone slab, much like the inner sanctum where the Grandmasters of the order convened. Chasca, Cusi, Acalan, and Tullu, along with the Inca spiritual chanters, stood at the base of the ritual grounds next to the altar.

Aside from the chants, no words were spoken.

Aside from the flicker of the torches, no movement was made.

Such is the way of the Blooded.

Such is the way of death.

Laid atop the altar, wrapped in white cloth, and curled around a bed of flowers, Rumi's earthly incarnation departed from Kay Pacha, the mortal realm of men, and joined the gods in Hanan Pacha.

A dominant and powerful screech echoed through the cool night sky as a grand eagle soared across the mountainside and joined a large host of other eagles. The birds encircled the ceremony and looked down upon their human counterparts.

While the chants from the holy men still resonated through the air, Chasca stepped forward and kissed the forehead of the man she loved. Taken by a combination of his wounds and the sickness that was brought to the land by the foreign invaders, Rumi's spirit ascended to the heavens. Chasca hovered over his body as a single tear fell from her eye and dripped upon the cloth on his face.

Cusi paced around to her daughter's side before whispering into her ear. "He watches over you, now, my child."

"Why must the gods be so cruel?" Chasca asked in the same low tone, lifting her head towards her mother and wiping a new set of tears from her swollen eyes.

"Countless men and women for countless ages have attempted to understand the will of the gods," replied Cusi as the flame from her torch flickered in the wind. "It is a fruitless endeavor, a wasted one. Accepting their will, not understanding it, is the only path."

"And what about your path, mother?" Chasca questioned with a slight scowl, abruptly changing the subject and taking Cusi off guard. "Why are you here? Why did you leave us all those years ago? I was only an adolescent, a young one at that. I needed my mother more than ever."

Cusi veered away from Chasca, pondering her response with great care before turning back to face her daughter. "I left because this is my calling in life. I loved your father, yes...I still do...but it was never my intention to be the wife of an emperor, rotting away in some palace while others get their hands dirty."

"But we thought you were dead," Chasca continued in a whispered tone. "Why didn't you tell us where you were going? Why didn't you tell us you were right here on this mountain all along?"

"To avoid the very thing that has now happened, Chasca. To avoid you abandoning your life and your father to come find me. I knew if the gods wanted our paths to cross again, they would make it so. And here we are, fates intertwined once more."

"And these men?" Chasca asked while subtly gesturing towards Acalan and Tullu, who stood nearby but just out of earshot. "Do you trust them?"

"With my life, child," Cusi responded with conviction. "I met these men around eight years ago in Cuzco. Acalan, the Aztec, had just escaped his dying world, and Tullu had the determination of the gods about him. I knew they shared the same calling as I, the same willingness to carve out evil from this land and truly make a difference. So we left Cuzco, left our former lives behind. We recruited others to our cause and found our purpose here, on this mountain, in this fortress of Machu Picchu."

Chasca nodded in acceptance of her mother's words, and the grudge she held against her for leaving began to fade as Chasca finally got the answers she had sought for many years.

"For what it's worth," Cusi continued, her eyes swelling with emotion, "I'm sorry for leaving you during your time of need, Chasca. I have forgiveness to ask of you."

After a brief pause of hesitation, Chasca bowed her head once more in sorrow as more tears flowed down her face.

She grabbed hold of her mother's robes and pulled her close, embracing her for the first time in many years. Chasca's show of affection caught the Grandmaster off guard, who was unaccustomed to showing emotion, especially in front of others. However, Cusi made an exception that night. On that grassy plateau on the highest peak in the Inca world, Cusi wrapped her arms around her ailing daughter, comforting the young woman and forgoing her usual role of stoic Grandmaster.

Acalan, who had watched in silent observation at Cusi's rare show of public emotion, paced towards the altar and removed the hood that shrouded his face. All eyes fixed upon the relatively young Aztec Grandmaster, a man now in his early thirties who had miraculously avoided being put to the sword on the shores of Tenochtitlan over a decade before. Acalan's wisdom and influence, despite his youthfulness, commanded the highest levels of respect.

"Brothers! Sisters!" Acalan shouted in Quechua to his Blooded brethren, all of which listened intently to his every word. The chanters ceased their songs and dances upon hearing the Grandmaster's call. "We gather here on this night to celebrate the life and death of Commander Rumiac Kachi, or Rumi as known by his peers. While I did not personally know this man, his bravery and renown are legendary amongst these lands. From his time serving under Huayna Capac, Huascar the Cruel, and finally to his defiance of the Spanish devils, Rumi has served his people with honor, and thus should be treated with honor in death. Although he was a valley dweller and not a member of our order, his mortal body will still be entombed amongst our own fallen, treated with the respect he deserves. If any man or woman has cause to oppose this notion, step forward and let your voice be heard."

Silence. Only wind and flames.

None opposed the words of the Grandmaster, though all had a right to do so.

"Let it be so," Acalan continued, taking their silence as confirmation. "In addition to the commemoration of this man's passing, we also induct another member into our order today. Where there is death, there is also life. This is the balance. This is the way of the Blood."

"This is the way of the Blood," all members of the order repeated in unison.

Acalan then stepped aside and let Tullu replace him next to the altar. As chief inductor into the order and living conduit of the gods, Tullu was tasked with conducting the Ceremony of the Blood that all men and women, regardless of age or ethnicity, had to undergo to call themselves Blooded.

Tullu pulled a small but razor-sharp dagger from the band on his robes. Chasca regained her composure and turned her sadness into determination as Cusi led her by the arm to Tullu's side.

"Come forward, warma," Tullu said softly to Chasca, prompting her to step towards him and examine his blade that glinted in the light of the torches. "It's time for your new life to begin."

All three Grandmasters gathered around Chasca as Rumi's lifeless, mummified body rested beside her on the altar.

Tullu continued speaking, this time in an elevated voice so that all could hear. "Chasca of Quito, daughter of Cusi Ocllo and Atahualpa, granddaughter of Huayna Capac, with this ceremony, your former life is now over. While you may retain the name of your past, you will now be reborn in the Blood and through the image of the gods. Repeat my words and be heard."

Tullu spoke the words of the Blooded creed, and Chasca repeated them with pride in her voice.

I am Blooded, and this is my creed.
I am warrior, and this is my sword.
I am shadow, and this is my cloak.
I am darkness, bringer of light.
The whisper in the wind.
The order in the chaos.

I am son to my father.
Daughter to my mother.
Bane of the wicked.
Guardian of the innocent.

My blood is strength from weakness.
Bravery from cowardice.
Hope from despair.
Truth from illusion.
Life from death.

I commit my blood to the earth.
Not for myself.
But for those whose blood has been shed unwillingly.
For those whose sacrifices have been ignored.
For those whose mortal lives have been stolen.

I am the blood, and the blood is me.
From this breath until my last.
I am Blooded, and this is my creed.

Upon Chasca's recital of the Blooded creed, Tullu took her hand and slid his blade across it from one side of her palm to the other. The sting of the dagger reminded Chasca of the oath that she had just taken. Tullu then guided her hand over Rumi's body and the exposed stone of the altar, and Chasca's blood dripped over it like a faucet. The holy men continued chanting, their voices rising louder and louder as Chasca felt a wave of divine energy flow through her body. Rumi's white robes ran dark red with the blood of the woman who he loved more than life itself, and it was only fitting that Chasca bestowed a part of herself upon him as he exited the mortal realm.

"On your knees, warma," Tullu commanded. "You will now be purified in the Blood."

Chasca stepped away from the altar and knelt at Tullu's feet. A holy man approached and handed the Inca Grandmaster a large bucket, and Tullu accepted it with a nod. He lifted the container into the air as the chanters bellowed even louder now, mixing their voices with the beat of small drums that hung from their necks. The hundreds of other members of the Blooded order then joined in the chants, and the night sky echoed with a deafening and synchronized howl of voices and drums.

The eagles screeched overhead and cawed with intensified energy. Tens turned into hundreds. Hundreds turned into thousands. The swarm of eagles became so large that it blocked out any small degree of illumination provided by the moon.

Tullu closed his eyes for a moment and raised his head to the sky in homage to the gods. Acalan and Cusi did the same. When Tullu's eyes opened, he turned the bucket down towards Chasca, who still knelt at his feet. Full to the brim with goat's blood, the bucket emptied upon Chasca's head and body, enveloping her in a thick, crimson coating. She gasped for air as the blood ran down her face, but she found her breath as quickly as she lost it.

"Rise now! Rise now, child of the Blood!" Tullu ordered, prompting the blood covered Chasca to ascend to her feet. "Rise and be seen! Rise and be heard! For you are now Blooded, from this day until your last!"

All at once, the chants and drums ceased and were replaced by a mighty and thunderous roar from the Blooded. They stomped their feet and yelled so loud, the residents of Cuzco could hear them all the way from the bottom of the mountain...or so the legend states.

Chasca swallowed the pain of losing Rumi and was reborn into something more than flesh and blood. She stood resolute in the face of her new existence, ready to cease the day and enact justice upon those who would threaten her lands and her people.

On the highest peak of the mountain, surrounded by her new family, Chasca smiled through the goat's blood that still coated her from head to foot and made her unrecognizable. Acalan, Tullu, and her mother, Cusi all glared at Chasca with approval, accepting her with open arms into the order.

"You must now travel alone to the High Temple of the Apus," Cusi informed her daughter, leaning in closer as the others still shouted and roared. "It is a week's journey that will test your bravery, your skills, and your resolve in the face of danger. Upon your return from this pilgrimage, we will go to Cuzco and release your father and our people from the shackles that bind them."

Chasca nodded at her mother in acknowledgment of this command. The lights of Cuzco shone brightly from the distant valley below as the young Inca fixed her gaze upon the city where her father was being held hostage by the Spanish invaders. The young Inca, now remade in the Blood, pursed her lips together and readied her sword arm.

There would be no peace with these devils.

No negotiation.

Only blood.

Only death.

The fires of war beckoned, and the Blooded would answer the call.

Volume III, Part IV
The Scribe and the Warrior

"Get down there, boy! Scrub harder!"

A thick leather whip wielded by a burly, foul-smelling Spanish guard cracked upon Chimalli's back, tensing his body and causing a painful expression to cover his face. The whip dug into the Aztec boy's flesh and left a bloody imprint from his right shoulder down to the left side of his lower back.

Chimalli tried to release his mind from the pain, but the deep cuts from the lashings that now stacked atop each other and turned his back into a bloody mess were impossible to ignore.

As Chimalli continued to scrub the dirt and grime from the floor of his prison cell in the city of Veracruz, his mind drifted to thoughts of Kelia. He hadn't seen her for many months since they were separated at the port and she was stowed away on a slave ship headed for Cuba. For all he knew, she could be dead somewhere or enthralled to a pig-headed Spanish lord.

And then there was Ohtli...poor child. He would never know the love of his family and his people. Chimalli only hoped the boy wasn't ill-treated in the hands of that psychopath, Francisco Pizarro, but deep in his mind, he knew this was unlikely. Pizarro's hatred of the Aztecs, of Rodrigo and Chimalli, ran too deep for him to treat Rodrigo's child with anything less than the worst possible disdain.

Instead of allowing his mind to escape, these memories and fears only proved to dampen Chimalli's resolve further, so he welcomed the next whip (somewhat) that came down upon his back and removed his thoughts from Kelia and Ohtli.

"Holy mother of Jesus, Gonzalez, do you ever bathe?" a Spanish voice from the prison cell next to Chimalli's rang out towards the guard with the whip. "You smell like the dogs."

Gonzalez, the half-wit guard on a serious power trip that used his authority to treat the prisoners in whatever manner he pleased, turned his attention towards the man who just insulted him and brought his whip down hard upon the metal bars. The inmate in the cell removed his hands out of the way just before the lash could connect with them.

"Too slow, big boy," the prisoner proclaimed with a cocky demeanor while Gonzalez charged around to enter his cell.

"Gonzalez, time to lock up! Let's go!" the voice of the commanding officer on duty echoed through the cell block.

The fat, ugly Spaniard stopped at his superior's command just before his key could unlock the insubordinate prisoner's cell. Gonzalez slammed Chimalli's cell door and stormed off, clearly angered by his inability to enact his version of justice upon the other inmate.

"Better luck, next time, el gordo!" the Spanish prisoner called out to the guard once more in defiance.

As the metal door to the outer section of the prison slammed shut for the night, silence filled the air, at least for a moment.

"You have to start standing up for yourself, little guy," said the inmate, a confident-looking Spaniard in his late forties with medium height and build. The man's thick, black beard covered most of his face, and the long, messy hair atop his head appeared strown about like an overgrown garden of weeds. He looked like he hadn't washed himself in many moons, and knowing how the prisoners here were treated, Chimalli expected this to be so.

Chimalli curled into a ball on the floor of his new cell, where he had just been transferred after months of isolation from the other prisoners. The light from a few torches outside the cells provided the only illumination along the entire block, which was otherwise shrouded in darkness.

"Courage, how you find?" Chimalli finally mustered in the Spanish language, struggling his way through the few words he had learned from Rodrigo. Chimalli's knowledge of the language was quite impressive considering his age and lack of consistent exposure to it.

"Courage?" the prisoner questioned with a confused expression. "I do not see it as so. Merely defiance. So they hit me if I mouth off to them? So what? Pain is simply a form of weakness, planted by God to test us. I revel in the pain. It makes me feel closer to Him, like I'm alive and He still has a purpose for me. It's when the pain stops...the feeling stops... that I will begin to worry."

"I wish confidence for me," Chimalli replied, hanging his young head in sadness and trying to hold the conversation in Spanish. He picked himself off the floor with a grimace at the pain of his wounds. "What is name?"

"Ahh, I thought you'd never ask!" the strangely energetic and possibly insane Spaniard exclaimed as he jumped on top of his bed to display a lighthearted sense of self-importance that was as imaginary as the audience he looked down upon. "I am Bernardino de Sahagun, legendary poet and author of the greatest manuscript that has ever been or will ever be! You may simply call me Sahagun, though, if it pleases you."

"Sahagun," Chimalli repeated. "I am Chimalli. Umm, what is author?"

"Writer, you could also say."

"Writer? What you write?"

Sahagun perked up once more at Chimalli's question. "I never thought you'd ask that either!" The spritely inmate, who looked like a wild cave man with a severe case of the crazies, hopped down from his bed and proceeded to pull out a large stack of papers and an ink quill.

"This, my very young friend, is my masterpiece, my life's work, my Magnum Opus, one might say. This..." he paused for dramatic effect as he held the papers into the air, "is the Florentine Codex."

Sahagun's words, even the ones Chimalli could understand, meant nothing to the young boy, but he saw the passion on the Spaniard's face as Sahagun grinned from ear to ear with pride.

"One of the guards is a friend of mine," Sahagun continued while pacing around his cell. "We fought next to each other during our time in the army. He slips me paper and ink so I can continue my work."

"You soldier?" Chimalli asked as his attitude towards the Spaniard became cautious. "You kill my people?"

Sahagun ceased his incessant strides back and forth around his cell, and his energetic demeanor transformed into a serious and stoic one. He put down his manuscript and turned to face the young Aztec boy, placing his hands on the bars between the two cells. "I was," he mustered, "a soldier that is. I fought at Cholula three years ago. I watched as Cortes ordered the execution of the entire city, all the men and women and the babies too…all gathered in the square like sacrificial lambs."

Chimalli remained silent as many of the words spoken by Sahagun about the events at Cholula were the same ones he had heard from Rodrigo. Chimalli knew that was a dark day in the history of the Aztec people, trumped only by the defeat at Otumba and the fall of Tenochtitlan.

"There was another Spaniard there at Cholula that caught my eye, a conquistador like me…only younger and lower rank," Sahagun continued, utilizing the gift of the gab that he possessed. "El Cid, they called him, descendant of a great Spanish war hero many centuries ago and son of one of Cortes's lieutenants. Cortes had a strange infatuation with making the boy join in the slaughter, but he refused. Got himself locked up at the top of the pyramid."

"El Cid," Chimalli said with a chuckle as he hadn't heard that name in quite some time. "El Cid my sister's…umm… husband. Rodrigo Diaz."

Sahagun emitted an elated smile, clearly impressed by the boy's knowledge. "That's correct, my little friend. You must have really known him. And he became your sister's husband, you say?"

"Yes, in Tenochtitlan. Great warrior. Great man."

"Fascinating." Sahagun's gaze veered off as he entered into deep thought. "I shall make sure to include this in the codex. You might just prove to be a valuable resource for my work. The world will need to hear your story."

"Ok, old man. What you want know?"

Sahagun grabbed his stack of papers and his ink quill once more as he sat on the bare cot in the corner of his cell. "Tell me something interesting that you've seen, that you've done, that you've –"

"I kill Spanish leader," Chimalli interrupted.

"Spanish leader?" Sahagun questioned with a grin. "Which Spanish leader?"

"Uhh, Cortes."

"You killed Hernan Cortes?!"

Chimalli nodded.

Sahagun burst out in laughter and rose to his feet once more to address Chimalli's seemingly outlandish claim. "You lie boy! Cortes was killed by a great warrior!"

Chimalli, still in pain from his wounds, stepped back to the center of his cell and flexed both arms to show off his muscles, which were practically non-existent since he was only thirteen. "Me, great warrior."

"No!" Sahagun shouted in a lighthearted fashion while still laughing hysterically. "No! No! No! It's not possible!"

Chimalli lowered his arms and shrugged his shoulders.

"If you killed him, then how did he die?"

"Stab. Through heart. My spear."

"And where did this happen?"

"Tenochtitlan, in city square by pyramid."

"And Pizarro, his nephew?"

Chimalli frowned at the sound of Pizarro's name. "He try kill me and Rodrigo. Rodrigo, umm, how you say, throw knife in leg. Peezaro run like coward."

Sahagun continued to listen with pure ecstasy plastered across his face. He could see there was no lie in the boy's eyes. The Spaniard had heard countless lies from people of all cultures, mainly his own, but this was not one. He knew in his heart that Chimalli spoke the truth.

Sahagun dipped his feathered quill in a small bowl of ink and began recording Chimalli's words on the parchment. The two prisoners of different ages and different backgrounds stayed up into the early morning hours sharing stories with each other. Sahagun was more interested in hearing Chimalli's tales than he was in narrating his own, but he did manage to inform the boy that he was imprisoned by Cortes after the massacre at Cholula. He and a few other conquistadors had refused to march with the army to Tenochtitlan after what they'd witnessed, and Cortes sent them back to Veracruz and locked them up for insubordination. Cortes threatened to hang them for treason, but after the Spanish leader's death, Sahagun and the others became forgotten men.

The days turned into weeks, weeks into months, months into years. The lashings were dealt less frequently and eventually stopped altogether as most of the tougher guards were transferred to the city watch to keep order within the growing sectors of Veracruz, which had become a Spanish stronghold and burgeoning hub for all trade into and out of the region.

Each passing moment between Chimalli and Sahagun proved to be a fruitful one over the next ten years. Chimalli informed the aging scribe all about the glamorous and horrific things he had witnessed during his time in Tenochtitlan and after its fall as well. Sahagun had been hidden away from the world since the events at Cholula, so his firsthand experience was severely lacking. He relied on the tales of others, especially Chimalli, to aid him in filling the pages of the codex.

When the young Aztec and the old Spaniard weren't working their minds, they were training their bodies to fight. Chimalli developed an impressive muscular frame as he progressed into his late adolescent years, and Sahagun's build was nothing to scoff over, especially for a man now well into his fifties. It also helped that Sahagun's friend within the prison staff often slipped them extra rations and essential items like hygiene kits and toilet paper, allowing the two prisoners to avoid malnutrition and squalor.

"As foul smelling as this is," Chimalli, now a young man of twenty-four years, stated in Spanish as he hauled a large bucket of fish off a Spanish trading ship and loaded it onto a horse-drawn cart, "I actually prefer it to the stench of the prison." Chimalli's knowledge of the Spanish language had been all but perfected over the years.

"It's only been a couple months since we were assigned to the docks," Sahagun replied with a chuckle, stowing his own bucket of fish next to Chimalli's. "Just wait until we've been doing this for a few years. We'll be begging for reassignment to the gardens or something a little less pungent on the nostrils."

"Speak for yourself, old man. There's nothing like being here, surrounded by the open air and the cool breeze rushing across the top of the water. If I die before you, unlikely I know, then commit my body to the sea. Don't throw me in some hole in the ground."

"I'll note your request," Sahagun jested as they walked back to the ship to retrieve more fish containers, "but as you said, very unlikely. If I have to smell another bucket of this shit, I might just die right here."

Chimalli, still wearing the rags of a prisoner but bulging out of it with arms and chest like an Olympian, jerked his head around abruptly to glare at Sahagun, who was also dressed in a tattered tunic but sported a more toned frame rather than a muscular one.

"When did this happen?" Chimalli asked with light-hearted confusion.

"When did what happen?"

"When did *I* become the optimist? What happened to the man whose spirit never dampens?"

Sahagun thought long and hard about Chimalli's claim. "My God, little one…err, big one," he said, restating his description of the Aztec's size. "You're right! What have these blasted fish done to me?! I've become a dreaded complainer!"

Chimalli bellowed with laughter at Sahagun's epiphany before remembering his status as a slave.

"Best not to show much emotion," the Aztec proclaimed, stifling his cheerful demeanor. "Actually, probably best not to be seen together at all. The guards would love the opportunity to jam a musket stock into your gut for laughing with a savage."

"Or yours for laughing with a traitor," Sahagun replied with one final smile.

"Indeed, my pale-skinned friend. Indeed."

As the two men reached the plank of the ship, they were halted by their supervisor, a crass Spanish lieutenant responsible for maintaining the work efforts and discipline of all prisoners at the dock.

"You two, inmates!" he shouted at Chimalli and Sahagun as saliva slung from his mouth. The officer had only been in charge for a few days, so he still didn't know their names… not that he would use them anyways even if he knew. "Get your asses over to Dock C. We've got a boat coming in from

Havana and we need all available hands to unload it. Move it! Now!"

The Spanish officer's tone was forced and comical, like he was overcompensating for his lack of actual leadership skills.

Chimalli suppressed a grin and turned away from the lieutenant, wiping the man's spit from his cheek. Sahagun followed behind while three young soldiers with muskets escorted them to their destination. The prisoners, who felt more like slaves with each passing day, were used to having multiple sets of prying eyes on them, especially when they were outside the confines of their cells.

Chimalli and Sahagun, along with their escort of guards, marched across the harbor towards the incoming ship, which was larger than many villages in the Aztec and Mayan worlds.

"That floating city looks familiar," said Chimalli, only half-joking about his description of the ship. The name *Hercules* was carved into the side of the wooden hull. "I think I saw it once when I was a boy."

"On the day you arrived here in Veracruz?" Sahagun asked.

"Yes, unless my eyes deceive me, this is a slave ship. The same one that took Kelia to the land surrounded by water."

"So we're offloading slaves? Wonderful. I'd rather smell the fish buckets. God would never sanction such barbarism as owning another human."

"Shut up! No talking, scum!" one of the conquistadors, a smooth-faced and likely low-ranking young man, yelled as he thrust his musket barrel into Sahagun's back, causing the old Spaniard to wince and stumble.

Sahagun regained his balance and glanced at Chimalli with an annoyed expression on his face, but he chose to remain quiet and not escalate the situation further. He knew they could overpower the inexperienced Spaniards if they wanted to, but the harbor was crawling with more guards. The satisfaction of killing a few conquistadors fresh out of the training yards would be overshadowed by their inevitable demise, and Chimalli and Sahagun certainly didn't want this chapter of their lives to be the last.

"Onto the pier! Now!" ordered the young guard, who felt the need to assert his dominance by giving the prisoners basic commands that they already knew to do.

"Yes, sir!" shouted Sahagun in a sarcastically elevated tone. The old Spanish scribe was likely around thirty-five to forty years older than this hot-headed prison guard and his two equally youthful cronies, and taking orders from a boy felt a bit strange to him. Most of the other Spanish soldiers were bearded men, or at least something that resembled men in appearance, if not in their actions.

As the large ship nestled into the port and the dock hands roped it onto the support studs on the pier, Chimalli and Sahagun noticed something a bit odd about the vessel, namely the people on it, or lack thereof. While they couldn't see over the deck due to the ship's size, the boat was close enough now that the shouting of a captain and the commotion of busy crewmembers should have been distinct.

But it wasn't.

No sounds emitted from the ship at all.

Other than the ongoing bustle of the other docks in the distance and the seagulls bellowing their melodic tunes, the air around the ship was eerily still.

The trio of young Spanish guards, who also sensed the strange silence, perked up when the ramp that was supposed to connect the ship to the dock was not immediately extended.

"Lower the ramp, ship mates!" yelled the conquistador who had struck Sahagun in the back.

Silence. Only seagulls.

"Lower it now! Do I have to get the comman—"

The guard's words were interrupted by the squeaking sounds of the wooden ramp being slowly lowered down on its hinges, though there was no audible confirmation from the crew.

Just as the ramp impacted the surface of the pier with a thud, a Spaniard emerged from behind the railing of the ship. The ship mate was sweating profusely and looked noticeably shaken, as was his voice when he spoke.

"C-come, gentlemen," the *Hercules* crew member beckoned as he ushered the guards and prisoners up the ramp. The slaves are...umm... ready. Ready to be offloaded. Come."

"Move!" the Spanish escort barked at Chimalli and Sahagun, prodding them up the ramp with his musket.

When Chimalli's feet creaked across the ramp's wooden surface, an instant feeling of uneasiness came over him. He didn't know whether to feel elation or fear, but in his heart, he knew that something was amiss. Something in the air wasn't right about this ship.

The prisoners, both wide eyed and ready, stepped foot onto the deck of the *Hercules*, followed closely by the guards. Not a soul was in sight other than the sweating man that greeted them at the ramp.

"Where is the rest of the crew?" questioned the young conquistador, raising his musket in alarm. "Where are the slaves?"

The crew member shuffled nervously in his stance before responding to the guard. "I'm sorry, amigos, I have a family."

At the conclusion of the man's sentence, a small blade soared through the air and connected with the young conquistador's neck, piercing his windpipe and causing his eyes to widen in pain. As he slumped to the deck of the ship, the other guards were ambushed before they could cry for help or fire off their muskets. A group of hidden natives, who appeared to be the slaves from the ship, emerged from behind various boxes and barrels and pounced upon the guards with relentless force, slitting their throats and spilling their blood on the deck.

Chimalli and Sahagun froze in their stances while the carnage ensued around them. They had no way of knowing the slaves' intentions or if they planned to slay the prisoners as well. Sahagun was, after all, as white as the guards who they had just slaughtered.

Out of the chaos, which only lasted for mere seconds, a gorgeous, mesmerizing young native woman with long black hair stepped forward and caught Chimalli's wondering eyes. Despite her ragged clothes, the beauty and raw seductiveness of her face and frame swallowed the energy around the ship's deck.

"Woah, woah, easy now," Sahagun pleaded with the woman in Nahuatl, presuming her to be the leader of the revolt. "We're not with these men. We were their prisoners, sent only to do their bidding."

"Relax, old man," the young woman replied, her voice as captivating as her appearance. "You're not our enemy. We're here to rescue a b–uhh...man named Chimalli. Do you know a young Aztec with this name?"

Sahagun stood in silence once more as his lips formed into a wide grin and his thick mustache curled up around them. Chimalli brushed past the giggling Spaniard, who gladly moved out of his young friend's way. The muscular Aztec, whose heart seemingly pounded out of his chest, presented himself before the native woman who appeared to be around the same age as him.

Chimalli swallowed anxiously and mustered a response. "Kelia?"

Volume III, Part V
Prison Break

"Chimalli?!" Kelia asked, her face beaming with excitement at the sight of the man who she hadn't seen in almost ten years since he was a boy. "Is that really you?"

"I could ask you the same question, ikniutli!" Chimalli replied. The two Aztecs leaned in to embrace, but both moved their heads to the same side at the same time, causing their lips to draw close to each other in an awkwardly romantic exchange. "You're a woman now."

Kelia maintained her grasp on Chimalli's waist while drawing her top half back to get a better look at him. "And you're certainly a man now," she proclaimed as she ran her fingers slowly down the curve of his large bicep. The two Aztecs grinned from ear to ear at one another.

Sahagun raised his eyebrows as he and several of the other slaves from the ship stared at their prolonged embrace and giddy dispositions. Chimalli and Kelia almost seemed like they forgot they were being watched by around twenty other sets of eyes. Neither of them appeared to care though, only existing in their bubble of laughter and light touching like a couple of smitten lovers. It was certainly a side of Chimalli that Sahagun had never seen, and based on the stunned reactions from Kelia's entourage, it was a side of her that they had never seen either.

Just as Sahagun (yes, that's me for anyone who hasn't been keeping up) prepared to step in and interrupt the mushy reunion of old friends that looked like it might be needing a private room to continue any further, one of the other slaves caught his eye and caused him to forget all about the young, inexperienced grovelers that were currently sucking all the energy from the deck of the *Hercules*. Standing before the only Spaniard left alive on the ship, other than the terrified Spanish crewman who was only spared so he could operate the ship, was an older Aztec woman of unrivaled beauty. She appeared to Sahagun like a golden-brown goddess with flowing black locks that extended down her back all the way to her rear end (which was also sculpted in the image of the gods). Even more mesmerizing than her appearance was the woman's charm, her energy, the way she carried herself with grace and elegance. And this was all before she even made a move or a sound. She hadn't even hardly looked at Sahagun yet, but it mattered not. He knew perfection when he saw it.

Slicking his messy hair back behind his ears, the Spaniard stepped forward to address this goddess that sprouted from the sea like the daughter of Poseidon. "Well, hello th–"

Before he could finish his sentence, the woman pulled a blade from beneath the cloth that covered her breasts and pressed it to Sahagun's throat while pinning him to the railing of the ship. "Back white devil!" she shouted. Her display of dominance only served to heighten Sahagun's interest in her. He thought that if there was ever a blade to be welcomed into his throat to end his life, it would be wielded by a woman like this. A caramel complected princess with the beauty of a siren and the strength of a lion.

Love had never entered Sahagun's heart up to that moment, but standing there on the deck of a Spanish ship, surrounded by dead bodies, smiling at this slave woman with a knife at his throat, coughing at the force she was using on his windpipe, knowing that there would never exist a maiden more fair, love never again left the heart of the aging Spaniard.

"Erandi!" Kelia hollered, finally snapping out of her trance that Chimalli had put her under. "Put the knife down. This one will not die today, at least not from our blades."

Erandi slowly lowered her blade and released some of the tension on Sahagun, allowing him to pull himself off the rail. Her adherence to the words of her much younger counterpart, who lacked decades of experience in comparison, signified Kelia's high level of respect from her peers.

"How have you all come to be here?" Chimalli questioned as he paced around and addressed the entirety of the ship's remaining inhabitants. "How did you escape?"

The slaves who spoke Nahuatl and understood Chimalli's words, which not all of them did, gestured in the direction of Kelia and Erandi.

"Them," another slave woman replied while pointing at the two Aztec women. "They saved us."

Kelia chuckled as she glanced up towards an eagle flying overhead in the bright, clear sky. "We couldn't have done it without the help of our feathered friend, who I'm fairly certain has followed us all the way from Havana. At least I think he's the same one. Brought me a key to the armory at the Governor's mansion, like it was meant to be. So I split the Governor's head into two halves and we stowed away on this ship. Didn't take long to free the rest of the slaves and kill the guards. And now here we are."

"Just like that?" Sahagun asked with an impressed smile at Erandi.

"Just like that," Erandi replied, but with an annoyed frown towards the Spaniard's hungry eyes.

"We have to get out of here, Chimalli," Kelia continued. "We make for Inca lands in the south. There is nothing left for us here."

"Agreed, let's go," Chimalli stated.

"Wait!" Sahagun suddenly shouted before jolting to attention. "You must leave without me, my dark-skinned brothers and sisters. I must return to the prison and retrieve my codex. It is my life's work and the only reason God has not forsaken me."

"Fine, safe travels," Erandi said dismissively while pacing away from Sahagun.

"No, I'm not leaving without him," Chimalli declared. "I owe my life to this man. He has been my greatest friend for many years."

"But there's no time!" Erandi yelled. "We must go now!"

"She's right," said Kelia. "It won't be long before this pier is swarming with more Spaniards wondering why this ship hasn't been unloaded with slaves. We cannot wait."

"I understand," Chimalli replied reluctantly. "But if that's the case, you must sail without me. I can't leave him to die here."

Kelia paced in anxious thought across the ship's deck, pondering her response. "Ok," she finally said, locking her fingers inside Chimalli's. "If you two must go back, then I go with you. I'm not losing you again."

"Gods preserve us," proclaimed Erandi while rolling her eyes.

"Erandi, can you prepare the ship for departure?" Kelia requested. "If we're not back by nightfall, leave with the others."

"If you think I'm letting you run off by yourself with these strange men, conetl, you better think again. If you go, I go too."

"So it's settled," Kelia said as the three Aztecs and one Spaniard stood around each other in a circle. "We go together, but we must hurry." The others nodded in agreement, and Kelia broke away to speak with the other slaves about readying the ship.

"I've instructed the others to leave if we're not back by sunset," Kelia informed the group upon returning. "There's an abandoned village just south of here. Should we not make it back to the ship tonight, they're to wait for us for three days outside that village."

"And if we're not there in three days?" Chimalli asked.

"If not, then this suicide mission probably didn't work and we're all dead anyways," Kelia replied with a shrug.

"Just how do you plan on getting in there, pinotl?" Erandi asked Sahagun in a scolding manner. "It's a prison, right? You think they're just going to let you scroll in and scroll out?"

Sahagun pondered the Aztec woman's words for a moment while stroking his thick beard. Erandi was right, as always.

"Don't you worry about that, my honey blossom," he responded with a wide grin plastered across his face. "I've got that covered."

Erandi sank her hands into her face in frustration. "May the gods deliver me from this little hairy white man," she declared to Kelia, who chuckled alongside Chimalli at their older friends' exchange. "I can't tell if he's just patronizing me or if he actually thinks I would ever be his…honey blossom, whatever that means."

"Give it some time, ketsaltik," Sahagun replied, shuffling his fingers through the hairs on his face. "The beard will grow on you. And so will I."

Erandi once more pulled her knife and held it towards Sahagun. "If I see anything growing over there, I'll cut it off." She pointed the blade downwards below his waist.

Kelia struggled to hold back her laughter as she lowered Erandi's arm and tried to turn the conversation back to a serious one.

"Enough, you two," she said. "There will be plenty of time to squash this sexual tension later after we set sail." Kelia's comment produced a famous Erandi eyeroll along with a disgusted grumble.

"I would very much like to know what this plan of yours is," intervened Chimalli, who had also been fighting back laughter at the sight of Sahagun's sheepish grin.

"As would I," declared Kelia.

Sahagun shuffled his feet and gazed at his Aztec companions as if they weren't going to approve of his plan. "You three are going to be my prisoners, and I'm going to dress myself in the least bloody set of Spanish armor I can find on one of these lovely corpses we have scattered around here."

"No, no way, it'll never work," proclaimed Chimalli. "Look at that ragged beard. You'll never pass for a conquistador. You also smell like the dogs."

"Easy now, my young friend, you'll embarrass me in front of my bride-to-be," Sahagun responded with a smile that prompted yet another sneer of derision from Erandi. "Do you have a better plan, hmm? Do any of you have a better plan?"

Chimalli, Kelia, and Erandi all glanced at each other, but no one could produce a more sensible idea.

Through his grin that seemed like it never faded, Sahagun chuckled with a single "Ha!", followed by, "Let's get a dead guy naked!"

Without any further resistance, the Aztecs accepted the Spaniard's plan and prepared themselves to carry it out. Sahagun undressed one of the guards and strapped on his armor while Chimalli, Kelia, and Erandi all hid daggers beneath their tattered slave rags.

Once they made all preparations, the four-headed ensemble hastened down the ship's ramp and off the pier towards the inner city of Veracruz. They were able to slip past several patrols unnoticed thanks to Sahagun's fake outbursts and overtly racist comments towards his "savage, monkey-fucking prisoners" whenever they would pass by other guards. These comments were often followed by a slight giggle from Sahagun (and Chimalli) once they got out of earshot of the guards.

"You know I didn't mean all that stuff about you guys copulating with the forest creatures, right?" Sahagun added with a smirk as the foursome slipped into a back alleyway just outside the confines of the harbor.

The three Aztecs all glared at him with the same annoyed expression.

"I think you were enjoying that a little too much," Kelia replied lightheartedly.

"And did you have to shove your musket into my back so hard?" Chimalli added.

"I had to be convincing," Sahagun defended himself with a shrug. "It was necessary boy, I assure you."

"Sure didn't feel necessary," Chimalli said with a grimace, holding the spot on his back where Sahagun had struck him with his musket stock. "I think you had been waiting to do that all these years."

"Perhaps," Sahagun admitted as he chuckled and pretended to thrust his weapon towards Chimalli. "Perhaps we will never know."

"Which way from here?" Erandi interrupted, changing the subject as the group used the cover of the narrow alleys to move swiftly.

"We take the next left, then through the market and around the barracks," Chimalli replied. "The prison is just a short walk from there."

The three Aztecs and their Spanish "master" completed the rest of the journey in relative silence, weaving in and out of any patrols they came across. Veracruz had grown from a small outpost to a loud, teeming stronghold of trade and military coordination in the ten years since Chimalli and Sahagun had been imprisoned. Europeans of various nationalities and skills, including soldiers and civilians alike, now packed into the city in hordes. The dense crowds in the street made inconspicuous movement easy, as the sight of Spanish soldiers leading indigenous slaves was no rare occurrence.

"We're here," Sahagun declared as they approached the gates of the prison.

"Great, what's the plan, now?" Erandi scoffed. "Just walk right past the guards? I count seven of them, and those are just the ones we can see."

"Faith, little dove, faith," Sahagun commented. "This is all part of the plan." In Sahagun's mind, he knew he was making everything up by the minute, but he maintained his false confidence in front of Erandi and the others. Chimalli, however, could see straight through his so-called "plan."

"Keep your blades ready, ladies," Chimalli said. "I have a feeling we're going to need them very soon."

"You sure could use some faith too, you little fairy," Sahagun jested with Chimalli, prompting a light shove from his young Aztec friend. "Alright, let's go."

The band of friends and reluctant acquaintances stepped forward into the clearing outside the prison. The Aztecs held their hands behind their backs, pretending to be bound at the wrists while Sahagun marched behind them and prodded them forward.

"Halt!" one of the guards, a sergeant, shouted as they approached. "State your business, soldier."

"I'm here on the orders of Warden Santiago," Sahagun stated while attempting to hide his face behind the Aztecs so the guards wouldn't recognize him. "The two female prisoners are to be reassigned to this station, and the male is already an inmate here."

"Females?" the guard questioned. "This is not the female quarters, soldier. Your orders are mistaken. The women should be admitted to the building around the block. That way."

Sahagun shuffled in his stance while trying to maintain his composure. "They already came from the female quarters, sir. These broads were too tough for the other women. Spitters and biters, these ones. My orders were to find them a place amongst the male quarters."

"Well I haven't heard anything about these orders. I'll have to check with my–" the guard's words tailed off as his tone became suspicious. "Hold a moment, why are you alone with three prisoners, soldier? Prisoner escort is to consist of no less than one guard per inmate. Where are your comrades?"

"Uhh, they umm," Sahagun stumbled through his words, struggling to find a way out of the predicament. Chimalli, Kelia, and Erandi also felt the tension in the air and braced themselves for a fight, one in which they would be heavily outnumbered and outgunned. "They were called away on urgent duty just before we arrived. We were so close to the prison gates when they left, I assumed it would be a non-issue."

"You assume too much," the Spanish sergeant countered. "Come closer. Do I recognize you from somewhere?"

"I, uhh, have been a guard at the women's facility for a couple years," said Sahagun shakily.

"Do they not make you shave that filth on your face over there?" the guard questioned further. "You look like a wet dog."

"Ha!" Sahagun chuckled a bit too hard.

The guard laughed back while maintaining his elevated level of suspicion. He and Sahagun exchanged a series of uncomfortable and overly dramatic laughs as the other guards joined in the outburst.

"No, no," the guard interjected and abruptly ceased his laughter, transforming his lighthearted expression to a humorless and serious one. The others stopped laughing as well, and Sahagun knew his cover was blown. "Not the women's prison. I've seen you here, in this one, but never in that armor."

Sahagun and the prison guard both pursed their lips and scowled at the other in a silent stare down. The brief stillness was deafening, and all parties held their breath for the chaos that was mere moments from erupting.

The sergeant thrust his hand across his body to reach for his sword, but Kelia's lightning-fast reaction beat him on the draw. She removed a small throwing knife from inside her waist cloth and slung it towards the guard in one clean motion. The blade penetrated through the man's hand before he could unsheathe his weapon, causing him to cry out in pain.

The other guards, who were behind the writhing sergeant, sprung to action and drew their swords and muskets. Before they could attack, though, Chimalli surged forward and took hold of the sergeant, placing a knife at his throat.

"Stay back! Back, back, back!" Chimalli threatened in Spanish as the guards remained in their defensive stances. Kelia, Erandi, and Sahagun tightly positioned themselves behind Chimalli and his hostage to avoid the line of fire of the Spanish muskets.

"I'll spill this man's blood all over his shiny little suit of armor if anyone takes a single step forward!" Chimalli shouted, strengthening his grip on the wounded sergeant's neck. "Where are the gate keys?!"

No one responded.

"Keys! Now!" Chimalli tightened his hold so hard against the Spaniard's throat that his eyes bulged and his breath began to give out.

"They're in his pocket!" one of the guards finally hollered, pointing at the sergeant and attempting to save him from Chimalli's wrath.

Erandi reached over into the guard's pocket and removed a large set of metal keys. "Which one opens the gate?" she shouted.

"The b-big brass one," the sergeant muttered through Chimalli's death grip.

Erandi cycled through the endless keys on the circular ring until she came to the only brass key she could find.

"This one?! Speak!" she exclaimed as she held it in front of the Spaniard's face.

"Y-yes."

"Move!" shouted Kelia to the other guards as the Aztecs, along with Sahagun and their Spanish captive, paced around to the gate. This forced the guards to pivot with them like a swinging pendulum.

Erandi placed the key inside the hole, and much to the group's relative delight, the gate to the prison swung open. They rushed in quickly, and Chimalli booted the sergeant back towards his companions before closing the fence behind them. The gate locked back into place, stranding the guards outside with no keys.

"Go, go, go!" Chimalli yelled as the Spaniards fired their muskets through the holes of the fence. The group was far enough away, though, that the inaccurate Spanish muskets had little chance of connecting with their targets. "Into the cell block!"

By now, the sound of the gunfire and the shouts of the guards echoed around the complex, drawing many other Spaniards to the commotion. Kelia glanced back to see dozens of other guards closing in around them.

After fumbling with the keys for a moment, Erandi finally found the correct one and unlocked the door to the prison cell block. Chimalli thrust his muscular shoulder into it and burst through with force.

"Hey, stop right n–" a Spaniard on duty in the cell block began to shout before Chimalli caved his head in with a lethal blow that sent him careening into the wall.

"This is mine," Sahagun stated to Erandi as they made their way over to the cells. "Please find the key with haste, little bird. I suspect our lives depend on it."

Chimalli and Kelia worked together to overturn a large crate to bar the door as the Spanish guards outside shouted and kicked at it.

"It's only a matter of time before they bring up someone with another set of keys!" Chimalli shouted, his shoulder pressed against the door with all his strength. "I won't be able to hold them all back!"

Sahagun sprinted to the rear door on the other side of the cell block, but as he veered off to find something to barricade it with, two musket-wielding guards rushed through and readied their weapons to fire.

"Erandi! Look out!" Kelia yelled at her friend as the guards both raised their weapons towards the Aztec woman who was the first to enter their vision.

Erandi, who had just found the correct key to Sahagun's cell, stared blankly at the guards and their guns. Exposed and powerless to stop the musket balls from soaring through the air at her, she awaited her fate in a fleeting moment of shock.

As the guards both pressed their fingers against the triggers to kill Erandi, a sudden and aggressive flurry of attacks from Sahagun thwarted their efforts. Erandi, Kelia, and Chimalli watched in amazement as Sahagun used his musket to blow a hole in the stomach of one of the guards before slamming his rifle stock into the head of the other with graceful and dominant precision. The grizzly Spaniard fought like a man half his age, moving his body and twisting up his opponents with deadly effect.

Once the guards were thoroughly dispatched and Sahagun barred the rear door, he paced into the cell next to Erandi that she had just opened. The normally humorous and smiling Spaniard stared at her with the most serious expression he had used in many years before muttering a single phrase. "Nobody points a gun at my woman."

Erandi stood wide eyed and shocked, not disputing Sahagun's words or giving one of her signature eyerolls. She possessed the look of a woman who had just fallen in love without even realizing it.

"Here it is," Sahagun continued, grabbing a stack of papers and ink that were hidden in a secluded cutout underneath his cot. "My two great loves, both existing right here in the same room." His two great loves, of course, were a reference to Erandi and his self-labeled Florentine Codex.

"Fantastic!" Chimalli hollered sarcastically while he and Kelia still held firm at the door. "What do we do now?! There's no way out of here!"

Sahagun stroked his beard in deep thought while pondering their escape plan. Like clockwork and typical of the aging Spaniard, a bright idea once again entered his brain.

"You guys aren't going to like this," he said cryptically as he chuckled and secured his codex in a small pack that he retrieved from the guards' office. "There's a hole in the floor at the back of this facility that leads into a sewage tunnel. They just recently installed it in the last couple of years. Supposedly it's a more sanitary way to remove feces than throwing it into the streets."

"Is there no other way out?" Kelia questioned with a disgusted look on her face.

Sahagun shook his head. "I'm afraid not, young one."

"He's right," added Chimalli reluctantly. "It's either that or stay here and die."

The others grimly accepted Sahagun's idea with unpleasant looks on their faces. The jangling of a key ring resonated outside the door and expedited their plan as the guards prepared to assault the building.

Sahagun laughed heartily and regained his usual merry demeanor.

"Who's ready to get covered in shit and piss?!"

Volume III, Part VI
Pleasure within the Pain

"Look away, little hairy white man."

Erandi strolled in the opposite direction but glanced back at Sahagun with the slightest hint of a smile, still attempting (and failing) to present a guarded demeanor towards the Spaniard.

"I sense much less disdain in your voice, my dove," Sahagun replied with a wide grin that displayed his usual levels of elation while in the presence of his mortal goddess. "Perhaps you are no longer revolted by the sight of me."

"Perhaps," Erandi confirmed, expanding her smile ever so slightly. "But you still don't get to feast your eyes on all this."

After exiting the sewage tunnel on the outskirts of Veracruz, Chimalli, Kelia, Sahagun, and Erandi traveled a safe enough distance to let their guard down before reaching a blissful oasis of trees and flowing water. Now several thousand paces from the city and clearly out of the search area of the Spanish guards, the ensemble settled on the banks of a river that contained the clearest blue water they had ever seen. Even with the stench of feces that still coated their bodies, the majestic view and sounds of nature at its purest were enough to overshadow the filth of the intruding humans.

Kelia and Erandi rounded the corner of a large rock and dense brush that led to a bend in the river. Just before they slipped out of Chimalli and Sahagun's sight, they both began removing their clothes in preparation to bathe.

The two men, looking more like starry-eyed puppies in that moment, stared at the women with a mesmerized glow in their eyes. Despite their differences in age and ethnicity, Chimalli and Sahagun both found a common and tantalizing interest in the seemingly seductive strides of their female counterparts.

The women's tunics both slid down to their waists and exposed their bare backs before they retreated out of view, prompting a synchronized groan from Chimalli and Sahagun.

"I never thought I would be so entranced by a woman covered in human excrement," Chimalli said while removing his own clothes. "There must be something wrong with me."

"I think that's called love, my young friend," replied Sahagun. "I believe I too have been struck by Cupid's arrow. I fear my heart will burst and I won't make it to the ship tomorrow."

"Cupid?"

"Never mind that. Let's talk about your cock for a moment."

"My cock?"

"Yes, yes, your little ding dong, your prick, your pichinku."

Chimalli scoffed. "Stay away from my pichinku, old man."

"Ha! You should be so lucky to have a lover like me. Unfortunately for you, my talents are reserved only for the señoritas, the ladies."

"Then why are you asking about my..."

"Try to keep up, idiota. I've known you since you were a little conetl. I know you've never felt the warmth of a woman's embrace."

"I've embraced a woman before," Chimalli retorted.

"The fact you thought I was talking about a hug only strengthens the need for this conversation."

Chimalli possessed an anxious expression on his face and sighed heavily, knowing Sahagun's words to be true. "It's not like that with Kelia and me. We're just friends."

"Wake up stupid!" countered Sahagun. "You're not a little kid anymore, and neither is she. Once you scrub that shit and sweat from underneath your balls, she's going to mount you faster than you can thank your gods for bestowing life's greatest pleasure upon you."

"I do not think—"

"It'll probably happen tonight!"

"Tonight? Really?"

"Trust me, I know the look on a woman's face when she wants you. She practically undressed you with her eyes when she saw you on that ship. And you looked like a love-sick schoolboy."

Chimalli pondered Sahagun's words before abandoning the flimsy veil of "only friends".

"What do I do if she comes after me?" Chimalli questioned nervously. "Tell me how to use my pichinku."

"Easy tiger," Sahagun responded, "you can't just instantly start waving that little worm around. You have to heat up the kiln before you stick in the boar. You understand what I'm saying?"

"I guess."

"Let me put it to you this way. You want her rain to fall long before you try to enter her chamber. Take your time. Have fun with it. Try not to be nervous. Women love a confident man."

"But I'm not confident. Not in the slightest."

"I know that, upa. You just have to make sure *she* doesn't know that."

Chimalli took a deep breath before responding. "Right. Confident. I can do this."

Sahagun chuckled at his young, inexperienced friend who waded into the river with only one anxious thought on his mind. "You could ask your gods for their help, and I will pray to my God just in case yours aren't listening."

Sahagun, now also stripped naked, splashed into the river alongside Chimalli and washed the filth from his body with the help of the crystal blue waters that turned brown upon receiving the unwanted gift from its visitors. The aging Spaniard continued sharing advice and stories of his own exploits with the young Aztec, who had the build of a mighty warrior but the innocence of a child when it came to matters of women and the proverbial heart.

Meanwhile around the bend of the river and out of sight of the men, Kelia and Erandi also exposed their nude bodies, basking in the warmth of the evening sun and the cold chill of the trickling stream, albeit in a much more delicate manner than the grimy, hairy men.

Erandi chuckled as the two Aztec women moved their hands along their arms and breasts to remove the waste that had accumulated on them in the sewage tunnel. "Do you think those idiots realize they're downstream from us and all this lovely cuitlatl is flowing directly at them?"

Kelia laughed with the older Aztec woman that had been her closest friend over the last ten years. "I imagine they haven't thought about it. Or perhaps they don't care."

"I know the white man doesn't," Erandi replied. "He looks like he hasn't washed in years."

"Don't act like you're not intrigued by his advances," commented Kelia. "You forget I've known you for quite some time. And I saw your face when he saved your life at the prison."

Kelia then changed her voice to imitate Erandi. 'Oh thank you, strange little hairy foreign man. How ever can I repay your kindness?'

Kelia's impression of Erandi forced another scoff and eye roll from the older woman, who quickly changed the subject. "I know why you persist on teasing me about the Spaniard. You do it to take the focus off yourself and your feelings for that boy."

Kelia cowered at Erandi's claims and didn't even attempt to deny them. "Is it that obvious?"

Erandi smiled at the young Aztec, who was now a woman and just as inexperienced as Chimalli. Kelia's adolescence and the few adult years of her life up to that point were spent in the shackles of slavery, and the only sexual experience she had was that which was forced upon her by old, wrinkly men. To Kelia, romance was a foreign concept. She felt its cold sting on her heart for Chimalli, but she had no knowledge of how to act upon it the correct way.

"Such a mighty young woman, brave and resolute, brought to heel by something as trivial as a man," Erandi joked and laughed.

"I cannot stifle my affections, Erandi," Kelia responded with a yearning grumble as she thought about Chimalli bathing nude just around the corner. "I have adored him since we were children, and now," she paused, widening her eyes and expanding her tone for dramatic effect, "he is ALL man."

"Would you even know what to do with that boy, that man?" asked Erandi.

"Well, yes. I would, umm. I would...no, I have no idea," Kelia admitted, usually confident but now hanging her head in romantic anguish. "I've only ever pleasured those who I did not wish to lay with, hollow shells of men that were more akin to beasts."

"A man is the simplest creature that walks this earth, my young friend. Fighting, humping, feasting, drinking. Men think they hold all the power, that they control the world, but they're wrong. They're so wrong. Once you understand the mind of a man, which isn't a difficult task, you begin to hold the power in your hands."

"How do I do that?"

"With that slit between your legs, of course."

"I don't want to *force* Chimalli to fall in love with me just by having sex with him. Besides, sex never led any of those men in Havana to love me, nor would I want it to."

"That was rape, child, not sex. It's important to understand the difference. If Chimalli is a good man, as good as you've always claimed him to be, then sex can be used as a sort of...test, if you will, an assessment of his feelings for you."

"I don't follow your logic," replied Kelia with a confused expression.

"The few minutes right after a man climaxes are the most honest and sincere moments of his life. If he truly loves you, and I don't mean in a lustful, obsessive type of way, you will know it in those moments."

"That must be why the men in Havana always hit me or stormed out or both, right after they...you know."

"Precisely, young one," Erandi confirmed with a nod. "Now you're catching on. My husband, gods cleanse his spirit, was one of the kindest, gentlest men I've ever known. *Especially* after sex."

"You have given me much to think about, Erandi. Thank you."

"Of course. You're a magnificent young woman, and you deserve to be with an equally magnificent young man. And if he's not, I'll snap his cock off myself and throw it in the river."

"What a lovely image," Kelia said as the two women laughed and finished bathing.

"Shall we check on the boys and make sure they haven't withered away without us?" Erandi joked after stepping out of the river and putting on a clean tunic. The pack that Sahagun retrieved on their way out of the prison fortunately contained enough dry clothes for all four of them to change into.

"Ready when you are," Kelia replied, already dressed and eager to meet up with Chimalli.

The two women gathered what few belongings they had and made their way around the large rock on the river bend.

"You know, I always–" Erandi stopped her sentence when she spotted Sahagun, emitting a sensual stare at the Spaniard's toned form. Sahagun had also shaved the thick beard from his face, revealing the skin around his neck, cheeks, and jaw line for the first time in many years.

Kelia, too, was put into a trance upon observing Chimalli, taking in every bit of his nude form that disappeared below the water at his waistline.

Sahagun spotted the two women's prying eyes as he smiled at them while tying up his long hair atop his head. "See, they just couldn't resist," he joked with Chimalli.

"Put those little things away so we can come back over there!" Erandi shouted. She and Kelia kept their gazes fixed around the corner but stayed mostly secluded behind the rock.

"You mean *this* little thing?" probed Sahagun, wading out of the deeper water and exposing his full nakedness. Sahagun's brash gesture prompted the women to giggle like gawking courtesans and scurry back behind the rock.

"Quetzalcoatl save us," Kelia declared to Erandi. "Nobody wants to see that."

"Speak for yourself, young one," Erandi replied with a shrug.

"Erandi!" Kelia countered with a wide grin. "Behave yourself!"

"Oh, I think not. I think the time for behaving ourselves has long passed, for both of us," Erandi asserted with a wink. "That little white man is getting the ride of his life tonight, and you better give that boy something he will never forget."

"Oh my," the embarrassed Kelia said, placing her hands against her face. "I have a feeling we're both in for quite the night."

"Yes we are, my friend. Yes we are."

■■■■■■■■■

Chimalli opened his eyes just as the sun began its ascent over the horizon. Gradually regaining his wits and smiling towards the clear morning sky, he dared not move a single muscle in his body, lest he wake the sleeping Kelia, who rested her head atop his chest and within the grip of his arm.

The cool breeze lightly brushed against Chimalli's young face. He could smell the sweet scent of Kelia's hair that curled up towards his nose. The touch of her bare skin against his own sent an elated shiver up his spine. For the first time in his short twenty-four years of life, Chimalli finally discovered what Sahagun had been talking about all those years when he spoke about the warmth of a woman. To be wrapped inside Kelia's embrace, to run his fingers along the smooth perfection of her skin, it was unlike anything he had ever experienced.

Chimalli leaned in to kiss the young Aztec woman's forehead, and just as his lips contacted her skin, Kelia opened her eyes and raised her head to meet his gaze.

"Perhaps your lips can find another place to rest," Kelia declared with a smile, leaning towards Chimalli's mouth before planting upon him the softest, most stimulating kiss either of them had ever experienced.

"I never want this moment to end," Chimalli asserted when their lips finally parted after several seconds.

"Nor do I," replied Kelia, locking her fingers between Chimalli's and lingering just above the surface of his face. "So let us allow this moment to last an eternity, never fading, never faltering."

"It is an impossibility that my love for you could ever falter, a task even the gods could not accomplish."

"Your love for me?" Kelia asked, her smile widening with each new word that Chimalli spoke. "Are you saying you love me?"

"I am," Chimalli proclaimed. "I have loved you since I laid eyes on you, ever since you told me your name on that boat as we left Tenochtitlan. It was like one chapter had closed and another had opened. Like a flower had wilted, only to be replaced by an even more colorful, more beautiful one. I knew from that moment that our destinies were intwined, that the gods had brought us together for a reason, that we would be together forever, both in life and death."

"Your words are intoxicating, like honey in my ears," Kelia responded as she closed her eyes and soaked in Chimalli's voice. "I too fell in love with you all those years ago, a love that has never waned."

With full hearts and an overwhelming sense of erotism coursing through their veins, the two young Aztecs pressed their lips together once more, moving their hands along the length of each other's bodies. The friends turned lovers laid with each other as passionately as they had the night before. Along with the pleasures of the flesh that each provided the other, Chimalli and Kelia both felt a sense of hope; hope for a kindling romance, hope for true happiness, hope for a brighter future.

After finishing up their morning wake up call, Chimalli and Kelia dressed themselves and discovered that Sahagun and Erandi also had an eventful evening of raucous lovemaking, or at least some version of it. Atop a blanket they had retrieved from Sahagun's pack, both of them sprawled naked across each other on the other side of the river bend. With a wink from Sahagun and a shrug from Erandi upon waking, the four fugitives, still on the run from their Spanish pursuers, laughed and reminisced about a night well spent before setting off towards the coast.

That night on the riverbank would remain in all four of their minds and hearts, for not only was it a turning point in two budding love stories, it was also the last night that Sahagun and the Aztecs would ever spend in the land of the Mexica, the Aztec homeland.

With the Spanish guards from Veracruz still searching for them, the ensemble made their way to the abandoned village the next day to rendezvous with the *Hercules*. Much to their surprise, the ship and its crew were still there, anchored in the bay and awaiting Kelia and Erandi's return.

Now safely aboard the ship that would deliver them to their new lives, the foursome stared blankly from the stern at the Mexica coastline that faded from view for the last time.

Chimalli took Kelia's hand, Sahagun took Erandi's, and Kelia and Erandi locked their grip in the middle to form a chain, an unbreakable link of friends and lovers that could never be broken...not even by death.

Codex Volume IV
❀❀❀
Two Worlds Unite

Volume IV, Part I
Unwelcome Visitors

"There's a foul odor in the air," remarked Chimalli as he paced through the intricately designed dirt paths of the Inca city of Quito.

"Maybe you just need another bath," Sahagun replied, tugging at the strings of the pack on his back that contained his codex pages.

"I'm serious. This place smells like death."

"Apparently anywhere my countrymen go, that stench follows them like a plague."

"Either it follows them or they create it, not sure which is worse," Chimalli commented as he and Sahagun observed several Spanish units patrolling the city. "If I had known you wouldn't be the first ugly white man to step foot in this land, I would have never come here."

Sahagun shrugged. "At least the locals are already used to seeing faces like mine, so they maybe they won't tear mine off and eat it or whatever they do here."

"These people don't eat faces, you idiot."

"Maybe *your* people don't eat faces, but these aren't your people, are they? These are Incas, not Aztecs. Entirely different brand of caramel. Besides, I know *your* people just stick to eating hearts."

"You really are an intolerant bastard," Chimalli half-heartedly joked.

"Oh, so I'm the intolerant one for acknowledging the difference between two cultures that live in two totally different parts of the world?" Sahagun countered. "Yet most anyone else that looks like me can't find the slightest difference between you and them. You're all blood-sucking savages to them."

"Hard to argue with that," Chimalli replied as the two of them continued strolling amongst the dense crowds in the busiest district of Quito.

"Look at this architecture," Sahagun remarked, marveling over the craftmanship of the Inca stone masons. "Truly fascinating, is it not?"

"No more fascinating than Tenochtitlan. Can't say I ever recall you gawking over the Aztec architecture."

"You forget I never laid eyes on Tenochtitlan," retorted Sahagun, "only Cholula, which I admit was quite the sight to see."

"How do I always forget that?" Chimalli questioned. "Cholula is a marvel, for sure, especially the Great Pyramid. But Tenochtitlan...oh I wish you could have seen Tenochtitlan, my friend. There's nothing like it in the world; or *was* nothing like it."

"I think it's ironic that my countrymen have the audacity to place the 'savage' label on Aztecs, Incas, Mayas, basically anyone that looks different. But you can't walk through the streets of our largest cities without stepping in shit, literal shit. It's not perfect here but at least the people take pride in keeping their cities clean. Unlike Europe, which is a cesspool of filth and sickness. There was a plague a couple hundred years ago, some called it the Black Death, wiped out a full quarter of the world's population, at least the world as we knew it back then."

"I fear the sickness brought from your homeland will be the end of us, the end of our way of life," Chimalli proclaimed as an Inca peasant passed them on the street, retching and coughing as he went. "Disease and death are a part of our world now."

"I share your fear," Sahagun confirmed, "and I share the blame, for I once dressed myself in that shiny armor they love to flaunt around."

"Nonsense, old man. It's men like you that give our people a chance. The ones that stand up to tyrants like Hernan Cortes and Francisco Pizarro. You share none of the blame for what has happened to our lands."

Sahagun turned to face Chimalli while still pacing alongside him, nodding in appreciation of the Aztec's words.

"Probably wasn't the best idea to separate from Kelia and Erandi," Chimalli continued. "Both of them speak this Inca Quechua language and neither of us do. I have no idea what the hell anyone is saying."

Sahagun chuckled. "Definitely wasn't our smartest plan."

"In any case, our mission still stands. We've got to find out more about this Blooded order. If the Spanish hate them so much, they must be exactly who we need to find."

"Did you hear that Spanish newsman yelling in the street back there?" Sahagun asked. "A thousand gold coins to anyone with information leading to the location of the Blooded hideout? They must be desperate to get rid of them."

"Yeah, we've got to be careful asking just anyone about them," Chimalli claimed. "Lots of people would jump at the opportunity to turn in a few Blooded sympathizers just for a chance at that gold."

Sahagun nodded in agreement with his younger Aztec counterpart. "Perhaps we should visit the local tavern. Barkeeps usually know all the best gossip."

"What's a tavern?" Chimalli questioned with confusion.

"You know, a bar, la taberna."

Chimalli stood silent and shrugged his shoulders, still not comprehending the Spaniard's terms.

"A place where people go to get drunk and forget about their wives who are riding some other guy while they're away at work or war or wherever," Sahagun explained bluntly.

"Places like that don't exist in our world," Chimalli countered, "at least amongst the Aztecs, and I imagine it's not dissimilar here."

"No bars? My God, no wonder you guys are so serious all the time. Even Jesus turned water to wine."

"I'm not sure who this...Jesus is, but no, there are laws against public drunkenness. When I was a boy in Tenochtitlan, one of the high shaman's assistants continuously indulged in drinking pulque and would wail in the streets all night about how the gods were angry with the people and how our world would soon be at an end. Freaked all the people out with his rants. The first offense he had his head shaved in public and his valuables stripped from his home. The second offense he forfeited his life."

"Sounds like the poor guy was on to something with his predictions," said Sahagun. "I guess someone should have listened to him."

"Perhaps."

"So no bars, what about a brothel?"

"You mean the place where men go to pay for sex from women who pretend to like them?"

"Precisely."

"Are you trying to get us killed by our women?" Chimalli asked, only half-joking. "I've heard Erandi speak multiple times about removing our pichinkus."

"She certainly has a way with words, doesn't she?" Sahagun displayed a facetiously worried expression on his face. "But no, my friend, I think we'll be safe from my love's wandering blade, as we wouldn't be there for pleasures of the flesh. The only person with more information than a barkeeper is a whore. A man will admit to all sorts of things after laying with a woman, even one that's paid for."

Chimalli stopped and pondered Sahagun's plan as the residents of Quito still flooded around them in the busy streets. "Alright, but not a word to the women about this, agreed?"

"I wasn't born yesterday, boy, my God."

Chimalli and Sahagun set off towards the various produce shops in the market to ask the locals about the nearest brothel, hoping this request would be met with less suspicion than inquiring about the Blooded. The information came freely and without much prying from the first business they visited, although they had to decipher the shopkeeper's hand gestures instead of his Quechua words. Much to their surprise (especially Sahagun's), the whorehouses of Quito were prohibited from resting inside the city walls. Such was the way of the Incas, as unbridled sexual proclivities were looked down upon as unclean in their society. Therefore, all brothels, regardless of their level of class, were resigned to the fringes of the city, often enjoying seclusion amongst the nearby forests.

"This is certainly much different than the kitty cat houses back in Spain," Sahagun remarked as he and Chimalli reached the entryway to the closest brothel they could find outside the city.

The adobe walls of the structure were built into the hillside, forming a symbiotic joining of the natural landscape and manmade architecture. The "doorway" was a series of colorful beads that hung down like a curtain, guarded by two brutish looking Incas with large spears.

"Hand over all weapons and sharp objects," one of the guards commanded while motioning to the daggers on their waistbands and displaying a needlessly angry stare at the two potential customers.

Chimalli and Sahagun both handed over the blades they had retrieved from the *Hercules* on their seafaring journey. Once they were thoroughly inspected by the intrusive and aggressive thumpers, they were ushered inside the beaded curtains.

Upon entering the facility, the two men felt like they had entered a new realm altogether, a land of mystery and seduction. The sounds of the forest creatures were replaced by those of sensual pleasures and erotic moaning. The smell of vanilla and cinnamon filled their nostrils and put them into a trance-like state. Chimalli and Sahagun progressed down the long corridor as their vision became clouded and hazy, both struggling to maintain their wits.

"We should not…umm…linger," Chimalli remarked. His head spun in a thousand different directions, and images of his sexual encounters with Kelia, both on the river and on the ship that brought them here, flashed through his young mind. "We're supposed to meet the uhh…our women…in the market…by uhh…in the market by nightfall."

"Yes, our women…the market," Sahagun confirmed, his eyes wider than the ocean as he too experienced disorienting flashes in his mind.

"Well, aren't you two handsome?" commented an older woman in Quechua while Chimalli and Sahagun exited the hallucinogenic hallway into a larger room that appeared to be a staging area to display the courtesans. The woman, presumably the madam of the establishment, dressed in a scantily clad outfit with her breasts barely hidden behind a thin piece of ornate cloth. Her grass skirt flowed down to the floor but was transparent enough to expose the full length of her legs. "What pleasures of the flesh do you seek on this fine evening?"

"Amo Quechua, no Quechua," Chimalli attempted to respond in Nahuatl while still experiencing the effects of the psychotropics.

"Ahh, is that Nahuatl I here?" the madam replied in the Aztec language. "You're a long way from home, good looking."

"You speak Nahuatl?" Chimalli questioned.

"I do, I speak many languages, but don't tell anyone that," she said with a wink. "Most men don't care for an intelligent woman."

"Your secret...safe...uhh with me," Chimalli replied, still slurring his words. "Now please, information."

"On to business so soon?" the madam asked as she grazed her finger gently down the skin on Chimalli's arm. "Business can wait."

"Girls!" the madam called out before Chimalli or Sahagun could protest. "Come and give these two stallions some options for this evening."

"Woah, umm...no, no," Sahagun remarked, attempting to regain his focus as several beautiful, nude women emerged from behind a lavish curtain. Adorned with ornamental jewels, necklaces, and bracelets, the courtesans exposed their breasts to their male visitors and giggled amongst each other at the sight of the two men.

"Not...necessary, please ladies," Chimalli pleaded with the women as they approached him and Sahagun, grinding their bodies against the unsuspecting men and moaning in unison with one another. Both Chimalli and Sahagun attempted to remove themselves from the seductive grip of the courtesans, but the hallucinogenic trance they had been placed under made it nearly impossible to escape.

"I have gold," Chimalli continued, reaching for the sack of gold coins that he had taken from the cargo hold of the *Hercules*. Chimalli's declaration only fueled the women's desires further when they realized the men were just as affluent in coin as they were in charming looks. "No, no, for information...I have gold...for information."

"What information could be better than a woman's flesh?" the madam asked as she stood back and watched her girls tempt the two men with the warmth of their bodies.

"Blooded...must find...the Blooded," Chimalli bellowed, forgetting his need for subtlety.

As the women still carried out their acts of seduction, Chimalli's words dissolved the older madam's smile and caused her lips to purse in concern. She approached the two men, staring them up and down with a great uneasiness in her demeanor.

"Girls, why don't you return to your quarters for now?" the madam said. "I need to speak to our new friends for a moment. Off you go."

Much to the relief of Chimalli and Sahagun, the courtesans abandoned their seductive moans and flirtatious advances, scurrying away behind the curtain and into the back rooms of the establishment.

"Drink this tonic," the madam instructed, revealing two cups in her hands, one for each of the men, both filled with an unknown liquid. "Your minds will return to their natural states, and then we'll have a little chat together."

With heads still spinning from the drugs, Chimalli and Sahagun glanced at each other to gauge their respective opinions on consuming this mysterious drink, although they didn't possess much of an option if they were going to get the information they sought. Both desired to exit their trances and regain their senses, so they each took the cup in front of them and drank the tonics at the same time.

"That's it, every last drop," commanded the madam, tilting both cups upwards to drain them thoroughly down the men's throats.

Chimalli and Sahagun both coughed and gagged after finishing the foul-tasting drink, prompting a grin from the madam.

"Alright," Sahagun stated when his fit of retching finally concluded. "Now about that inf–" Sahagun's words tailed off abruptly. He expected to feel clarity of the mind, but his hallucinations were replaced only by a sense of light-headed dizziness. Sahagun gazed at Chimalli, discovering that his Aztec friend had already collapsed to the floor.

The madam said nothing, waiting patiently as the Spaniard stumbled and emitted one final groan before blacking out and joining Chimalli on the floor.

■■■■■■■■■

An unknown, distorted voice echoed through Chimalli's barely conscious mind.

The young Aztec struggled to open his eyes as a hooded figure emerged through his blurred vision. Chimalli's head still felt disoriented but in a different way than he experienced from the hallucinogens. His grogginess began to wane, though, as the figure in front of him, cloaked in black robes and masked to hide the person's face, became clearer.

Beside the hooded figure was the madam from the brothel outside Quito, still dressed in the same garments as before. She spoke to the hooded one in Quechua, preventing Chimalli from deciphering her words. The cloaked figure gave no reply but nodded at something the madam was saying.

Next to Chimalli laid Sahagun, who, like Chimalli, also struggled to lift himself off the hard ground and regain his consciousness. Neither of them knew where they were or how much time had passed since their psychedelic encounter at the Inca brothel.

"Where are we?" Chimalli managed to muster in Nahuatl as the landscape around him came into view. Giant, elaborate statues of what appeared to be gods sat around a large plaza complex made of stone in the shape of a square. The altar at the foot of the largest statue and the extravagant columns around the complex were carved with various effigies and tribal inscriptions. Surrounding Chimalli, Sahagun, and their two captors was an encapsulating system of mountains that reached to the clouds on all sides of where they rested, and only a small, narrow path etched between two of the mountains. The complex was simple but powerful, like a spiritual presence could be felt amongst them.

A large eagle flew overhead, squawking and cawing rapaciously through the clear morning sky.

"This is the High Temple of the Apus, the gods of the mountains," the madam responded. "And you have now entered the realm of the Blooded, just as you requested."

"Perhaps we could have our ropes removed if it's not too much trouble," Sahagun requested as his and Chimalli's hands and legs were bound together tightly.

"Oh, did you think we brought you here for your benefit?" the madam responded with derision. "You come barging into my establishment, prying and asking about our order after Pizarro puts a sizable bounty on us, and you expect our trust? Stupid old man."

"I'm no older than you, dried up old puta," Sahagun snarked at her, prompting the madam to strike him across the face and send him crashing to the ground.

"You will hold your foul tongue in the presence of this holy place," ordered the madam, "something a foreign devil like you would do well to remember."

"Please, we mean you no harm," Chimalli pleaded with the madam, attempting to calm the situation. "You two are Blooded? Both of you?"

"We are, my young, respectful friend. Perhaps you could teach *your* friend some manners."

"I will do so," Chimalli agreed, glancing at Sahagun with a wide-eyed stare as his Spanish friend picked himself off the ground with an annoyance on his face from being struck.

The hooded figure stood stoic in the face of the commotion, remaining silent while still wearing the mask that concealed his or her identity.

"Who are you?" Chimalli continued to the madam.

"I am Madam Koya, leader of the Quito branch of the Blooded order. We use the cover of our brothel to gather information on Spanish troop movements, supply shipments, and anything else that might be of interest to the order."

"I see, and who is your masked, tongue-tied accomplice, here?" Chimalli asked.

"This," Koya replied, pausing to consider whether or not to reveal her partner's identity, "is someone of no concern to you."

The secrecy of the hooded figure intrigued both Chimalli and Sahagun, but neither of them chose to continue their pursuit of discovering the person's identity.

"We need to get back to Quito," Chimalli changed the subject. "There are others waiting for us. They'll be worried about our safety."

Koya chuckled at Chimalli's words. "So handsome, so manly," she said, "but not so bright, are you? We're many days from Quito now. You and your friend have been unconscious for quite a while. And as for the others back in Quito whom I assume are Spanish spies like yourself, they *should* be worried about your safety, for you've seen your last sunrise, at least in this mortal realm. Your bodies will be sacrificed to the Apus when we grow tired of speaking to you."

"Woah, woah, wait a moment," Chimalli asserted, "we're not spies. We've come to help you, to join the cause."

"Come to help, huh? To join the cause?" the madam questioned suspiciously. "You travel with a Spanish devil who looks too old to fight in Pizarro's army but still old enough to spy for him. Neither of you speak the language of this land, and you're carrying a large stack of papers with endless amounts of writing in that barbarian Spanish language. You want me to believe you both are here to help?"

Chimalli swallowed nervously before responding. "Umm, yes?"

"You see over there? That row of pikes with skulls atop them?" Koya asked ominously as she leaned in close to Chimalli and pointed towards the entrance to the complex. "Those pikes are reserved for spies like you, little rats sent by Francisco Pizarro to find out information about us."

"We're not spies!" Sahagun interjected, although his words carried even less weight than Chimalli's due to the paleness of his skin. "We have no love for Pizarro and his conquistadors!"

"Says the man who looks like he could have been a conquistador in a former life!" Koya barked back at the Spaniard.

Sahagun shrugged, "Well, you have a keen eye and you're not wrong, but–"

The madam shoved a gag into the Spaniard's mouth before he could finish speaking.

"That's enough from you," she proclaimed. "It's time to meet your god, little man."

"Same goes for you, my dashingly handsome, friend," Koya continued as she gagged Chimalli as well.

The two men struggled and attempted to wiggle out of the ropes that bound their hands and feet, but their efforts proved fruitless. The madam grabbed Sahagun, and the hooded figure took hold of Chimalli. The two Blooded captors dragged their helpless prisoners behind them towards the altar, which, as they approached, Chimalli and Sahagun could see had copious amounts of dried blood plastered across it.

Both called out through their gags, but the defeated men could only watch as their demise loomed large. The captors tossed them against the blood-covered stone altar, which had several notches for heads to be placed inside. At the base of the altar slots were a series of buckets, each one with more dried blood. These, presumably, were meant to catch the dripping blood of whichever poor soul was being sacrificed to the gods.

Both Madam Koya and the unknown hooded figure began chanting in Quechua as they removed daggers from their sheathes and waved them through the air towards the sky. Much to Chimalli and Sahagun's surprise, the voice of the hooded figure was that of a woman's, not that it mattered at this point, seeing as their end was near.

Chimalli and Sahagun gave each other one final glance and nodded to show respect to one another. Sahagun then closed his eyes and began communing with God in his head, asking forgiveness for his sins while his small wooden cross dangled from the string around his neck. Chimalli also focused his mind to communicate with the gods, albeit a different set of deities than the one Sahagun prayed to, and the two men prepared for the cold sting of the blade.

When the two women concluded their chants, they both reached down simultaneously and placed their blades to the throats of Chimalli and Sahagun, whose hearts raced wildly at the feeling of obsidian grazing against their skin.

Just before the daggers could spill the blood of their victims, the executioners stopped abruptly.

Two voices echoed across the complex of the High Temple.

Not just any voices.

The voices of women.

The voices of Kelia and Erandi.

"Hands off my man, bitch!" Kelia shouted in Quechua to the hooded woman.

"You looking to get sliced up, whore?!" Erandi yelled at Koya as she pointed her spear at her.

Koya and the hooded woman, both taken off guard by the intruders, took up defensive stances and readied themselves for combat.

"Do you know who we are?!" the hooded figure shouted back.

"All I see is an imbecile who can't tell when someone is following her for days, and a dead bitch in a hood who touched the wrong man," Kelia countered while her and Erandi approached with weapons drawn.

"Many call me the bane of Huascar, but you can simply call me…" the woman declared, wielding her axe and removing her mask and hood, "…Chasca."

Kelia smiled and gripped her sword.

"Let's dance, Chasca."

Volume IV, Part II
A Clash of Titans

A red sun descended behind the mountains and bled its rays across the High Temple of the Apus. The stone statues of the Inca gods stared down at the mortal inhabitants that gathered in their most sacred complex, weeping for the blood that was to be spilt on that day. A veritable clash of the titans awaited the High Temple, its hallowed stones transforming into a battleground of death and chaos.

The combatants held tight to their weapons, preparing themselves for absolution, a release that would render either victory or death. The four women readied their sword arms to pierce the flesh of the opponents that stood before them. The strong and courageous Aztecs, Kelia and Erandi, against the steady and unbreakable Incas, Chasca and Koya. Each woman was as brave as she was beautiful. None of them backed down in the face of danger, choosing instead to meet their destinies at the edge of a blade, whether it be their own or their enemy's.

Chimalli and Sahagun, normally at the forefront of every engagement, both knelt helplessly at the altar where they almost had their throats slit mere moments before. The two men, still bound at the hands and feet, observed as the women now took up arms in their stead.

Kelia and Erandi dressed themselves in tattered cloths that covered their breasts and upper thighs but exposed their arms and abdomens. Kelia's headband consisted of mostly green feathers, while Erandi's feathers were blue and purple. Both women wielded steel Spanish weapons that were confiscated from the *Hercules*, a sword for Kelia and a spear for Erandi.

Chasca removed her thick black robes of the Blooded order to reveal a golden breastplate, a flowing and beaded skirt, and ornate jewels that adorned the bands on her arms and legs. The Inca's light, colorful armor indicated her high status as a warrior and allowed her to move more nimbly than she would in her Blooded robes. Koya still wore her revealing madam's outfit with only a thin breast cover and slotted skirt. The madam's obsidian-tipped spear contrasted the steel-pointed spear that Erandi possessed, and Chasca carried her preferred copper-headed axe, although she had lost the one that had gained her such renown during the civil war against Huascar.

"Spanish weapons?" Chasca asked the Aztecs with a chuckle. "No doubt a gift from Pizarro. He sure doesn't hide his spies very well."

"Oh, don't worry," replied Kelia. "I'll slice open Pizarro's neck with it as soon as I send you to meet your ancestors. That pretty armor you've got there won't save you."

"There's a nice warm spot right here where you can place your sword," Chasca smiled while rubbing a spot on her exposed belly where her armor didn't reach. "Plant that blade in my gut and make your Spanish overlords proud, if you can."

"I'm going to thrust this metal straight into your eye," Kelia countered. "That'll be an improvement on that ugly face of yours."

While Kelia and Chasca exchanged insults, Erandi grew tired of Koya's smug expression and condescending eyes bearing down on her. Without warning, she lurched forward at her opponent, thrusting her spear at Koya and attempting to skewer her like a wild boar.

Just as Koya sidestepped Erandi's spear, Chasca swung a powerful blow against Kelia, prompting the young Aztec to raise her sword in defense. With the sound of copper impacting steel, the Battle of the High Temple began.

Kelia shifted her stance to negate Chasca's formidable strikes, parrying them and countering with a flurry of her own. Both warriors wielded their weapons with great skill, neither of them gaining an advantage over the other.

Meanwhile, the spear duel between Erandi and Koya raged on a short distance from where their younger counterparts fought. The two older women slashed and stabbed with precision, each one narrowly avoiding the tip of the other's spear on multiple instances. Koya took an aggressive approach and backed Erandi onto a pile of stones that ramped up onto a second level of statues just off the flat surface of the ground. The two women, although both now standing on an uneven surface, still fought with grace and passion, allowing their footwork to synchronize with the strokes of their weapons.

Closer to where Chimalli and Sahagun still rested at the altar, Kelia swept Chasca's feet from underneath her, crashing the Inca to the ground. The dust from the stones was disturbed by the impact, and Kelia moved swiftly to finish off her opponent. She swung her sword downward at Chasca's neck, but the agile Inca dodged the attack and rose to her feet before Kelia's second strike could land. The two young women, both with a stout yet toned frame and standing at similar heights, wasted no time in charging back into the fray with an epic clash of sword and axe that echoed across the temple complex.

The fight persisted forward, the hot sun bearing down on the four women of comparable skillsets. None had an edge over their opponent, and each warrior was a single mistake away from meeting their end. Although silent to the mortal ear, the drums of combat and melodic tunes fitting of a grand battle reverberated through the High Temple. The bards bellowed their songs of death and pain, and the keepers of the immortal realm guided the fighters' weapons with a stylistic beauty unrivaled by any other bout of combat ever to grace the land.

Erandi's fight with Koya continued on the second layer of uneven rocks and boulders that ramped higher and higher off the ground. Koya's relentless strikes pushed Erandi further and further up the stones as the Inca grunted and cursed with each stroke. The Aztec waited patiently for her moment to strike, backing her feet into the best possible positions and parrying each of Koya's attacks. The Inca gave no opening, though, showing no signs of weakness in her technique.

On the other side of the complex, Kelia backed away from her opponent and panted as she took a moment to catch her breath. Even with her youthfulness and high level of conditioning, the young Aztec had never been forced into a sustained engagement of this magnitude, especially against a warrior this skilled. The hot midday sun bore down heavily on Kelia, and the rigors of a long fight began to take its toll.

Chasca, on the other hand, was no stranger to prolonged stints of combat. She had fought in numerous battles, some of them lasting hours at a time. The sweat from her forehead paled in comparison to Kelia's, whose strength weakened with each swing of her sword.

"Wearing down a bit, I see," remarked Chasca, who also panted but not as vigorously as Kelia. "You're a skilled fighter, no doubt, but you've now shown your weakness."

Kelia hunched over and placed her hands on her knees to try and regain her stamina, but this task proved difficult for the young Aztec. She chose to save her breath by not responding to the Inca's attempts to bait her. Instead, Kelia gritted her teeth and surged forward to exert dominance and prove to Chasca that she would have to work for this kill, that the Inca would not easily wet her axe with the Aztec's blood.

Now atop the highest platforms of stone, Kelia and Erandi swung their spears with the same zeal as they had at the beginning of the fight. Erandi climbed up the head of a nearby statue and attempted to gain an advantage over her foe with the use of higher ground, but Koya maneuvered and ascended to the same level before Erandi could strike her down. Jumping from head-to-head of several compact statues that sat shoulder-to-shoulder against each other, Erandi eluded Koya while the Inca remained hot on her trail. On each statue head, the fighters exchanged blows and thrusts before bouncing to the next statue. Neither woman lost a step as both probed the other for gaps in defense.

Nearby, Kelia fought with a second wind, a renewed sense of vigor after her moment of rest. She knew her endurance wouldn't hold up as long as Chasca's, though. Realizing the necessity of ending the fight soon if she was to emerge victorious, Kelia worked through Chasca's guard and slit her thigh with a small cut. The Inca winced backwards in pain, keeping her feet but stumbling off balance.

Chasca looked down at the wound that Kelia had just inflicted. The Inca was shocked at the Aztec's successful strike, as she felt like the superior fighter all the way to that point. A sense of rage coursed through Chasca as she gripped the handle of her axe tighter than before, and the sight of blood flowing from her leg spurred her onwards even harder now. The Inca warrior reigned down a series of mighty blows on Kelia, who once more began to weaken under the weight of her decreasing strength. Chasca was relentless, like a goddess that wielded a divine instrument of death. Each successive strike hit with greater impact than the last, and all Kelia could do was hold her sword in the air and block Chasca's attacks with every trace of power she had left.

In the blink of an eye, like a flash of lightning across the sky, the dynamic of the battle changed as one of Chasca's strikes finally penetrated Kelia's waning defense, sending her sword careening out of her hand and onto the ground. After stripping the Aztec's ability to shield herself from the onslaught, Chasca thrust the heel of her sandal into Kelia's chest and caused her head to bounce off a nearby stone.

Kelia's world went red. The young Aztec became dazed and lost after the impact. With wide, desperate eyes, she searched frantically for her sword...but to no avail. Her mind manipulated the stones around her, and a crimson haze cast over her vision. She heard Chimalli's distorted voice cry out to her as she crawled aimlessly along the ground.

"Get up, Kelia! Get up!" Chimalli's distant Nahuatl words echoed through Kelia's mind. "Kelia! No!"

Chimalli's pleas with the woman he loved were lost though, as Kelia finally accepted her fate and rolled over to face her opponent with dignity. She raised her hands, not to block Chasca's incoming attack, but to reach for the red sun that gleamed down on her.

As Kelia's fingers wrapped around the sun, an eagle flew into her fading view, nestling into her grip. The Aztec took hold of the sun and the eagle and pulled them into her soul, becoming one with their spirits.

The stroke of Chasca's axe whipped through the air.

A bright light gleamed across Kelia's face, encapsulating her with its warmth.

And then...darkness. Nothingness. An empty void, unfilled by the mortal realm of existence.

But, wait, Kelia's detached mind wandered. *Darkness, emptiness, but also warmth. How could this be? Not only warmth, but heat. Where is the cold embrace of death? Where is the release? By the gods, so much heat.*

It was at this time that Kelia realized her darkness came not from death, but merely from the closing of her eyelids. When she finally opened them, the Aztec awoke to the sounds of unrestrained shouts and the rapid squelching of flesh.

Kneeling beside Kelia was her closest friend, Erandi, who cursed and screamed wildly as she plunged her dagger into her target. The Inca gargled and choked on her own blood while Erandi skewered the flesh from her gut.

Kelia then brought her mind to the realization that the eagle she pulled into her grasp wasn't an eagle at all. Erandi had leapt from the top of the nearby statue to crash down upon Chasca and rescue her friend. Kelia had pulled Erandi into her heart, allowing life, not death, to surge onward through the darkness.

"Koya!" shouted Chasca, lifting herself off the ground and rushing to her companion's aid.

Upon hearing Chasca's voice, Kelia was stunned to discover that Erandi's kill was not Chasca, but Koya, who had jumped down behind Erandi and injured herself before the Aztec turned to finish her.

As Chasca lifted her axe to strike Erandi, Kelia rose to her knees, pulled a small dagger from her waistband, and slung it towards the Inca. The blade struck the center of Chasca's gold breastplate, not piercing it deep enough to kill her, but still connecting with enough force to halt her movement and send her collapsing to the stone surface of the temple.

Chasca's axe slipped from her hands. The mighty warrior princess, victor of countless battles, lay defeated in the shadow of the Aztecs who bested her. Madam Koya, leader of the Blooded in Quito, closed her eyes one last time and faded into the blackness that Kelia had expected for herself.

"Kill me and finish this," asserted Chasca as she wriggled in pain and smiled through her blood-stained teeth. "The gods will have their vengeance on you, on all of you."

Kelia regained her focus as her mind cleared from the fog that had clouded it. "I won't kill you. Not yet. I will not betray my honor for the likes of you."

"A traitor with honor?" questioned Chasca. "I've seen it all now."

"The most amusing part is how you still think we're traitors," remarked Erandi as she paced around Chasca. "Your blindness has now gotten your friend killed."

"She wasn't my friend," Chasca claimed, still lying on the ground and wincing in pain. "I only met her today, a couple hours ago actually, when she brought your two friends here with her. But she was Blooded, like me. This fact alone demands respect."

"Agreed," Kelia said. "Which is why we will allow you to perform a ritual for her passing."

"We will?" Erandi asked with a smirk, still cleaning Koya's blood off her sword.

"Of course," Kelia replied, glancing at Erandi scornfully. "Don't let your anger strip you of your honor."

"I'm sorry, my friend. You're right. As always, your discipline and patience has far surpassed my own, despite your youthfulness."

"I am no priest. I can perform no ritual," Chasca stated while ascending to one knee. "We will place her body on the altar and let the gods take her soul to Hanan Pacha."

"As you wish," nodded Kelia with respect for her dead opponent.

"That accent," Chasca continued, "neither of you are from here, are you?"

"No, we are Mexica, Aztec," answered Kelia. "Our greatest city was burned to the ground by the Spanish eleven years ago. My mother was raped and murdered in the room next to me while her attackers reveled in their barbarism. They almost did the same to me. I assure you, we are no spies. It is my life's goal to kill every last foreign devil who steps foot on our lands. We only possess these barbarian weapons because we commandeered one of their ships to get here."

"Aztec?" Chasca inquired with interest. "You are not the first Aztec I've met this week. Such a strange coincidence."

Kelia perked up and matched Chasca's interest. "There's another Aztec here? In these lands? So far from our home?"

"There is, a man. A great man. He and my mother sent me here to the High Temple of the Apus as part of my initiation into the order. And like you, I hear he escaped the sack of the city all those years ago."

"What is this man's name?"

"I'd rather not say," replied Chasca, still suspicious of the band of Aztecs who traveled with a Spaniard. "But I hear he evaded certain death on the shores of your city. His legend grows in these parts. They say a great spirit saved him from many Spanish swords and lifted him to safety. It's whispered that he rode on the back of an eagle all the way here, though I'm not so sure I believe everything about the tale."

"Could it really be him?" Kelia spoke softly to herself and wrestled with her thoughts. "No, it's not possible."

"What is it, Kelia?" Erandi asked after seeing her friend's confusion. "Who are you thinking this man is?"

"Do you remember how I told you about my escape from Tenochtitlan?" Kelia spoke to Erandi. "The man who saved us, who sacrificed himself so Chimalli and Ohtli and I could escape?"

"Yes, I remember, Emperor Cuauhtémoc's friend. You said he was swarmed and killed by the Spaniards as you watched from your boat."

"That's right. Chimalli told me that before he died, he wanted to make for these lands, that this was the only safe place left in the world for our people. His words were the reason we came all this way."

Erandi and Chasca both glanced at the young Aztec with confusion.

"If I say his name, will you take us to him?" Kelia asked Chasca. "Will you believe me that we're here to join your cause and not spy on you?"

"His name is only known to the Blooded, the ones who dwell on the mountain," Chasca replied. "If you know his name, then you must know his spirit. So yes, I would take you to him and let him decide your fate in this land."

"Is he the former ruler of a city called Texcoco, near Tenochtitlan?" Kelia questioned. "A man who answered only to the Aztec emperor in his past life? Is his name Acalan, son of Cacama?"

Chasca rose to her feet with a renewed vigor and a glimmer in her eyes, like she had finally pulled the veil back from these foreigners and discovered the truth of their intentions.

"He's alive?!" Kelia prodded with excitement. "Acalan is alive?! Here, in the land of your people?!"

Chasca's nod of approval caused Kelia's eyes to widen. She turned towards Chimalli and Sahagun, who both still laid idle on the ground near the altar. The two men could hear the women's conversation but were ignorant to their words due to a lack of knowledge of the Quechua language.

"Chimalli!" Kelia shouted in Nahuatl. "He's alive!"

Volume IV, Part III
Union of Heroes

"Tu honras su," Sahagun said to Chasca in Spanish as he watched the Inca glance back nervously towards Koya's body that had been laid at the altar of the Apu. Chasca had placed her at the base of the largest statue in the High Temple, giving her the most respectable sacrament of death that she could offer without the presence of a Willaq Umu, a high priest of the sun.

"What nonsense does the white man speak to me?" Chasca asked the other women in Quechua, turning her head in the opposite direction. "You should tell him to hold his tongue. His barbarian words are offensive to this air."

The unlikely band of warriors, consisting of three Aztecs, one Inca, and one Spaniard, rode away from the complex on the backs of three Spanish horses. Chasca had brought the twin white mares, Lilly and Lyla, on her journey to the temple. Chasca rode Lilly, Chimalli and Kelia rode Lyla, and Sahagun and Erandi rode a grey horse that Koya had used to pull her cart from Quito to the High Temple.

"He means no offense," Erandi countered in defense of the man who she had come to love. "He praises the way you handled the body of your companion. He says you honor her."

"Oh," Chasca responded with a surprised expression. "Tell him thank you for his kindness, but please ask him to use the Aztec language and refrain from using the words of his homeland. The atrocities I've seen from men using that tongue would tame even the bravest of warriors."

Erandi nodded and translated Chasca's words to Sahagun in Nahuatl, prompting him to gesture in respect of the Inca's wishes.

"How is it that both of you know our language," Chasca asked the Aztec women, "but neither of your men do?"

"Erandi and I were enslaved on a large island called Cuba for ten long years," Kelia replied. "There was a woman there, an Inca like you, who taught us the language during that time. We thought it would be useful since our plan was always to break free and make it here to this land. Turns out the gods steered us on the right path."

"And your men weren't with you during this time of enslavement?" Chasca prodded further.

"No, it was the most difficult time of my life being away from Chimalli. We finally reunited a few months ago after we escaped and rescued them."

"*You* rescued *him*? How romantic...like a tale of long-lost lovers," Chasca commented genuinely, her smile beaming and her mind wandering to her own past.

"I suppose you could say that," Kelia muttered while smiling at Chimalli. "The gods were not ready to finish our story."

"I have a story like that myself," Chasca said as her tone waned to sorrow. "Rumi was his name. He was a great warrior, and he loved me like no other."

"You will meet him again," Kelia responded, prompting Chasca's shock over the compassion of the woman who she had just fought to near death the day before.

"What do you think they're talking about?" Chimalli whispered to Sahagun in Nahuatl, pulling his horse close to Sahagun's so his voice didn't travel.

"They're women," replied Sahagun. "I'm sure they're talking about the smell of the flowers or something."

Erandi, who had been listening to Kelia and Chasca's ongoing conversation, overheard Sahagun's comment and rolled her eyes at the Spaniard.

"Are you crazy?" Chimalli asked. "Did you not see them try to hack each other to pieces yesterday? These aren't the dainty women you have back in your country, my friend."

"You misunderstand me, amigo. I certainly am not accusing them of being dainty, as you say. But even the toughest of women still have a soft side, a part of them that makes them one of God's most elegant creations. It's what allows them to be better than us in almost every way. A man fights, kills, feasts, and dies, rarely stopping to admire the beauty that surrounds him. A woman can live two lives: one of bravery and perseverance, but also one of compassion and sensitivity. It's a talent that most men are unable to master."

"How can you be such a dick but such a good person at the same time?" Chimalli questioned lightheartedly.

"I agree with Chimalli," Erandi interjected with a grin. "Your moral complexity is astonishing."

"Such a man is needed in times like these," Sahagun said playfully as he raised his shoulders and smirked like a gawdy nobleman.

"Might want to throw him off that horse and save yourself while you can, Erandi," Chimalli joked.

"Another comment about smelling flowers and I'll make sure he's face down in a whole meadow of them," Erandi jested in return.

Sahagun grinned and imitated Erandi's eye roll. "I'll have you both know that I'll be writing down everything you say in the codex. The world will know how cruel both of you were to poor Bernardino."

"I prefer Sahagun," Erandi quipped, "or simply chontalli."

"How fitting that I'm being labeled a chontalli, a foreigner, in a land where you Aztecs are just as foreign as I am."

"Nobody is as foreign as you," Chimalli commented with a smile, "in mind or in body."

"Alas, Sahagun is doomed to wonder this world alone," Sahagun continued, referring to himself in third person, "a foreign devil with no home and no one who loves him."

"We'll see if you still feel that way tonight," Erandi remarked, reaching her hands around Sahagun's torso and grabbing him in a place that made his eyes stand at attention, along with other parts of his body.

"Previous comment rescinded," Sahagun replied instinctively as Erandi and Chimalli both laughed at the Spaniard's witty humor.

Over the next several days, the mounted ensemble trotted onwards over the mountains, stopping only to sleep, hunt, or relieve their bowels. The original group of four developed a sense of respect for their newly acquired Inca comrade, especially after hearing of Chasca's noble background. Kelia and Chasca, in particular, began to form a bond between each other, both realizing they were much stronger as allies than enemies.

After a week's worth of travel and battling much colder temperatures than they were accustomed to, the group finally reached the walls of Machu Picchu. The majestic stone gatehouse stood before them, and even the Aztecs, who were no strangers to grand architecture, observed in awe the splendor of the mountain fortress.

"I am the Blood!" Chasca shouted while Lilly neighed and trotted towards the gate.

"And the Blood is me!" the Blooded guard called back in response. "Who walks this path with you, Chasca?"

"These are friends, come to join our ranks," Chasca answered. "Grandmaster Acalan will vouch for them, and so will I. Bring him here, if you will. Tell him I've brought him a few old friends."

The guard, standing atop the stone wall by the gate, appeared suspicious of the outsiders but retreated to fetch the Grandmaster.

"If you all have been lying to me this whole time and you really are spies," Chasca said while turning to face her companions, "then may the gods take mercy on my foolish heart."

Chasca's comment was only half-serious, but bringing outsiders to the gates of Machu Picchu carried a significant weight and a substantial breach of trust if anything went wrong, especially since Chasca herself had only recently been inducted into the order.

"This is good stuff," Sahagun remarked, jotting down on his parchment Chasca's words that Erandi translated for him. The Spaniard had become quite adept at riding and writing simultaneously. "–mercy on my foolish heart," he repeated as he wrote.

A few moments later, much sooner than expected, a familiar voice rang through Chimalli and Kelia's ears, instilling a sense of excitement in them. The two young Aztecs grabbed each other's hands and smiled at one another.

"Old friends? I don't have any old friends, none that are still alive at least," Acalan rambled to the guard in Quechua as he climbed the stone gatehouse. The Aztecs outside the gate could vaguely make out his words from their position at the base of the walls.

"Who is this, Chasca?" Acalan called out as he peaked his head over the stones. His black hood silhouetted his face, but Chimalli and Kelia could still make out the face of the man who they hadn't seen in over a decade. "You must have a good reason for bringing outsiders to our walls."

Chasca opened her mouth to reply, but Chimalli held his hand out towards her, spurring Lyla forwards and gesturing that he would handle a response.

"Time has not been kind to you, my old friend," Chimalli jested to Acalan in Nahuatl as Kelia held tight to his waist on the back of the horse.

"Is that—" Acalan squinted his eyes, his mind clouded with uncertainty.

"I guess we've grown quite a lot since the last time you saw us," Kelia stated, leaning around Chimalli to present her face to Acalan.

A realization came over Acalan's face, a moment of clarity, like a veil had been pulled back and his confusion was swept away.

"Chimalli? And...the girl from Tenochtitlan? By Quetzalcoatl, it cannot be."

"By Quetzalcoatl, it is," Chimalli replied while his and Kelia's smiles grew wider. "Her name is Kelia, by the way. I can't remember if you had the time to learn her name before we got separated."

"Chimalli and Kelia! It's really you!" Acalan bellowed with excitement and grinned from cheek to cheek. "Open the gates! Now!" he directed towards the Blooded guards, who pulled the levers to pry open the large stone entrance.

Acalan jumped down the backside of the gate and sprinted towards the waiting Aztecs with open arms. "How can this be?! It defies all conceivable odds! Where have you been all these years?! I haven't seen either of you since you boarded that boat on Lake Texcoco and drifted out of my sight forever...or what I thought was forever! When was that, ten years ago?!"

"Eleven!" Chimalli returned the excitement as he and Kelia took turns hugging Acalan. "Eleven long years! We've had quite the journey to get here, needless to say. First, we were on the run in the Mayan jungles, then we got taken in by a Mayan fishing village, then we got captured by Pizarro and imprisoned for ten years, and then we escaped and sailed here on a stolen Spanish ship before these two (Chimalli gestured towards both Kelia and Chasca). engaged in one of the most awe-inspiring battles I've ever witnessed. You know, the typical story of any average person in this new world."

Acalan widened his eyes at the depth of Chimalli's words, each line spurring the older Aztec to an even greater level of shock. "Truly fascinating..."

Meanwhile, Sahagun dipped his quill in a small container of ink that Erandi held by his side, maneuvering it furiously across the parchment at every word spoken. The Spaniard's face beamed with the same degree of delight as his Aztec counterparts, soaking every minor detail into his codex.

"But enough about us," Kelia commented. "*You're* the one who's supposed to be dead. We saw you get overtaken on the shores of Tenochtitlan. How did you survive?"

"Didn't you hear?" Acalan replied with a lighthearted twinkle in his eye. "I was lifted out of there and brought here by a convocation of eagles. At least that's the tale the bards sing."

"So, what *really* happened?" Chimalli asked with a chuckle.

"The tales are exaggerated, but only the part about me being lifted to safety. There were eagles, though, lots of them. I've never seen so many creatures willingly aid a human in distress quite like this. Just as I prepared to meet my end, a whole army of eagles swooped down upon the Spanish soldiers. They screeched and clawed at my attackers until I was able to find an opening to escape. I was forced back into the city and hid in an old storage cellar for three days with no food or water. I finally found my opportunity to run, and run I did...or swim, more like it. I jumped in the water at nightfall of the third day and swam the entire distance to the mainland."

"You swam across the whole of Lake Texcoco?!" Chimalli questioned in disbelief. "That's almost like an ocean to itself!"

"It *felt* like an ocean," Acalan confirmed, his mind harping back to that fateful stretch of time when Tenochtitlan crumbled and died. "I chose the shortest route across the south part of the lake. I still needed help from the gods, though, and they answered my call for aid. The same eagles that attacked the Spanish and saved my life were also the ones that flew overheard for several hours while I forced my body to move forward. It was truly a divine moment. About a year later, after trudging through the jungles to get here, I finally arrived in Cuzco and met Tullu and Cusi, this one's mother. We founded The Order of Blooded Natives to fight back against the foreign invaders."

"I can't understand your strange words," Cusi remarked to Acalan in Quechua as she stepped through the gatehouse. The Inca Grandmaster referred to Acalan's use of his native Nahuatl, which she hadn't heard him speak in many years. "But I know my name when I hear it in any language."

"Mother!" Chasca exclaimed, embracing her tightly.

"I'm so happy you've returned safely, my child," Cusi commented as she sunk into the arms of her daughter.

Tullu emerged from the gate as well with a wide grin on his face. "Welcome back, warma," he said to Chasca. "I see you've returned with a few friends. They are friends, I assume?"

"They are," Chasca stated while returning a smile. "Although it didn't begin that way. I met up with Madam Koya of Quito at the High Temple. We thought these people were spies and a fight ensued. Koya was killed."

"Koya is dead? At the hands of these people?" Cusi asked as she observed the Aztecs and their Spanish companion with suspicion. "Which one of you struck the blow?"

"I did," Erandi stated as she and Sahagun were the last to dismount from their horse.

"You killed Koya?" Cusi questioned, prompting a nod from Erandi. "Her death will disrupt our efforts in Quito, but I can't say I ever had any love for the woman. Owner of that insufferable establishment of loose women."

"You all travel with a barbarian," Acalan remarked in Nahuatl, changing the subject and referring to Sahagun. "Explain his presence."

"The way we all felt about Rodrigo is the way I feel about this man," Chimalli replied. "His skin is pale like the clouds, but I trust him with my life."

Acalan glanced upon Sahagun with apprehension, just as Cusi had done, but he ultimately let his guard down after pondering Chimalli's words. "Rodrigo is the only foreigner from across the great blue sea that I've ever trusted, but if you vouch for this man, then we shall trust him as well.

Tullu and Cusi weren't thrilled about taking in the Spaniard, or even the other Aztecs for that matter, but Chasca and Acalan's approval of the outsiders was enough to sway them, as both Grandmasters reluctantly nodded their heads to welcome the foreigners into Machu Picchu.

"Come," Cusi continued, pulling Lilly and Lyla by the reigns and leading the horses into the fortress. "It's getting late. We must find beds and food for our new guests."

Kelia translated any relevant Quechua words to Chimalli, and Erandi did the same for Sahagun. Conversely, Acalan converted the Aztecs' Nahuatl language back to Quechua for Tullu, Cusi, and Chasca.

"Thank you, ma'am," Chimalli said in Nahuatl. "Your hospitality is much appreciated."

"You all have arrived during the calm before the storm," Tullu remarked as the group entered the stone gate of Machu Picchu and gazed upon the fortress with the typical amazement of someone who had never laid eyes upon it. "Every son and daughter of this land must be willing and able to drive these devils back across the water."

"Indeed," Cusi confirmed. "Tonight, we feast and prepare. Tomorrow, the fate of our people will be decided when we go to Cuzco to rescue my husband, the emperor. Our scouts confirm he's being held in the dungeons below the royal palace."

"What Pizarro is doing to your husband is the same thing his uncle did to our emperor back in Tenochtitlan," Erandi said. "The Spanish will never relent. No matter how many you kill, they will always return even stronger."

"Yes, I've heard such tales from Acalan," Cusi replied to Erandi's statement. "But what would you have us do, Aztec? Give up? Let our villages burn and our people die? That will never be an option."

"I fear we are the last hope for our people," Tullu commented. "The emperor's forces are scattered and lack the leadership necessary to fight back against the Spanish. The defeat at Cajamarca decimated the morale of the valley dwellers. The people have nearly given up hope."

After the Quechua words of the Inca Grandmasters were converted to Nahuatl for Chimalli and Sahagun, a brief silence came over the group as they pondered the events to come.

"I forgot to ask before," Acalan said to Chimalli in Nahuatl, breaking the silence. "What has become of Ohtli, your nephew? Where is Rodrigo and Atzi's child?"

"Taken," Kelia replied with sadness, as not a day had gone by that she hadn't thought about her time as a family with Chimalli and Ohtli. "Stolen by Pizarro and sent back to their homeland across the water. Pizarro even claimed he was stripping Ohtli of his name and giving him a Spanish one, but we forgot what he said it was."

A suspicious look plastered across Acalan's face as he stopped in his tracks, prompting the others to do the same.

"What is it, my friend?" Chimalli questioned.

Acalan switched to Quechua as the group huddled around the Aztec Grandmaster. "Chasca, what did you say that boy's name was? Pizarro's son? The one in Cuzco right now with darker skin than the other boy?"

Chasca thought for a moment before the boy's name re-entered her mind. "Umm, Alejandro, I believe. Why?"

No translation was needed for Chimalli and Kelia. Their eyes widened upon hearing the name Alejandro, as it jarred their memories from ten years before, back to when Pizarro snatched Ohtli from their arms during the raid on the Mayan village of Chinquila.

And what shall we call you? Pizarro's words echoed through their minds just as clearly as they had all those years ago. *Your savage name will no longer be appropriate for the son of a Spanish nobleman. I know, how about...Alejandro?*

"Alejandro?" Kelia asked, staring into Chimalli's eyes.

The two young Aztecs both shouted the boy's real name at the same time.

"Ohtli!"

Codex Volume V

The Crimson Sky

Volume V, Part I
The Long Night

Alejandro stared through the clear night sky towards the towering peaks of the nearby mountain range. From where he stood on the balcony of the royal palace in Cuzco, the Andes Mountains stared back at him and gently kissed the clouds from below.

Growing up in Spain, Alejandro was no stranger to rolling hills and high mountains. He had seen the Pyrenees, the Sierra Nevada, and several other ranges during his short twelve years. Such was the life of a noble's son. Traveling was one of Alejandro's few positive experiences from his time in Spain. Unfortunately, though, that's where his fond memories faded. Many people in Spain scoffed at him because of the savage blood flowing through his veins. He had learned very quickly that looking different meant he would also be treated differently, a cruel part of life that he had accepted long ago.

"Just be lucky father lets you sleep here in the palace," Valentino sneered, barging into the upstairs common room and interrupting Alejandro's peaceful evening. "If it were up to me, you would be in the dungeons sleeping in a bucket of your own filth, just like that savage king or emperor or whatever he calls himself."

Alejandro closed his eyes and took a deep breath before responding to his revolting, arrogant half-brother. "Shouldn't you be torturing some helpless animal? Or perhaps you need more herbs to help your poor little mangled hand?"

Valentino gritted his teeth and seethed at Alejandro. The young Spaniard looked down at his hand that now only possessed three full fingers after he was attacked at Cajamarca a few weeks prior. His other two fingers, the ring and little one furthest from his thumb, had been severed about midway down and were wrapped together with a small white cloth.

"That's what happens when you try to kill someone, idiota," Alejandro continued with a chuckle. "You got what you deserved."

"I tried to kill a savage, an animal like you, a plague upon our world," replied Valentino.

"But you're not in *your* world, are you?"

"And you are, dog? You think you belong here?"

"More so than you."

Valentino laughed as he stepped closer to his brother, close enough to lower his tone to a near whisper. "You belong nowhere, you half-breed rat. You're a freak, a son of a whore who spread her legs for any weary traveler that happened across her. The only thing you are is lucky. Lucky that father was foolish enough to lay with that puta and create such an unholy spawn."

Rage bellowed inside Alejandro at his weasel brother's insults towards his mother, but he maintained his outward composure, knowing that striking Valentino would only make things worse for himself.

"If I pushed you over the edge of this railing," Valentino continued, staring out over the balcony to the large, open terrace below, "no one would miss you. You think father cares if you live or die? Especially after your cowardice in dealing with the locals. If you had done your duty and killed those savages, I would still have all my fingers."

"My only regret from that day," Alejandro responded while sustaining his eye contact with his brother, "is that the Inca didn't take your entire hand. Or your life for that matter. The world would surely be a better place without you."

Valentino grinned from ear to ear as he produced a dagger from his waistband. He held out the handle of the blade towards Alejandro, attempting to bait him into taking it.

"If you think me better dead, then go ahead, take my life...dog."

Everything within Alejandro wanted to thrust the knife into his brother's flesh. Nothing would have been more satisfying for the young boy who had been bullied and ridiculed his entire life simply for looking different. Alejandro knew the gallows or the pyre would await him if he did, but he hardly cared. Death seemed like a sweet release from the cruelty of this world.

"Soon," Alejandro declared, "very soon." He pulled away from Valentino and marched out of the room at a brisk pace, removing the temptation of gashing open his brother's gut. Valentino's sinister laugh echoed behind Alejandro as he slammed the door shut.

Alejandro placed his head against the adobe bricks of the hallway and chided himself for allowing his brother to get under his skin. Tears flowed down the boy's face as he struggled to control his emotions. The curse of being different weighed heavily on Alejandro, and in a small way, he knew Valentino was right. He didn't belong anywhere. The Spanish hated him for being native. The natives hated him for being Spanish. His mixed heritage felt like nothing more than a burden, a problem with no solution.

As Valentino's footsteps approached the common room's trapezoidal-shaped doorway (typical Inca architectural design with a wide bottom and narrow top), Alejandro quickly wiped his eyes and scurried down the hallway to his quarters. The less he had to interact with his brother, the better. Alejandro entered his room and closed the door behind him, putting to rest yet another stressful evening.

Valentino smirked as he marched into the hall and heard the hinges of Alejandro's door clicking into place. The Spanish boy, older than Alejandro by only two months, prepared to enter his own bed chambers but abruptly stopped when he heard a shuffle of footsteps down the hall. The steps sounded rushed, moving quickly in the opposite direction.

"Who's there?!" Valentino questioned loudly.

There was no response, but as Valentino trotted forward into the next dimly lit corridor, he saw the tail end of a dark figure scurrying away from him around the subsequent corner. The bottom of the shadowy character's black robe caught the boy's eye. Whoever this was, he or she clearly didn't want to be spotted.

"Hey you! Stop!" Valentino shouted, sprinting down the hall. Normally the cowardly boy would have never chased after a mysterious figure sneaking around amongst the darkness, but his false bravery had peaked that night after his run-in with Alejandro. There was also a certain curiosity about a person fleeing that forced the boy to give chase. Valentino pursued the hooded man (or woman) through the elaborately constructed hallways of the royal palace, always a step behind the fugitive, never getting a good look at his or her face.

As the chase led down a flight of stairs towards the dungeons below the palace, Valentino abruptly halted his movement when he rushed into the room that possessed the jail cells. Laying in a pool of their own blood on the ground in front of him were two Spanish guards, both of whom had their throats cut. Two hooded figures stood next to Emperor Atahualpa, who had just been freed from the confines of his cell. Everyone paused and stared at the young Spanish boy in shock for what seemed like an eternity.

Just as Valentino prepared to cry for help, the figure that he had been chasing rushed from behind the door and placed a hand over his mouth.

"That's the wrong kid!" Chasca hollered in a muted tone so as not to alert any of the other guards. She and Cusi removed their hoods to reveal their faces.

Tullu, who was out of breath from sprinting through the palace, fought with the wriggling Spanish boy and struggled to keep him still and quiet. "You said to take Pizarro's kid right?! How many kids does he have?!"

"He has two!" Chasca replied once more in a hushed but stern manner. "I said to get the dark-skinned one! This one is white as the snow on the mountain peaks!"

"I agree the boy deserves to be rescued," Cusi asserted, "but not at the expense of the cause. If he's not here, then we must go without him."

"I saw his eyes at Cajamarca," Chasca continued. "That boy had a chance to kill me and didn't. He saved my life, and I owe it to him to save his."

"Why do you think he needs saving?" Tullu questioned as he still wrestled with Valentino. "He's one of them, a Spaniard, is he not? Just like this little rat!"

"A half-Spaniard in blood, perhaps," countered Chasca, "but not in spirit. You heard what the outsiders said about him, didn't you?"

"She's right," added Atahualpa, who had been bloodied and beaten by his captives. The emperor propped himself up with the help of his daughter and his wife. "I too saw the boy at Cajamarca. His heart is no more Spaniard than yours or mine."

"That may be so," Cusi said, "but there's no time. Acalan and the others wait for us in the courtyard."

Chasca nodded in agreement with her mother. "We'll get father outside to Acalan. Then I'll come back for the boy."

"So be it," Tullu conceded to Chasca's wishes while Valentino still wiggled in his grasp. "What about this little pale devil?"

"Gag him and take him with us," declared Cusi, prompting Valentino to widen his eyes in fear. "He may prove to be a useful bargaining tool, especially if we can't find Pizarro's other son."

Tullu wrapped a cloth through Valentino's mouth and bound the boy's hands behind his back.

Just as the group prepared to exit the dungeons, a hand emerged from one of the cells on the far side of the room, accompanied by a muffled groaning sound.

"What about him?" Chasca questioned her father.

The emperor veered towards the prisoner's outstretched hand as he pondered his next move. The man's face was still shrouded in darkness, but his moans sounded more and more desperate as time passed.

"We don't have time for this!" Tullu emitted with a whispered shout. "He's a traitor! We should cut his throat and be done with him."

"He's my brother!" Atahualpa snapped back at Tullu as he shot the Blooded Grandmaster a harsh glare. "You may be a leader atop the mountain, but down here in the valley, this is my domain. You will learn your place."

Tullu scowled but held his tongue as Atahualpa hobbled over to Huascar's cell.

"Looks like we both lost our titles," the emperor said with a chuckle to his brother, the same man whose tongue Atahualpa had ripped from his mouth after defeating him in battle.

Huascar grinned at his younger brother for the first time in many years. No words were spoken, but only because he no longer had the ability to speak. His facial expressions did the talking for him, and in Atahualpa's mind, his brother appeared to be a broken man filled with sorrow for his past grievances.

"These demons have taken the seat of our father, the seat that rightfully belongs to us," Atahualpa continued as he held out his hand, gesturing for Huascar to take it within his own. "Fight with me, brother, and after we rid our lands of this plague, we will rule together, side by side."

Chasca, Cusi, and Tullu glanced at each other in confusion upon hearing Atahualpa's proclamation. As misguided as it seemed to be, he was still the emperor, even in this current state of turmoil. His words and wishes still held enormous weight.

Huascar looked at Atahualpa with a fire in his eyes, one that indicated to the emperor that his brother had now returned to him. He grabbed hold of Atahualpa's outstretched hand and squeezed it with a warrior's grasp.

"Atahualpa," Cusi interrupted as her husband unlocked Huascar's cell. "This man fought against you. Against our daughter. Against your father's dying wishes. I do not think—"

"It is not your decision!" Atahualpa once again snapped, clearly harboring a resentment towards his wife who he hadn't seen in years. "You lost the ability to influence my decisions when you left us! When these blood people became more important to you than your own family!"

Chasca veered away at her father's disturbing words, and Cusi stared into her husband's eyes in shattered silence.

"Did you spread your legs for this man?" the angered emperor continued to press, motioning towards Tullu. "What about the Aztec? Did you lay with him too?"

Cusi's expression turned to one of disgust upon hearing Atahualpa's insulting claims. She raised her hand and swiped it across her husband's face, causing him to wince back from the force of the slap.

"You stocked your bed with a new whore every night when I was here," Cusi retorted, "yet you accuse me of laying with these men with no evidence but your own foolish jealousy."

Atahualpa said nothing but stared blankly at his wife as Huascar exited his cell.

"This was a mistake," Cusi declared. "We should never have come here. You and your traitor brother can find your own way out. I'm leaving."

"Mother, stop!" Chasca pleaded to no avail as Cusi marched out of the dungeon with Tullu and Valentino behind her.

"Come, father! Quickly!" Chasca hollered, turning her attention towards Atahualpa and Huascar. Her uncle's calm expression was unlike anything she had ever seen from him, especially in the moments when "Huascar the Cruel" had earned his nickname. Now though, he looked like less of a cruel tyrant and more of a whipped dog, a hollow shell of the authoritarian despot he used to be.

The three Incas hurried out of the side entrance to the prison, passing by another set of dead guards they had dispatched on their way in. They followed closely behind Cusi, Tullu, and their young Spanish hostage, all of whom already approached the central terrace of the palace complex.

"What took you so long?" Acalan whispered when Cusi and Tullu reached the large, open plaza, which was illuminated only by a few torches placed on sconces around the ornately designed columns. "The others are waiting by the stables. They've stolen a wagon so we can make our escape—Who's this?" Acalan asked, sharply changing the subject upon seeing Valentino. The Spanish boy continued to squirm and moan in a futile attempt to break free from his captors.

"Pizarro's son," Tullu replied. "One of them at least."

"This little shit is pale as a ghost," commented Acalan, "I wanted the other one. You said he had a child of mixed blood, right?"

"I'm going back for him," Chasca cut in as she, Atahualpa, and Huascar stepped onto the terrace.

Acalan sent a scathing glare towards Huascar upon seeing him alongside the emperor. "Is that—"

"Yes, Aztec," Atahualpa interrupted. "This is my brother, Huascar."

"You vouch for this man?" Acalan asked with caution.

"I do, obviously," Atahualpa responded without hesitation. "I appreciate you all coming to my rescue, but Huascar is a changed man. You must trust my judgment."

"As you wish," Acalan reluctantly conceded to Atahualpa, although he maintained his aura of suspicion. The Aztec was no stranger to witnessing poor decisions from emperors. His time with Montezuma in Tenochtitlan had shown him that weak leadership was enough to topple an empire.

"Let's go, Chasca," Cusi said, prompting Atahualpa to frown at his wife's attempt to bond with their daughter. "I'll come with you to get the other boy."

Chasca nodded in approval, but just as they set off to reenter the palace, a sinister laugh resounded through the dark on the other side of the terrace, causing the ensemble to halt in fear.

"Off so soon, ladies?" Pizarro's menacing voice echoed; his face dimly lit by the flames of his torch. "You're going to miss all the fun!" After Pizarro finished his cryptic introduction, more torches appeared around the plaza, all held by the Spanish commander's steel-clad conquistadors.

Chasca, Acalan, Cusi, Atahualpa, Huascar, and Tullu (still holding firm to Valentino) all took up defensive positions around the complex, using the various columns as cover from the Spanish muskets that fixed upon them.

The palace doors were then slammed shut and barricaded by more Spanish guards, cutting off any hopes of escape for the band of Incas (and one Aztec).

"We're surrounded!" Chasca shouted. "Tullu, hold a knife to the boy's throat!"

"Stay back!" Tullu yelled in Quechua at Pizarro and the conquistadors that closed in on them. "I'll kill this little waqati!"

"While I would certainly prefer that you did not harm my son," Pizarro replied, not understanding the Inca's words but rather the implications of his aggressive gesture, "do so at the peril of the one you came here to retrieve."

Much to Chasca's dismay, she watched as Pizarro yanked Alejandro from the concealment of the shadows and held a dagger to his throat, just as Tullu did to Valentino.

Acalan also peered at the Spaniards from behind his column, resting his eyes on the one called "Alejandro". The darkness shrouded Acalan's vision, but he needed no sight to feel a connection to the boy.

"If you kill my son," continued Pizarro, who was oddly calm despite both the boys he raised having blades pressed against their necks, "I kill the little savage who you so desperately wish to save...for some reason."

"Father, why are you doing this?!" Alejandro cried out with tears in his eyes. He struggled to understand his father's actions as Pizarro's knife gently grazed his skin.

"Silence, boy! You are no son of mine!"

Acalan listened intently to the family drama unfolding before them as he was the only non-Spaniard in the courtyard who could speak the Spanish language. Even Valentino stopped wiggling in Tullu's grasp long enough to hear his father's words.

"I lied," Pizarro declared to Alejandro, although his voice was loud enough for the entire palace complex to hear. "I never slept with a native whore, at least not one that bore me a child. I rescued you from those savage kids, Che–muli and some other little girl–I forget all your ridiculous barbarian names. I hoped that with a proper Spanish upbringing, you would grow into a good, decent young man. I know now that this was never possible. That savage mindset is buried deep into your thick skull."

Placed into a state of shock at Pizarro's claims, Acalan settled his eyes upon the boy who he hadn't seen in over a decade since they were separated on the shores of Tenochtitlan. "Ohtli…" he whispered to himself.

Ohtli rested still and silent in Pizarro's persistent hold, tears flowing down his young face at the realization that his whole life had been a lie. "W-where are my real parents?" he finally mustered through his sobbing.

"Ha!" Pizarro bellowed. "Your father, that traitor Rodrigo Diaz, and his savage whore are dead. I personally strung their bodies up on the causeway at Tenochtitlan for the world to see."

If Ohtli's true identity hadn't been confirmed already, Pizarro's reference to Acalan's good friends from his past life, Rodrigo and Atzi, certainly cemented it.

"I'll make you a deal!" Acalan shouted to Pizarro during his first encounter with the Spaniard in over eleven years. "An exchange! This boy for that one! Then we leave Cuzco for good, never to return!"

"Do I know you, savage? I never forget a voice," Pizarro remarked, still unable to see the man he spoke to.

"You put a musket ball in my shoulder about thirteen years ago after I killed all your Tlaxcalan sycophants on the edge of that cliff! I guess you were afraid to fight me man to man!"

"I'll be damned!" Pizarro exclaimed while laughing hysterically and still holding tight to Ohtli. "That *is* you, isn't it?! Then you spent the next two years in captivity getting the piss beat out of you, right? You must be one tough hijo de puta if you survived all that! I almost felt bad for you! Your face looked like a mangled mess!" Pizarro paused briefly, taking a moment to intensify his laughter. "Although as I recall, I think I landed a few blows myself on that ugly barbarian face of yours!"

"No matter!" Acalan replied, "I took my revenge on your horse that night on the causeway at Tenochtitlan! Did he die from that arrow?!"

Pizarro immediately ceased his laughter and transformed his demeanor to one of anger. "You fired that arrow?"

"Straight through the beast's neck! Sent you crashing to the ground and squealing like a little girl if I remember correctly!"

Pizarro forced a smile once more at hearing the Aztec's words. "At last, I meet a man worth killing! These Incas have been dreadfully boring and too easy to kill!"

Acalan began to regret his decision to trade insults with the Spanish leader after he returned to his senses and remembered the predicament they still faced. "I am willing to put the past behind us, though! How does the expression go? Let bygones be bygones?"

"You speak our language well...for a savage," Pizarro responded. "I'll give you that much. And you seem like a worthy foe. For this, I shall let you all live tonight as long as you promise not to harm a hair on my son's head."

"How do I know you won't shoot us the moment he's returned?"

"You have my word as a fellow warrior," Pizarro declared, placing his hand over his heart as a gesture of good faith. "Release my son and you will be allowed safe passage from the city."

"And the other boy?" asked Acalan. "The Aztec?"

"Take him and go. He's dead to me."

Acalan pondered Pizarro's proposal, wondering if the Spaniard would betray his offer of peace the moment he retrieved his son. The Blooded Aztec Grandmaster relayed Pizarro's message to the Incas in the Quechua language so they could all understand what was about to happen.

"They'll kill us all the moment we release that boy!" Chasca shouted at Acalan while the other Incas all grumbled in agreement with her.

"What choice do we have?!" Acalan snapped back. "Kill the boy and be killed along with him?! We've come too far to die like this."

"I will make the exchange," Cusi remarked, reversing her decision and siding with Acalan. "He's right. What other choice is there?"

"I'm growing impatient with all this savage mumbling!" yelled Pizarro, mocking the Incas with a clicking noise and a sarcastic impression of the Quechua language. "Bunta, bunta, bunta! My offer expires in ten seconds! Then we start shooting!"

"He says we have ten seconds before they kill us all," Acalan relayed the message. "We must go now."

Without hesitation and before anyone could interject, Cusi pulled Valentino away from Tullu's grasp and marched him towards the Spanish line. She ushered the boy forward by the collar of his tunic while still holding a blade to the back of his neck. The others all held their breath as they waited to see if Cusi's bold move would save their lives.

Now exposed to every musket in the plaza and with a young boy as her only cover, Cusi stared out at her Spanish foes that gathered in a semi-circle around them. In the middle of the Spanish line stood Pizarro, who seemed eager for the return of his son.

"Release the boy," Cusi stated, pointing at Ohtli, "and I'll release this one."

Much to Cusi's surprise, Pizarro instantly freed Ohtli from his grip and shoved him forward. Ohtli glanced back at the man who had stolen him as a baby and raised him as his own child.

"Did you ever love me, father?" Ohtli asked, still accustomed to addressing Pizarro in this manner.

Pizarro barely budged at the question posed by the boy whom he had called his son for ten years. The uninterested

Spaniard could only mutter, "I'm not your father, savage," as he kept his eyes fixed on Valentino.

Ohtli wanted to cry, to scream, to break down. He spent his whole life seeking approval from a man who was willing to cut his throat and abandon any semblance of love that Ohtli had so desperately sought. A tear ran down the boy's face as he turned around to face Cusi and the others. Despite the Incas' attempt to rescue him, they were still strangers to Ohtli, much like his own name (which he still thought to be Alejandro).

With no other options, Ohtli marched forward to the waiting arms of Cusi, who had just released Valentino. The two boys passed each other, and the normally vain and cruel Valentino stared ahead at his father with wide eyes and a whimpering expression, likely brought on by the fear of being so close to death.

When Ohtli's "brother" and all the other Spaniards were now at the Aztec boy's back, he felt a small measure of hope in the face of his Inca rescuers, who all stared at him intently.

Unfortunately for Ohtli, like most traces of hope in his life, his optimism faded quickly when he saw one of the other Incas approach Cusi from behind. It all happened so fast, like a gust of wind sweeping through and destroying any chance of peace.

"Huascar, what are you–" Atahualpa bellowed, but it was too late.

Huascar's knife was already lodged in Cusi's back.

The Blooded Grandmaster, only moments away from grabbing Ohtli's hand, widened her eyes in shock and pain when the blade entered her flesh again and again. Huascar stabbed relentlessly and without mercy, propping up Cusi with one hand while the other held the dagger that split open her back with each new stroke.

"Mother, no!" Chasca shouted in terror as she sprinted towards them. A Spanish conquistador fired his musket and hit the young Inca in the shoulder, dropping her to the ground just before she could reach her mother.

"Cusi! Chasca!" Atahualpa hollered upon witnessing his wife and daughter sprawled motionless on the terrace. Tullu held the emperor back as Atahualpa frantically struggled to come to their aid. "Let me go! Let me go!"

Huascar shoved Cusi to the ground, her body impacting with a loud thud. Chasca groaned in pain at her gunshot wound but mustered the energy to look into her mother's eyes one last time. Cusi gargled and spit blood from her mouth as she glared back at her daughter. The two Incas, separated for many years and finally reunited, shared one final moment together before Cusi's spirit faded from her earthly form.

"You bastards!" Acalan shouted as Huascar grabbed Ohtli by the throat and forced him back to the Spanish line. "You said no harm would come to us! You said you would give us safe passage from the city! You gave your word, you snake!"

Pizarro chuckled, welcoming Valentino into his arms before responding to the Aztec. "I'm not responsible for the actions of your own people! It was not I that broke our truce, savage! And that little bitch charged us!" he yelled while pointing at Chasca. "I will not subject my men to danger! It's *your* people who have broken our deal! And now you will all die for it!"

Still covering themselves behind the large, elaborate columns of the plaza, Acalan and Tullu glanced at each other with brave yet hopeless expressions upon hearing the Spaniard's proclamation.

Atahualpa sheltered alongside the remaining two Blooded Grandmasters, but the look in his eyes indicated a broken man. The emperor had just lost the empire that his ancestors fought so hard to build. His people suffered under the oppression of foreign invaders. His wife had just been brutally stabbed to death by his own brother who betrayed him and broke his trust. His daughter laid shot and injured on the ground in front of him, likely to meet her own death once the Spanish muskets opened fire again.

Bloodied and bruised from her injuries, Chasca struggled through the pain and rose to her feet with a look of determination in her eyes. Pizarro, Huascar, and the musket-wielding conquistadors all laughed as Chasca drew a blade from her robe, held it towards the Spanish line, and marched forward with the last bit of strength she had left.

In the darkness of the night, Ohtli, Atahualpa, Acalan, and Tullu all looked upon Chasca's courage with dread and respect. The brave young Inca, ready to meet her end and join her mother in death, emitted a deafening roar and charged ahead.

Pizarro grinned from ear to ear before giving the command to his men.

"Fire!"

Volume V, Part II
Smoke and Ashes

A voice rang through Ohtli's young mind.
"–Ohtli!"
Too distant to make out the words.
"–up, Ohtli!"
The sound in Ohtli's ears became clearer, and he felt a pair of arms wrap around his body.
"Get up, Ohtli!"
The ringing in the boy's ears suddenly halted and was replaced by sounds of anarchy and destruction. The outer gateway to the royal palace had burst open with a mighty explosion just moments before the conquistadors could unleash a volley of lead upon Chasca. The mortar that held the fieldstones in place on the surrounding wall had come loose by the detonation of a powder keg, and the stones soared in the direction of the nearby conquistadors.

Pizarro, Huascar, Ohtli, and Valentino, all far enough away to avoid death but still close enough to be affected by the blast, had been jolted to the ground in a display of explosive force that few Incas had ever witnessed.

Chaos ensued along the Spanish line. Smoke filled the air around the palace. Many of the conquistadors lay dead, and many others stumbled to their feet in a dazed and disoriented fashion.

Ohtli, still struggling to maintain his balance, looked up to see the dark complexion of a native woman's face. The woman pulled his limp body through the smoke and towards the palace entrance that had just been blown open by the explosion.

Next to Ohtli and his rescuer were three other warriors: a young native man, an older native woman, and an older Spanish man.

"Kelia! Keep Ohtli moving!" the young native man shouted.

"On your left, Chimalli!" Ohtli's female rescuer hollered back.

The young man, whom Ohtli deemed to be called Chimalli, sidestepped the sword of a Spanish conquistador and bludgeoned his attacker's head with a swift and brutal blow.

Several other conquistadors emerged through the smoke, and Chimalli and his companions maneuvered around their enemies' blades to make quick work of them. The older Spaniard found a gap in the armor of an approaching conquistador, piercing the flesh under his opponent's arm before opening the man's throat with a merciless slash of his sword.

"Sahagun!" Chimalli shouted after thrusting his dagger into a conquistador's neck. "We're almost there! The horses are right over there!"

"Come on! Let's go!" rang out the voices of Tullu and Acalan, who sat in the two drivers' seats of a small wooden carriage just outside the plaza. The wagon, which was just big enough to cram a few people into the back, was pulled by the twin Spanish mares, Lilly and Lyla.

"Where's the emperor?!" Kelia shouted in Quechua as they came upon the others, noticing that everyone except Atahualpa had made it to the carriage.

"I thought he was with you!" Chasca yelled while lying in the back of the cart and grimacing from the gunshot wound in her shoulder.

"He was right behind us!" Erandi hollered.

"I have to go back for him!" declared Chasca as she lifted her broken body to return to her father.

"I'll go!" Sahagun yelled after confirming Chasca's words with Erandi. "If I'm not back in one minute, leave without me!" Before Erandi and the others could protest his actions, Sahagun bolted through the smoke and back into the plaza with his sword drawn.

"Where is he going?!" Chasca questioned, not understanding the Spaniard's use of Nahuatl.

"He's going to retrieve your father," Acalan said, "but you can't – wait!"

Acalan's words were cut short as Chasca hopped off the cart with haste and grimaced through her injuries to follow Sahagun into the smoke.

"Warma, stop!" Tullu pleaded with Chasca to no avail.

More explosions erupted nearby as Blooded warriors continued to detonate barrels of gunpowder to cover their escape, but forming through the smoke on all sides of them was a rising battle cry of an approaching Spanish horde.

"Aztecs and Incas! Warriors of the Blood!" bellowed Acalan as the Spanish shouts grew louder and closer. "Draw your weapons and prepare to defend yourselves!"

"Find your strength, children of the gods!" hollered Tullu while placing a dagger in Ohtli's young hands. "Call upon Viracocha for his guidance!"

Chimalli, Kelia, Erandi, Acalan, Tullu, and several other Blooded fighters all took up defensive positions around the carriage and prepared for the weight of the Spanish attackers to bear down upon them. Ohtli sat in the wagon with his dagger pointing outwards towards the enemy, reminiscent of Chimalli at that age and when he first wet his blade in combat.

"Blooded! Warcry!" shouted Acalan, prompting the non-Blooded Aztecs to glance upon their hooded allies as their voices roared with a deafening chant to the gods. Tullu and Acalan raised their hands to the sky in the direction of the eagles that flew overhead, and many other Blooded slashed their blades wildly through the air.

Chimalli glanced into Kelia's eyes as she looked back into his. The two Aztec lovers locked their hands together, embraced, and shared a passionate yet short-lived kiss.

The first Spanish conquistador emerged through the smoke, and the Blooded chants were immediately replaced with the sound of clashing steel, copper, and obsidian.

"Prepare to meet your god!" Acalan yelled before parrying the Spaniard's attack and slashing his sword through the man's face.

More conquistadors, along with several native tribesmen that fought alongside the Spanish, flooded through the smoke and slammed against the waiting line of Aztecs and Incas. The explosions around the palace continued, and the chaos of battle ensued at the gateway.

Meanwhile, Sahagun and Chasca sprinted back into the plaza as they heard the chaos of battle emitting behind them.

"Father!" Chasca hollered, resting her eyes on the beleaguered emperor who sat on the ground beside his dead wife. Atahualpa stroked Cusi's hair gently, oblivious to the carnage around him.

"Emperor! Sapa Inca!" Sahagun shouted towards Atahualpa with a few Quechua words he had learned from Erandi and Kelia.

The emperor's tears flowed liberally down his face and landed on his wife's corpse. The look in Atahualpa's eyes was one of defeat, one of a man who had given up all hope.

"Father!" Chasca yelled once more. "We must go, now!"

"Leave me," Atahualpa said softly and with little emotion. "Supay is leading your mother into the afterlife, and I wish to join her in death."

"I don't know what the hell you're saying!" proclaimed Sahagun in Nahuatl, grabbing the emperor's arm to pull him away, "but the others won't last much longer! We have to leave, now!"

"I said leave me, you foreign devil!" Atahualpa shouted, changing his tone and elevating his aggressiveness towards the Spaniard. "Your kind has done enough."

"So be it," Sahagun said, understanding the emperor's gesture and retreating away from him. "Come on Chasca! There's no time!"

Chasca looked down upon her father one last time, settling her eyes on the shattered remnants of a once great man. The fight had left his soul, and he sunk into a black hole of oblivion. Chasca took a deep breath, wiped the tears from her eyes, and left her dead mother and broken father behind as the morning sun peaked over the nearby mountains.

When Sahagun and Chasca turned to embark on their journey back to the carriage, the sounds of battle suddenly halted, although the smoke still made it impossible to see what had transpired. A wave of uneasiness and fear rose inside the Spaniard and the Inca.

"Bind their hands! All of them!" Pizarro's voice rang out on the other side of the smoky film between them. The Spanish leader's words all but confirmed what Sahagun and Chasca had feared.

"You thought you could sneak into *my* city?! That you could take *my* son from me?!" Pizarro shouted as the sound of a musket pistol blasted through the air. "I am a living god amongst mortals! You all will kneel at my feet before your time in this world is over!"

Sahagun and Chasca crouched low and maneuvered their way through the smoke into a nearby thicket of bushes that had been unaffected by the explosions. The hiding place offered just enough vantage to see their Aztec and Inca comrades, all of which had been subdued with hands tied behind their backs. Many Spanish conquistadors and Blooded warriors lay dead on the ground while the survivors were forced to kneel before the seething Pizarro.

"Once more you have put my son in danger!" continued Pizarro as Valentino sat nearby on the ground with the tears of a coward flowing down his face.

"Papa, I want to kill them for what they've done to us," mustered Valentino through his sobbing while holding his three-fingered right hand that Rumi had disfigured. "Can I Papa, please? Can I kill them all?"

"You can kill one, but make it quick," confirmed Pizarro, who continued to pace and stroke his beard in thought.

Without pause, Valentino leapt from his seated position, unsheathed a dagger, and cackled as he jammed it into the heart of a kneeling Blooded warrior.

Chasca gasped at the sight of the young Spaniard's barbarism, but Sahagun placed his hand over her mouth to stop her from being heard.

Valentino then jumped into the carriage and pulled Ohtli down by his neck. The Spanish boy tossed his former brother (whom he now discovered wasn't related to him at all) onto the stone pathway with force. Ohtli grimaced at the pain of the impact, but he was helpless to stop Valentino's rage. The Spaniard mounted Ohtli and began slapping him in a childish yet cruel manner.

"Stop this savagery at once!" Chimalli pleaded with Pizarro in Spanish, attempting to abate the child's rage.

"Wait a moment, don't I know you, boy?" Pizarro asked Chimalli. "You look so familiar."

Chimalli remained silent as to not provoke Pizarro's rage, especially with Ohtli still being attacked by Valentino.

"No, it can't be..." Pizarro continued as he peered back and forth at Chimalli and Kelia. "Well isn't this just a day for reunions?! Che-muli and his little savage girlfriend! My, you've certainly grown into a fine young woman."

Pizarro leaned down and stroked Kelia's hair suggestively and beamed with perversion. Kelia winced backwards out of his grip and spit on his boots, prompting a sinister laugh from the Spaniard.

"Ahh, don't worry, young one," said Pizarro. "I would never soil my seed by entering you and creating another hybrid. Look how they turn out!" Pizarro gestured in the direction of Ohtli. "Even the slightest drop of savage blood will rot the soul. I see that now. The blood of our sons and daughters must remain pure. That's why I order my men to kill any savage whore they've mounted."

"How's your leg?" Chimalli questioned, abandoning his restraint. "What's it been? Eleven years? Eleven years since Rodrigo put that dagger in your leg in Tenochtitlan...since

I put that spear in your uncle's heart." The Aztec chuckled. "Two grown men, protected by steel and an army of sycophants, bested by a dying man and a twelve-year old boy."

Chimalli's words stirred a fire inside Pizarro. "Careful, boy. If you had seen what I did to your people and the bodies of your sister and her lover boy, you would hold your tongue."

"There's a special place in hell for those who mutilate the dead," Acalan asserted in Spanish. "Your god will condemn you and your men for all eternity for your actions."

"Foolish savages," Pizarro laughed. "*I* am the only god you need to concern yourself with. Invoke my wrath and you and everyone you hold dear will suffer a fate far worse than anything you can imagine."

Acalan and Chimalli heeded the Spaniard's warnings and remained silent. Pizarro was a coward but also a man of his word. From his time serving under Cortes in Mexico, to his years as the Butcher of Aztec and Mayan villages, and now to his conquest of the Incas, Pizarro's fury was widely renowned.

"Valentino, that's enough," Pizarro ordered his son to cease his assault on Ohtli, prompting a sniveling groan from the boy.

"Throw them in a cell until their day of judgment arrives," Pizarro directed towards his soldiers. "Let it be known that if you stand against your overlords, the bringers of civilization and culture to these barbaric lands, your life will be forfeited in full view of all."

"We have to get out of Cuzco and back to Machu Picchu," Chasca whispered in Quechua to Sahagun, who recognized the name of the Blooded's mountain fortress. "Regroup and come back with more men."

"Machu Picchu? You want to leave?" asserted Sahagun with a forceful whisper. "I will not leave Erandi and the others! I would sooner die than stand back while they're executed in cold blood!" The Spaniard's Nahuatl words clashed with Chasca's Quechua ones as the language barrier between them proved to be a deterrent for communication.

Suddenly, a thought sparked into Chasca's mind when she looked down and saw a dead conquistador a short distance from where they hid in the brush.

"Spaniard," she said, tugging at Sahagun's arm and directing his attention towards the dead man. "I think I know how we can get out of the city. Then we come back with every man and woman we can find that will help us."

Sahagun turned to focus on the corpse of the nearby soldier along with the man's trousers and glimmering suit of metal armor.

"Regroup and come back," Sahagun confirmed Chasca's plan.

As Chimalli, Kelia, Erandi, Acalan, Tullu, Ohtli, and the other remaining Blooded were marched away towards the dungeons, Sahagun pondered one last thought before he and Chasca pulled the lifeless conquistador towards them to remove his pants and armor.

"Never tell Erandi I got naked in front of you."

Volume V, Part III
The Pit

"Where are we?" Erandi asked in Quechua, wiggling her arms to release some of the tension from the ropes that bound her hands behind her back.

"I believe we're at the Moray amphitheater," Tullu responded, "in the Sacred Valley not far from Cuzco."

"The Moray amphitheater?" questioned Kelia. "Never heard of it. What are we doing here?"

"Well, you haven't been in this land very long, warma," chuckled Tullu. "Moray is used mostly for performances and agricultural research. I'm sure the Spanish didn't bring us here to watch a play, though."

"By the sounds of the crowd out there," Acalan added from his kneeling position inside the newly constructed Spanish stables, "if a performance is taking place, I'm guessing we're the stars of the show."

Kelia, Tullu, and Erandi all nodded their heads in agreement, and Chimalli did so too after Acalan repeated his words in Nahuatl.

"You knew my parents?" Ohtli asked Chimalli in Spanish, changing the subject with the only language he knew. "What were they like?"

"Yes," Chimalli confirmed, nodding his head. "Knew them is quite the understatement."

"Your mother was just as good of a sister as she was a mother. She would have forgiven me for failing you all those years ago."

"I don't understand," Ohtli admitted with confusion. "My mother was your sister?"

Chimalli nodded once more.

"So that makes you my uncle?"

"It does, conetl. I tried to do right by Atzi, and by your father, Rodrigo, but I fell short. I let that madman catch us. I let him take you from me. You were only a year old."

"Only a year? But that would have made you a boy like me?"

"Yes, I was," Chimalli responded. "Kelia and I were barely older than you when we escaped the ashes of Tenochtitlan. I remember carrying you on my back in a sling. Acalan was there too. He almost died to secure our departure."

Kelia and Acalan both turned their heads and smiled at Ohtli, reliving their own experiences with the boy and prompting him to stare back at them with an uncertain expression.

"I remember the last time I spoke to you," Acalan inserted into the conversation. "You could barely hold your eyes open. I strapped you to Chimalli's back before we entered Kelia's house to rescue her from the soldiers. I told you this would all be over soon. What you went through would have killed any other baby I've ever known, but not you. You were a fighter."

"And I remember the first time you ever curled up into my arms for comfort," Kelia added with a tear in her eyes. "I knew I could never take the place of your mother. She was the wife of Emperor Quetzalcoatl, after all. But I did everything I could to be a motherly figure to you, like a big sister if nothing else."

"Quetzalcoatl?" Ohtli questioned. "You mean the Aztec feathered serpent god?"

"Yes," Chimalli replied while the others nodded. "Your father was deemed by the people to be the return of Quetzalcoatl after the old temple devoted to him was engulfed by flames just before Rodrigo was executed. Of course, nobody knew that it was actually me that set the temple alight to save them."

"I was taught back in Spain that Quetzalcoatl was a monster, a demon from the depths of hell," Ohtli said.

"I can imagine why the Spanish would portray him that way," countered Acalan. "They wish to strip away everything that makes us Aztec, to wipe out our culture and traditions, much like they're trying to do here with the Incas."

"I don't know what to say," said Ohtli while lowering his head towards the ground in sorrow. "You've all been through so much for me. Sacrificed so much. I'm not worthy of it. I'm not strong enough."

"Look at me, nephew," Chimalli asserted in a determined voice. "You're stronger than you could ever imagine.

You might not be the son of a god, but you're the son of two of the greatest people I've ever known. The blood of El Cid Campeador, a great Spanish hero who lived many centuries ago, runs through your veins. You want to know if you're strong enough? After I stabbed Hernan Cortes through the heart, I hid from the guards in an old fish barrel with you. When I heard them coming for us, I placed my hand over your mouth and nose to stop you from breathing…to save you from the torment they would put you through. But even then, you wouldn't give up. Acalan saved us with his bow, and your lungs continued to pump air through them. So you see, conetl, the spirit of the jaguar lives within you, hidden by years of captivity and brainwashing, but it's still there, waiting to come out."

"But we'll all be dead within the hour, will we not?" asked Ohtli. "My fa– Pizarro…will take my life just the same as he will take all of yours."

"He may take our lives, young one," Kelia replied, "but he will never take our spirits. The bards will sing of our sacrifice for a thousand years."

"I'm so afraid," confessed Ohtli. "I don't want to die."

"As am I," Acalan agreed.

"But you're a great warrior," countered Ohtli, "you've fought in many battles, yes?"

"Yes, and every time I've drawn my weapon and stared down an approaching enemy, fear has gripped my soul. It is not the absence of fear that gives us courage. It's the ability to face your enemy in spite of it. Face your destiny with courage, and fear will not overtake you."

The rumblings of a large crowd echoed outside the stables where Chimalli, Kelia, Acalan, Tullu, Erandi, Ohtli, and Atahualpa knelt in captivity. The group of Aztecs and Incas, all with bound hands, sat in a row close to the entrance to the building. None of them had yet seen what awaited them on the other side of the door, but all of them breathed deeply in nervous anticipation of their fates.

"Whatever awaits us out there," Acalan continued to the whole group, first in Nahuatl for his Aztec friends and then again in Quechua so the Incas could understand, "serving beside all of you has been my life's honor. I can think of no better men and women to meet my death beside."

"We stand together, fellow Grandmaster," Tullu replied.

"Until the gods call us home," added Chimalli.

The rest of the troupe, other than Atahualpa, nodded with respect for the Aztec's words. The Inca emperor hadn't spoken or shown any signs of emotion since standing over his dead wife's body a week before. He simply knelt and stared at the ground with an apathetic expression.

Suddenly, the side door of the stables swung open, heightening the sounds of the crowd. Standing before them was Francisco Pizarro, the orchestrator of madness that had befallen the embattled Incas. Beside him pranced his son, Valentino, who, true to form, cackled like a schoolgirl at the sight of the captives.

"Look at them, Papa," Valentino marveled, "just look at them. All lined up perfectly like lambs for the slaughter. Oh how I can't wait to see their flesh ripped from their bones!"

"Patience, my son," Pizarro stated as he and Valentino marched over to the kneeling prisoners. "They will all be dead soon."

Chimalli glared at Pizarro while the Spanish leader squatted in front of him, the man's breath reeking of sour wine.

"I've waited a long time for this day," continued Pizarro in the direction of Chimalli, but his words were meant for everyone. "You all have been a thorn in my side for too long. Worthy enemies, perhaps," he glanced in the direction of Acalan, "but at the end of the day, nothing more than savage nuisances, obstacles on my path to eternal divinity. I will be revered for all time as the liberator of the southlands, just as my uncle was to the barbarian domains in the north. The world will know my name. I will be feared and respected from every corner of the map. Pity that none of you will be alive to hear the bards sing my tales."

"The world will know that good men and women stood against a tyrant, a bloodthirsty conqueror," countered Acalan in Spanish, prompting Pizarro to march over to the Aztec's side.

"You say that like it's a bad thing," Pizarro said with a sinister smile. "Tyrant, you say? I accept this title with pride. Tyrants restore order amongst the chaos. Without men like me, where would our world be? In the hands of weak savages like that worthless sack of shit over there that you people call your emperor.

Atahualpa said nothing and had no reaction to the Spaniard's insults towards him.

"And bloodthirsty conqueror?" Pizarro continued to Acalan. "That's ironic coming from those who tear the still-beating hearts from their enemies' chests. The blood I've spilt pales in comparison to the savagery your cultures partake in. No, my friend, I am simply a conduit of God, a divine messenger sent to cleanse the barbarians of their wicked ways."

"I'm not your friend," Acalan retorted with a disgusted look on his face.

Pizarro laughed audibly at the Aztec's claim. "No, I suppose you're not. Befriending a savage would be like trying to tame a wild animal. Eventually you'll always get bitten."

"Should we tell them, Papa?" Valentino beamed with delight. "Should we tell them about the beast?"

"Hush, boy," Pizarro replied as he rolled his eyes at his sniveling son, "it was supposed to be revealed to them as they entered the— fine, tell them, you simpleton."

Valentino leaned in towards Ohtli, drawing close enough that saliva slung from his mouth onto his former brother's face as he spoke. "I won't spoil the fun by revealing too much, but let's just say you Aztec savages are in for quite the... familiar...surprise."

Valentino then diverted his speech towards Ohtli directly. "I can't wait to see these barbarian eyes torn from your sockets and feasted upon like Sunday brunch."

Having heard enough of the weasel's incessant blabbering, Ohtli found his courage and thrust his head into Valentino's, busting open the Spanish boy's eye and drawing blood from it.

"Why you insolent little...!" Valentino struggled to form his words as he unsheathed his sword and attempted to strike Ohtli with it, though the boy was stopped by his father's hand just before his blow could land.

"Guard!" Pizarro yelled to a nearby conquistador who watched over the prisoners as he directed his ire towards Ohtli. "Gag this one and place a bag over his head. He will see nothing but darkness as he leaves this world."

Valentino wiped the blood from his nose and seethed at Ohtli's slight against him. The young Spaniard paced the stables from front to back, cursing under his breath as he strode.

"He's about to die. He's about to die," Valentino continued muttering to himself, attempting to abate an emotional outburst towards Ohtli. "Just keep calm. He's about to die."

Meanwhile, the guard aggressively shoved a cloth across Ohtli's mouth before placing a sack over his head. The boy's ragged, long-sleeve tunic and trousers matched the garbs of the other prisoners, but the bag now shrouded his world in darkness. Ohtli squirmed in panic at losing his vision and his voice.

"Fear not, conetl!" Kelia proclaimed, trying to calm the terrified boy's nerves. "We're still here with you! Never let them take your spi—"

Kelia's words were cut short as Pizarro slapped her across the face to stop her from talking.

"Quiet, savage!" Pizarro exclaimed.

"Don't touch her!" Chimalli yelled, rising to his feet and charging Pizarro before being instantly subdued by the guards.

"I grow weary of this banter," Pizarro asserted. "It's time for the cleansing to commence."

The Spaniard made his way to the two nearest horse stalls and began stroking the manes of Lilly and Lyla, who had both been recaptured during the failed raid on Cuzco. The Spaniard's touch caused the mares to recoil away from him. "By the way," Pizarro continued, "thank you for returning my horses to me. Such beautiful creatures, are they not? We'll have to break them of whatever savagery they've been exposed to, though. No matter."

Pizarro chuckled as he directed his attention towards Atahualpa. "Emperor! Oh revered, fearless leader of the people! Join me, will you not?"

Once more, Atahualpa gave no reaction and continued staring at the ground with the same blank expression as before.

"Fine, have it your way," Pizarro said with shrug, gesturing towards the guards. Two conquistadors marched over to the battered emperor and pulled him upwards by the shoulders before leading him out the side door with Pizarro.

The bright rays of the midday sun plastered across Atahualpa's face as he struggled to adjust his weary eyes to it. Before him stood a large crowd of people gathered inside the massive Moray amphitheater, many of them cheering and jeering at the sight of the bound emperor. Most of the onlookers appeared to be natives from other tribes, enemies of the Incas, brought in by the Spanish to dilute Inca influence and provide an audience that would cheer for their deaths.

At the base of the amphitheater sat an elevated wooden platform with the murdering usurper, Huascar, slouching across a makeshift throne. Atop the head of Atahualpa's treacherous brother was the Mascaipacha, a gold-threaded ceremonial headpiece designed only for the emperor of Cuzco. The false ruler, along with thousands of throat-slashing spectators, looked down upon the central terrace that had been walled off and transformed into an arena for blood sport.

Pizarro trotted down the sloped path at the head of the column and raised his hands to the sky like a god amongst men. With the beaten and bruised Inca emperor being escorted behind him, Pizarro relished the praise heaped upon him by the adoring crowd and laughed at their curses towards the emperor. Attempting to avoid any semblance of weakness, the Spaniard struggled through the pain to hide the limp he contracted from Rodrigo's dagger more than a decade prior.

"People of Tawantinsuyu and the lands beyond!" Pizarro shouted in Spanish as he climbed the platform that overlooked the fighting pit. A translator formed his words into Quechua for the crowd to understand. "Incas! Chanka! Chimu! All other noble clans that have joined together this day! We are gathered here to put aside our petty squabbles and usher in a new era of peace and prosperity! To witness the cleansing of a tyrant and his followers! To witness the power of your new god, me! Francisco Pizarro! Sent to this realm by my heavenly father to bring order and stability to a land engulfed in chaos and barbarism!"

Many of the Chanka and Chimu "visitors" were lifelong enemies of the Incas. Their deep-rooted hatred towards their stronger and more advanced neighbors fueled their desire to see them suffer at the hands of the Spanish conquerors. Instead of gathering for peace and unity, they had accepted Pizarro's invitation as a form of bloodless invasion into a once-strong land. Most of the Incas within the crowd knew the motivations of the Spanish and their native allies, but the threat of Pizarro's conquistadors and Huascar's royal guards that patrolled every corner of the complex prohibited them from taking action.

"Fear no more, brave warriors and citizens!" Pizarro continued. "Your liberation from oppression is finally here! It starts today! With the passing of the imperial crown!" Pizarro gestured towards Atahualpa, who was forced to kneel at Huascar and Pizarro's feet. "This man stole the birthright of his older brother, cut his tongue from his mouth, and supplanted his throne!"

Pizarro's claims worried the Inca citizens of the crowd, who had already suffered for many years under Huascar's rule. The only cheers came from the non-Incas, who were more than happy to see Atahualpa step aside in favor of his brother, a puppet to the Spanish.

"Kiss the feet of your new god and emperor, and you will be spared," Pizarro declared, leaning in close and lowering his voice so only Atahualpa and Huascar could hear. The translator continued to make the Spaniard's words known to all.

Atahualpa raised his head and formed a resilient look on his face for the first time since Cusi's murder. The emperor, now reduced to wearing the rags of a prisoner, said nothing but spit on the shoes of both men, first his brother, then Pizarro.

Huascar, adorned from head to toe in imperial garbs, scowled at his brother's defiance. He glanced at Pizarro, who sighed and nodded his head to the new emperor. With one fluid motion, Huascar thrust his sandal into Atahualpa's chest and sent him crashing into the large pit below with a forceful impact into the mud.

The Incas in the crowd gasped, but the Chanka and Chimu cheered loudly at the sight of Atahualpa being kicked into the arena.

"Bring out the rest of the prisoners!" Pizarro shouted to his men that guarded the top of the amphitheater by the stables. "Bring out the followers of this usurper! Bring out the members of the blood cult that dwells in the mountains!"

The side door of the stables swung open, and the captive Incas and Aztecs were ushered out one by one to meet their fates. The brightness of the sun stung their faces, much like it had done to Atahualpa. Acalan and Tullu led the group down the steps of the amphitheater with Chimalli, Kelia, and Erandi behind them. At the back, a Spanish conquistador shoved Ohtli along, forcing him down the long steps of the arena as the crowd jeered wildly. Still gagged at the mouth and bagged around his head, Ohtli fidgeted his way down the stairs while the guard continued to berate him.

Pizarro and Huascar looked upon the approaching prisoners with sinister smiles as the crowd began pelting them with squash, tomatoes, stalks of corn, and several other crops. The Aztecs and Incas closed their eyes and turned their heads to shield themselves from the assault.

"Don't lose faith, my brothers and sisters! This will all be over soon!" Acalan shouted to his comrades before a nearby conquistador jammed his musket stock into the Aztec's gut.

Chimalli attempted to reach back and touch Kelia's hands, but the ropes that bound them made it impossible to feel the comfort of each other's skin.

"I love you, Kelia!" Chimalli hollered over the jeers of the crowd and the continued hurling of food. "I will be with you always! In this life, or the next!"

"I love you too, Chimalli!" Kelia responded with tears streaming down her face. "If death comes for us, it is only the beginning! Our spirits will live on!"

When the prisoners reached the bottom of the open amphitheater, the guards positioned them around the side of the pit where Atahualpa still clung to life in the mud below.

"Bring the boy to me," Pizarro ordered, motioning for the guards to bring Ohtli to the platform where he and Huascar stood like divine beings presiding over a congregation of mortals. The conquistadors shoved the wriggling Ohtli up the steps towards the man who used to call himself the boy's father as the crowd continued to cheer for the events to come.

"Behold these brave men and women!" Pizarro shouted to the crowd while looking at the prisoners that encircled the fighting pit, "once mighty warriors, savage as they are, now reduced to nothing more than rats to be squashed beneath my boot!"

As Ohtli continued to squirm and wrestle with the ropes that confined him, the other five prisoners awaited their destiny with steady hearts, resting their eyes on a large wooden gate along the side wall of the arena.

Pizarro cleared his throat before emitting one final line to the crowd. "Citizens of Tawantinsuyu, I present to you this evening's executioner, The Beast of the Yucatan!"

When Pizarro finished his introduction, Chimalli and Kelia both dropped their jaws in horror when they saw what emerged from the gate. The Aztecs glanced upon the familiar fangs of a creature believed to be long dead as a large, ravenous cat trotted his way through the passageway and onto the fighting grounds.

"Chimalli," Kelia uttered, her voice cracking in shock. "Is that...?"

"Yes," Chimalli confirmed, "it's Khuno."

The aging jaguar that had accompanied the Aztecs through the Mayan jungles when they were children planted his feet in the muddy pit at the center of the spectacle of onlookers. Several native handlers followed Khuno into the arena and controlled the thick chain around his neck with a system of ropes.

Pizarro directed his words away from the crowd and towards Chimalli, Kelia, and Ohtli. "The three of you might recognize this beast that you once unleashed upon me and my men. Now, after all these years, I get to return the favor."

Khuno curled his lip and exposed the large fangs that protruded from his jaws as Emperor Atahualpa struggled to his feet with the last trace of energy he could muster.

"After we subdued the beast that night in the village all those years ago," Pizarro continued to the Aztecs, "we found him to be a formidable opponent in the ring. As you can see, he's never been defeated. All it takes is to deprive him of food for about a week, and this one is ready to tear the limbs from anyone who's unlucky enough to join him in there."

While Khuno's belly grumbled with hunger, the look in his eyes was that of pain and agony. His once beautiful fur now appeared patchy and unkempt, and the stress of a decade of servitude and fighting bore heavily on the jaguar. His caring soul had been stripped away and all that remained was a beast whose only value was to entertain a crowd.

"Look at him, Chimalli," Kelia said through her tears. "Look what they've done to him. He's pitiful. We have to do something."

"Not yet," Acalan replied from Kelia's opposite side, keeping his fellow Aztec grounded. "Stand ready and focused."

"Quiet!" a nearby guard commanded before striking Acalan in the back of the leg and dropping him to one knee.

"Emperor!" Pizarro exclaimed as Huascar threw a single spear into the pit next to his brother. "Defend yourself!"

The beast handlers waited anxiously for Pizarro's command to release Khuno onto the emperor. Atahualpa stumbled in his stance and looked down at the spear that laid in the mud beside him.

"I have not the strength or desire to wield this spear against this creature of the forest!" Atahualpa declared loudly, bellowing from the depths of his lungs. "Thus," he spread his arms and exposed his ragged form to the jaguar's claws. "I will die with the honor that remains in me, and I will leave this world with dignity!"

"Fight, coward!" Pizarro shouted, annoyed by the emperor's defiance.

Atahualpa said nothing in response, depriving the Spanish leader the satisfaction of witnessing his struggle to survive.

"As you wish," Pizarro declared, "release the beast!"

Upon command, the handlers loosened their grips on the ropes that all linked to Khuno's neck chain, and the jaguar surged forward with fury.

Atahualpa did not scream. He did not fight. He simply closed his eyes and accepted his fate as Khuno tore through his flesh. The hungry jaguar gave no quarter to his prey, feasting on the emperor with a rage that stemmed more so from the cruelty of his captors than a desire to kill his defenseless opponent.

Huascar chuckled from his seated position on the throne as his brother's body was ripped apart into a bloody, mangled mess. Pizarro, too, giggled and marveled over the slaughter.

"Unless you want this savage boy to experience the same end as your former emperor," Pizarro stated towards the prisoners as he grabbed Ohtli by the shoulders and held him over the pit, "I suggest one of you step forward and reveal the location of your mountain fortress. It seems to be the last bastion of resistance in these savage lands, and none of my scouts can seem to find it."

Chimalli, Kelia, Acalan, Erandi, and Tullu all held firm in their positions, glancing at each other but not conforming to Pizarro's demands.

"Not a word to this madman!" Acalan proclaimed to the others. "The cause is greater than one life, even a boy's."

Kelia continued to sob, and Chimalli peered at Ohtli in anguish. He too wept for the boy whom he had cared for since Ohtli was a newborn babe swaddled in his mother's cloth.

"I'm sorry, child," Chimalli declared. "This villainy will not go unpunished. Stay strong, just like we talked about."

"You think I'm bluffing?!" Pizarro questioned with unhinged anger in his voice. "I'll do it! Tell me where Machu Picchu is! Tell me now or this boy's blood is on your hands!"

With sadness and defiant resolve, the prisoners all stood silent in the face of Pizarro's rage. The Spaniard emitted a crazed shout that resonated around the amphitheater after the continued disobedience of his captives.

"Go to your savage gods!" Pizarro hollered into Ohtli's ear as he released the boy from his grasp. Ohtli's body crashed into the mud below, and the impact sucked the boy's breath from his lungs.

"Ohtli!" Kelia shouted as she and Chimalli attempted to jump into the pit to save him. The conquistadors restrained them though, preventing the Aztecs from rescuing Ohtli from his impending doom.

"Khuno! Please spare him!" Chimalli pleaded with the jaguar, but the Aztec's words scattered to the winds as quickly as he spoke them. Khuno had tasted flesh for the first time in over a week, and he was in no mood to stop now.

Accompanying an audible gasp from the crowd and the prisoners, the beast sprinted over to Ohtli's side and sunk his teeth into the boy's neck without hesitation. The savagery that commenced exceeded that which had occurred to Atahualpa's body. Chimalli and Kelia, along with the other prisoners, turned away in horror at the sounds of ripping flesh. Even most of the crowd, which had previously been thrilled at the sight of the emperor being killed, scoffed at the repulsive barbarism and murder of the young child.

"You hear that sound?!" Pizarro shouted in his continued frenzy as Khuno feasted uncontrollably on Ohtli's body. "That's the sound a savage body makes when it dies! It's unique, guttural, like a squelch that pierces the senses! Ha! Where's Valentino? He's missing all the—"

Pizarro halted his sentence abruptly after resting his eyes upon Ohtli's body, or what remained of it. Confusion engulfed the Spaniard and a sickness twisted in his gut as he focused his vision on the boy's right hand. Pizarro noticed a cloth around it on the spot where two fingers were missing. The paleness of Ohtli's hands, which were the only parts of his body that weren't covered by fabric, caused the Spaniard's eyes to widen in shock.

"Pull that beast back!" Pizarro shouted. "Guards, get in there and remove his hood! Now!"

The handlers tugged Khuno away from Ohtli, and a Spanish guard jumped into the pit to examine the body. A large convocation of eagles screeched and cawed overhead as a symphony of dread orchestrated inside Pizarro's loins. He panted and sweated heavily in the few seconds it took for the guard to reach Ohtli's body.

In a moment of absolution and clarity, Pizarro screamed in deranged terror when the guard removed the boy's hood and revealed that Ohtli had not been the victim of Khuno's fangs.

Not Ohtli, no, but Valentino instead.

Pizarro's son, the real one, laid mangled and almost unrecognizable as the sight of the dead Spanish boy drew exasperated mumbles from the crowd.

A persistent ringing sound pierced the soul of Pizarro and sent him into a daze. He could barely think. He could barely speak. He mustered every modicum of strength he could and shouted at the top of his lungs.

"Bring me that guard!" he emitted in a frenzy of madness. "The one who escorted the prisoners down here! Bring him to me now!"

The bards sung a melodic tune of vengeance...or perhaps justice, and the spirit of the jaguar rumbled in the hearts of every brave soul that surrounded the arena. As the other conquistadors all glanced at the guard that Pizarro sought, the Spanish leader rested his vision on the man's back plate of armor. When the soldier turned to reveal his face, Pizarro widened his eyes and gritted his teeth.

"I know your face," he proclaimed. "Where do I know you from?"

"Who? Me?" the guard answered facetiously. "I served you and your treacherous uncle a long time ago. I..." he paused and took a bow, "am Bernadino de Sahagun, and I curse the very ground you walk."

"Traitor! Seize him!" Pizarro yelled to his conquistadors.

"Chasca! Now!" Sahagun shouted in a tone that echoed across the entirety of the arena.

Without pause, the wooden doors of the stable at the top of the amphitheater burst open, and Chasca and Ohtli (the real one) surged through them with divine force.

"Lilly! Lyla! Lead us out girls!" Chasca hollered as she and Ohtli spurred on Lilly and Lyla, respectively.

The two white mares charged ahead and bolted down the steps of the amphitheater, and the prisoners below removed the ropes that had been loosely wrapped around their wrists to fool the Spaniards into thinking they were bonded.

"Now, warriors, fight!" Acalan shouted while he, Chimalli, Kelia, Erandi, and Tullu pulled hidden daggers from their tunics and struck the unsuspecting Spaniards with relentless aggression.

When the Spanish conquistadors began firing their inaccurate muskets at Chasca and Ohtli's approaching cavalry charge, most of the crowd scattered and panicked to avoid being caught in the crossfire. On queue, like a light in the storm, several hooded figures emerged throughout the amphitheater. The citizens dispersed as though a colony of ants had erupted, but dozens of Blooded warriors revealed themselves and stood resolute in the face of tyranny.

Pizarro and Huascar peered upon the unfolding events, drawing their weapons and preparing their soldiers for combat.

"Infantry, form up!" Pizarro commanded. "Protect me at all costs!"

The tongueless Huascar grunted and glared at Pizarro with disdain for letting their enemies surprise them with an attack.

"Watch the way you look at me, emperor," Pizarro stated with disrespect for Huascar. "Let's not forget who put you on that throne and who can remove you from it. Now help me repel this rabble!"

Huascar scoffed at Pizarro's words but turned to face the advancing horde of Blooded fighters.

"Stay tight, warriors! Keep the pressure on them!" Tullu shouted as the group of prisoners and their Blooded reinforcements slammed against the line of sword and buckler troops that formed around the side of the pit.

"Huascar! Pizarro!" Chasca hollered when she and Ohtli reached the bottom of the amphitheater. The Inca warrior, who had now lost her father and mother to the wrath of the Spanish leader and the false Inca emperor, pointed her axe in the direction of the two men. "I'm coming for you! I'm coming for both of you bastards!"

"Ohtli!" Kelia yelled after she finished thrusting her dagger into one of Huascar's warriors. "Stay close! Keep your blade ready!"

Ohtli, frightened at the ensuing carnage, dismounted Lyla and sprinted to the safety of his Aztec and Inca comrades, dodging incoming attacks from the soldiers of Pizarro and Huascar. "I'm scared, Kelia! The enemy are too many!"

"Have faith, nephew!" Chimalli shouted after dispatching an incoming native warrior with a vicious slice to the man's throat. "Search your heart for courage!"

"Push! Push! Push!" Acalan exclaimed while he, Sahagun, and Erandi led a charge against the shields of the conquistadors. "Drive them back!"

As Pizarro's men held firm against the Blooded assault, Chasca and Lilly soared through the air like a duo of conquering heroes to pierce the weakest part of the Spanish line. The conquistadors were caught off guard by the impact of Lilly's charge, and many of them careened into the nearby pit. Also caught in the charge were Chimalli and Kelia, who stumbled into the pit alongside the Spanish soldiers.

"Chimalli! Kelia!" Erandi shouted from above. "Look out!"

Chimalli, still dazed from the fall, rose to his feet just in time to sidestep an incoming strike and kill the Spanish attacker.

"Get up, Kelia! Get up!" Chimalli pleaded as he helped Kelia off the ground.

"Erandi! Sahagun!" Kelia hollered when she gathered her wits. "Protect Ohtli!"

Sahagun jammed his sword into an approaching conquistador and booted the man's corpse into the pit before turning to address Kelia. "With my life, child!"

Chimalli and Kelia both stopped in their tracks as the blood soaked Khuno, who had just finished tearing apart another Spaniard, prowled towards them through the mud. Neither of the young Aztecs raised their weapons, and just as the jaguar revealed his fangs and prepared to attack, Khuno recoiled and stared intently into their eyes.

"Hey there, old boy," Chimalli said to the large cat who they hadn't seen in over ten years. "You remember us?"

Kelia reached her hand nervously towards Khuno's bloody mouth, and the jaguar sniffed it thoroughly before forming a delighted expression on his face, likely for the first time in many years.

Kelia and Chimalli both grinned at Khuno's demeanor towards them, and the sight of the beaming creature brought them hope. Their feline friend brushed the tattered fur on the top of his head against their hands and relished the kindness they showed him.

For a brief moment, the reunion of man and beast was perfect, like none of the chaos around them even existed. That moment passed though, and it passed in a flash.

A spear sailed through the air and pierced the skin on Khuno's side, causing the beast to bellow and collapse in pain.

"No!" Chimalli yelled as the weight of the falling jaguar brought him to the ground as well. The Aztecs both looked up at the same time to witness the man who threw the spear, and neither were surprised to see Pizarro himself at the top of the platform. The Spanish leader grinned from ear to ear at his kill and took pleasure in the Aztecs' sorrow.

Chimalli propped up Khuno's head, and Kelia held his paw as the fire in the jaguar's weary eyes extinguished, his soul and the pain inside it passing from the earthly realm.

"Be at peace, my old friend," Kelia proclaimed, placing her hand across Khuno's heart.

Meanwhile, still on horseback, Chasca slashed her axe through several warriors before setting her sights on her father's mangled body in the pit. Rage engulfed the Inca, and she scowled at Huascar and Pizarro with hate in her eyes.

"Warma, wait!" Tullu shouted as he fought his way to Chasca's side. "We'll take them together!"

"I'm taking them now!" the brash Inca declared before surging Lilly forward.

"Warma, not yet!" Tullu pleaded, but Chasca was blinded by her hunt for vengeance.

Chasca and Lilly charged up the steps of the platform to reach their targets, but just as Lilly reached the top, Huascar overturned a nearby barrel and sent the horse and her rider crashing to the wooden planks. Chasca slammed against the boards with force, and the injured Lilly quickly rose to her feet and scampered away to safety.

Pizarro approached Chasca ominously as the wounded Inca reached for her axe that had slipped from her grasp during the fall.

"Not this time, princess," Pizarro declared, stepping on Chasca's arm just as her hand contacted her weapon. The Spaniard raised his sword in the air and swung it downwards at the helpless Inca. Instead of entering Chasca's flesh, though, Pizarro's attack was met with the sound of clanging steel as Tullu's blade clashed with the Spaniard's sword in mid-air.

"You will not touch her, you devil!" Tullu hollered, unleashing a flurry of attacks upon the Spanish leader.

Chasca leapt to her feet after Tullu's heroic rescue and grabbed her axe off the ground. Huascar surged forward at Chasca, attempting to catch his niece off guard before she could reestablish her balance. Despite her wounds, though, Chasca parried her treacherous uncle's attacks.

While Tullu and Pizarro continued to fight on the other side of the platform, Chasca's superior skills pressed the cowardly Huascar backwards and caused him to widen his eyes in fear. Reality set into the heart of the false emperor as a look of regret enveloped his face. Chasca maneuvered through his guard with ease before thrusting her axe into Huascar's leg. With a clean, subsequent stroke, she swung the axe around and planted it into the top of his head, splitting it open between his eyes.

Huascar, usurper of his brother's throne not only once, but twice, buckled and collapsed to the ground. The Mascaipacha fell from his head and landed in the pit next to the remains of Atahualpa. The traitor's death proved to be just as inglorious as his life, and the light from his eyes faded.

Chasca reveled in her victory for a short instant, but her joy was replaced with dismay when she heard the discharge of Pizarro's musket pistol. Chasca glanced over to see the swords of Tullu and Pizarro locked at the top of their swings, but Pizarro had drawn a pistol with his other hand and fired it into Tullu's gut.

The Blooded Grandmaster peered into Pizarro's eyes with shock as blood poured from the Inca's stomach. Tullu's defensive guard crumbled, and Pizarro smiled and thrust his sword through his opponent's neck, removing Tullu's head from his body.

"Tullu!" Chasca shouted in terror, sprinting forward to engage Pizarro.

The Inca's movement was halted though when she heard Erandi's voice behind her.

"Chasca!" her Aztec ally shouted, causing Chasca to turn in her direction. "Get out of there! Our lines are breaking! We must fall back!"

Chasca gritted her teeth as she looked back and forth between her friends and the Spanish leader that had just killed a Blooded Grandmaster. She could take Pizarro's life right here and now, but she risked being left behind as Acalan rallied his warriors, along with Lyla, for a full retreat from the onslaught of the Spaniards. The steel of the conquistadors proved too difficult to overcome, and the outmatched Blooded were pushed back.

Erandi and Sahagun helped Chimalli and Kelia out of the pit, and the group sprinted away from the encroaching Spanish swordsmen.

Pizarro's sword still dripped with Tullu's blood as he grinned at Chasca. The Inca grumbled with frustration before withdrawing from the platform. Chasca mounted the waiting Lilly just before the Spanish soldiers could catch her, and she retreated from the amphitheater with the others.

Pizarro's smile faded as he glanced around at the carnage around him. "Fucking savages, all of them," the seething Spaniard mumbled under his breath while his Inca and Aztec opponents faded from view.

The conquistadors had beaten the Blooded back, but their invasion right under Pizarro's nose proved his vulnerability. His son lay dead before him, the boy's limbs and throat torn from his body. Pizarro's puppet emperor was also dead, and he knew many of Huascar's men would likely abandon the Spanish alliance as a result.

"Sir!" one of Pizarro's captains shouted. "We have a civilian here that claims to know the location of the enemy encampment! He says it's only a three day's ride from here! If we give chase now, we can assault their fortress before they regroup their forces!"

"Good," Pizarro answered, his menacing eyes glaring towards the Andes mountain range in the distance. "Prepare your men for departure, captain."

"Yes, sir," the conquistador acknowledged.

"It's time to end this."

Volume V, Part IV
Enemy at the Gates

"Xiutla monan, Pizarro!" Acalan shouted in Nahuatl while overturning a table in the Great Hall at Machu Picchu. "We had them, Chimalli! We had them right where we wanted them! If only I had fought harder, maybe we—"

"You fought like a true warrior, you fool!" Chimalli interrupted. "Worthy of praise and respect from your people."

Acalan calmed his nerves and placed his rear on the stone slab in the center of the room beside Chimalli. The torches of the inner sanctum burned brightly, but the empty council seats hung over the Aztecs with an aura of darkness, bleak and devoid of hope.

"And yet here we stand," Acalan replied, slouching over and placing his hands around his face, "beaten and broken, fleeing back to the mountains like a whipped dog with our tails between our legs."

"We gave Pizarro a taste of his own cruelty, made him kill his only son," countered Chimalli. "That's got to count for something."

"It was satisfying to watch, yes, but I fear we've done more harm than good. I fear our defeat will show the people that defeating these foreign beasts is impossible. Even when we catch them off guard, even when we strike them where it hurts the most, they still prevail. We pound on the steel of their armor over and over, yet they manage to deflect our attacks and push us back every time. How can mortals like us stand up to such monsters? How much loss can we take before we crumble? Cusi, Tullu, Atahualpa, all great leaders...all gone now, crushed under the weight of the Spanish menace."

"Yes, they're gone," Chimalli asserted, "but *you* still remain, Acalan. Those men out there, the ones who have pledged their lives to this cause, they still fight for you. They would die for you and for this land without a moment's pause."

"What if I can't deliver them the world they fight so hard to build?" Acalan questioned, a single tear flowing down his cheek. "What if I'm not strong enough?"

Chimalli rose to his feet and stared at the older Aztec with determination in his eyes. "Even if that's true, you harbor your doubts and find the strength to fake it, if nothing else. Do you think Rodrigo was strong enough to rule beside Cuauhtémoc as a god among men? Of course not, but he knew the people needed him to be something he wasn't. He found his courage and did what needed to be done. So will you, my friend. You are the last remaining Grandmaster of this order, and if you can't discover your strength, then none of us will."

Acalan wiped his face and grabbed Chimalli's outstretched hand that lifted him off the hard stone surface of the inner sanctum. "Your mind has grown as strong as your sword arm, Chimalli, a far cry from the boy I knew in Tenochtitlan. You're already a better man than I could ever hope to be."

"Cease your praise, pinotl," Chimalli responded with a chuckle. "I've spent half my life in a prison cell while you've been making a difference in the world."

"The only difference I'm thinking about right now is the one we can make with that powder," Acalan stated while looking at a barrel of gunpowder that Sahagun and Chasca had carted back to the fortress after their escape from Cuzco. "We don't have any guns to use it with, but perhaps we can find a purpose for it."

"It does make quite a mess when combined with fire," Chimalli admitted.

Acalan nodded in agreement as footsteps scurried down the adjacent hall next to the inner sanctum.

"Chimalli! Acalan!" Kelia's voice rang out as she entered with Sahagun, Erandi, and Ohtli on her heels. "They're here!"

"Who?" Acalan asked with concern.

"Pizarro and the conquistadors," Sahagun replied, almost out of breath from sprinting to deliver the grave news to Chimalli and Acalan. "Along with a few thousand Chanka warriors that have rallied to his banners. Someone must have tipped them off about the location of the fortress."

"A few thousand?!" repeated Acalan, his stomach twisting at the realization of how vastly outnumbered they were. "After our losses at Cuzco and Moray, we have maybe five hundred able bodied Blooded warriors, and that's likely a generous estimate."

"We must put a sword and bow in every hand able to wield it," Erandi added. "Even the women and children. The conquistadors are only a quarter-day's ride from here."

"Hundreds of weeping wives fill the streets outside," said Acalan. "They still mourn for their fallen husbands, and now you want me to shove a weapon in their hands? In the hands of their sons and daughters? To bring more death and grief upon their families?"

"Death and grief are here, Grandmaster," Sahagun asserted, "if we don't fight, all of us, the Spanish will rape the women and cast the children from the side of the mountain."

"I don't need a Spaniard to tell me what atrocities your countrymen are capable of committing," responded Acalan with a look of disdain for Sahagun. "I've seen it with my own eyes."

"So have I," countered Sahagun in defense of himself, "and those men are no countrymen of mine. My place is here, Grandmaster, with you and the people of this land."

"Forgive my words," Acalan said, reversing his harsh demeanor. "The thought of losing yet another home weighs heavy on me. You have proven yourself loyal to our cause, and thus deserve to be treated as such."

"It pleases me to hear that," Sahagun replied, "but I wish to be more than just loyal. I wish to be one of you. We all do. We wish to become Blooded. To be washed in the Blood of the mountain."

"Is this true?" Acalan questioned his fellow Aztecs. "You wish to become a member of our order?"

"It is," confirmed Chimalli. A nod from both Kelia, Erandi, and even young Ohtli verified their intentions as well.

"So be it, my friends. We have little time for ceremony, though, and it must be performed by more than just me."

"I believe I can assist with that," Chasca's voice rang out as the hooded Inca entered the chamber carrying a large bucket of goat's blood. "We can do it here and now. You say the words of our creed, Grandmaster, and I will wash them in the Blood."

Acalan grinned and nodded in agreement. "Kneel, all of you."

"Won't we make a mess of this sanctum?" Chimalli jested.

"We will," Acalan replied as he retrieved his bright red cloak from the wall. "The Great Hall was the place where Cusi, Tulli, and I all took the oath for the first time. We cleansed our souls and these stones in blood over eight years ago. Seems fitting that you all will carry on that tradition, especially if we face our end on this night."

The ensemble of Aztecs and Spaniards, or a mixture of both in Ohtli's case, knelt at Acalan and Chasca's feet while the Aztec Grandmaster prepared himself to conduct the

Ceremony of the Blood, which was previously performed by Tullu before his death.

Acalan cleared his throat and placed his hand on each initiate's shoulder as he called their names. "Chimalli, Kelia, Sahagun, Erandi, and Ohtli, my brothers and sisters of the Blood, with this ceremony, your former life is now over. While you may retain the names of your past, you will now be reborn in the Blood and through the image of the gods. Repeat my words and be heard."

While there were no chanters or other witnesses to the ceremony other than Chasca, a great tune rumbled and vocalized within the minds of the initiates. The spirit of Khuno, the fiercest and bravest jaguar Chimalli and Kelia had ever known, flowed through their hearts and filled them with pride and honor.

Acalan sounded the words of the Blooded creed in Quechua, and even the non-Quechua speakers (Chimalli, Sahagun, and Ohtli) felt the power of the creed as they repeated it.

"I am Blooded, and this is my creed," the group all repeated in unison to finish their oaths.

Acalan concluded his speech before standing before each of the initiates, slicing their hands one by one as he went down the line, starting with Erandi and ending with Chimalli. Ohtli winced when the dagger ran across his hand, but the young boy held firm and brave despite his pain. Their blood committed to the stones of the Great Hall, and just like Chasca had felt during her induction, the sting of the blades reminded them of their vows.

"Now," Acalan commanded, "place your hands on the stones and be cleansed in the Blood."

Chimalli, Kelia, Sahagun, Erandi, and Ohtli all leaned over and placed their bloody hands upon the stone surface that rested at the base of the empty seats of the Blood Council. Four crimson handprints now coated the stones of the Great Hall's inner sanctum, but as Chasca maneuvered herself around the inductees and raised the bucket in the air, the handprints were swallowed by a river of blood that washed over the Spaniards and Aztecs. The goat's blood flowed down each of their faces and backs, enveloping them in a thick stream of crimson.

"Rise now! Rise now, children of the Blood!" Acalan shouted as the initiates all ascended to their feet while blood flowed into the cracks of the stones around the chamber. "Rise and be seen! Rise and be heard! For you are now Blooded, from this day until your last!"

■■■■■■■■■

It started with a drop. A single drop of rain fell upon Chimalli's new cloak that he had just received from being inducted into the order. The blood from the ceremony just hours before still stained his hair and face, but as more drops of rain plummeted from the night sky, the blood on his face, as well as the faces of his Aztec and Spanish companions, began to clear from their skin.

"Come, Ohtli," Chimalli instructed the boy of only thirteen years of age.

Ohtli, who wore the same robes as the other Blooded initiates, approached his uncle and awaited his orders. The sounds of Spanish and Chanka boots grew louder from their position atop the outer stone walls of Machu Picchu.

"Yes, uncle?" Ohtli questioned with a nervous hesitation, attempting to ignore the approaching horde of devilry.

Chimalli raised his voice to compensate for the increasing sounds of rain that muffled the voices of the Blooded defenders. "Do you know the first thing you did when you were born?"

"No, I suppose I was a bit young," Ohtli jested, prompting a grin from Chimalli. "I imagine I cried."

"That's the funny thing, though, you didn't cry. You barely made a sound other than a few whimpers. Your mother, Atzi, birthed you in a dark cellar beneath the soil of Tenochtitlan. When you emerged into the world for the first time, I rushed into the room with you. I was so eager to see my nephew, the boy from two worlds."

The Spanish and Chanka infantry outside the walls halted and gave a deafening war cry upon Pizarro's command. Ohtli turned his head to meet the shouts of their opponents, but Chimalli smiled and pulled the boy's face back towards his own.

"You laid on your mother's chest, swaddled and calm," Chimalli continued, ignoring the sounds of the encroaching attackers that lingered outside the walls. "I ran to my sister's side as fast as I could. I remember how dim it was in the room. One of the torch sconces had just gone out, and there was barely enough light to see your eyes staring back at me. I had never seen such composure. You weren't even scared. You looked into my eyes with a certain calmness, a tranquility that engulfed your entire spirit. I remember thinking to myself how strong willed you would be as you grew in this world. I swore from that day forward that I would dedicate my life to protecting you, especially after your parents were taken from us."

"I wish I had known them," Ohtli replied as he too blocked out the shouts of Pizarro's conquistadors.

"So do I, child, so do I. But you have their strength. Never forget where you come from. Never forget the power that flows through your veins. You are Aztec, one of us. And now you are Blooded. There is nothing this world can throw at you that you can't handle."

Ohtli fought back his tears and embraced his uncle like a son would embrace a father. The boy held tight to Chimalli's neck.

"Chimalli and I will be with you always," Kelia added with a smile as she glanced down at them. "Whether we meet our ancestors on this night or fifty years from now, we will all do so together."

Ohtli reached for Kelia's hand and pulled her close to join him and Chimalli in their embrace. The three Aztecs, whose story began when they were children fleeing in a small boat from the shores of Tenochtitlan, found themselves together once more, covered in goat's blood and devoted to a higher purpose.

"Acalan! So-called Grandmaster of this heathen blood cult!" Pizarro shouted from horseback at the front of the column as the Spanish leader glinted at the high walls of Machu Picchu for the first time. "Your fortress is lost! Order your men to lay down their arms, and they will not be—"

Before Pizarro could finish his speech, Acalan fired an arrow through the rain towards his target, piercing the flesh of the Spaniard's horse, just as he had done over a decade earlier on the causeway at Tenochtitlan.

Pizarro's steed collapsed and slumped to the wet ground, and the Spaniard's face planted in the mud in front of his men. The line of Blooded defenders atop the walls all wailed in laughter upon seeing the Spanish commander flailing on the ground as his men attempted to remove the dead horse that laid limp upon his legs.

"Dirty savages!" Pizarro shouted as he stumbled back to his feet. "Vile, grotesque, barbaric!" The Spaniard's rage enveloped him once again, just as it had done at Moray after he killed his own son by accident. "Release the prisoners!"

The Blooded laughter ceased after hearing Pizarro's orders as confusion set in amongst the ranks. That confusion soon turned to clarity, though, as the Spanish catapults behind the infantry line slung their payloads over the fortress walls.

Chasca glared in shock as the heads of her mother and father, as well as Tullu and dozens of other deceased Blooded warriors, planted in the mud behind the walls. The defenders gasped after witnessing the barbarism of the Spanish, though they expected nothing less at this point. With tears in her eyes, Chasca sprinted down the steps on the backside of the wall, slinging a cloth around her parents' heads to shield them from the pouring rain. Atahualpa and Cusi Ocllo, husband and wife, great and noble rulers of the realm of the Incas, were dishonored and reduced to projectiles for catapults.

Chasca lowered her head in sadness but raised it with determination. Still nursing the wounds she had received during the attack at Moray, she fought through her pain and gathered her composure for the fight to come.

"Archers!" Acalan yelled as Pizarro formed up his line of musketeers. "Nock arrows!"

"Tell your men to aim for the swordsmen!" Sahagun yelled to Acalan as he and Erandi ran down the line to alert the Grandmaster. "The musketeers can't fire their weapons in the rain! Their matchlock rifles won't work!"

"Are you sure of this?" Acalan asked when Sahagun reached his side.

"I am, Grandmaster. I fired these weapons many times during my time in Cortes's army. The rain will douse the firing mechanism."

"Draw and target the swordsmen!" Acalan ordered to his men, prompting the Blooded archers to turn their bows away from the musketeers and towards the sword and buckler troops.

The Blooded archers, including Chasca, Chimalli, Kelia, Sahagun, and Erandi, all pulled their bow strings back and awaited Acalan's command. The rain pelted their black cloaks and shielded their eyes from the hundreds of eagles that circled overhead. The birds screeched through the sounds of thunder as lightning bolts stabbed the night sky.

Every Blooded man, woman, and child that defended the walls of Machu Picchu all held their breath during the final calm before the storm. The chants of the holy men in the temple filled the air, and the mortal realm of men was beset once more by fire and blood.

"Loose!" Acalan ordered. In unison, a volley of hundreds of arrows released towards the Spanish sword line. While many arrows bounced off the Spanish armor, many others found their way around the steel, sneaking through the weak points at the neck, legs, and under the arms.

Several Spanish swordsmen, along with dozens of Chanka warriors, screamed in pain and fell to their deaths in the mud.

"Muskets! Fire!" Pizarro ordered, but much to Sahagun's prediction, only a few rifles discharged due to the heavy rain. The musketeers worked to fix their malfunctioning weapons, but before they could think, another arrow volley soared into the Spanish and Chanka lines.

"Press forward!" Pizarro ordered his captains as the conquistadors charged the walls with ladders in hand.

"Fire at will!" Acalan shouted as he picked up his bow and began firing with his men. The Blooded archers, led by Acalan and his superior skills as a bowman, unleashed a fury of death upon their foes, felling many of them before they could reach the walls.

"Prepare to repel ladders!" Sahagun shouted as he threw down his bow and locked his fingers inside Erandi's. "To the death, my little dove?"

"Only in death will we part, my hairy little white man," Erandi proclaimed, planting a firm kiss upon Sahagun's lips.

"Draw your sword, Kelia!" Chimalli yelled as the two Aztecs both stood in front of Ohtli, shielding the boy from harm.

"This is just like how we met!" Kelia shouted back before locking lips with Chimalli.

"How so?" Chimalli asked as a Spanish ladder crashed against the stone ramparts of the wall.

"With a thrust of our blades!"

A bearded conquistador emerged from the top of the ladder, yelling, cursing, and slashing his sword as he charged Kelia. The Aztec warrior woman ducked his attack and whipped her club through the man's face before Chimalli thrust his foot into the conquistador's chest, sending him crashing back to the ground.

"It's a bit more even now that we're not kids!" Chimalli jested and grinned as another Spanish soldier propelled himself up the ladder, only to be met with a heavy blow by Chimalli to the center of the head.

"Ohtli!" Kelia hollered after a few more kills and a short lull in the action. "Take my bow and stay in this corner. Do you know how to use it?"

"Umm, I took a few archery classes a couple years ago," the nervous and uneasy young boy replied, "but all I did was shoot at straw targets, not flesh."

"This is no different," Kelia proclaimed, moving quickly to prepare Ohtli for combat. "Just draw and release. If anyone comes up right here," she said while pointing towards the Spanish ladder that had been placed on their flanks, "you watch our backs and send an arrow into their black hearts."

Ohtli nodded anxiously as footsteps sounded near the top of the ladder.

"Here comes one now!" Kelia shouted through the noise of the rain. "Draw!"

Ohtli readied an arrow and took a deep breath before using all his strength to pull the bow strings back. He held shaky but firm in his stance for a brief second before the head of a Chanka warrior emerged over the ramparts.

"Release, Ohtli! Now!" Kelia commanded.

Ohtli centered the man's head in his vision and released an arrow straight through his eye. The impact of the arrow jolted Ohtli's target off the ladder and back to the ground below.

"You got him!" Kelia shrieked delightedly.

"Well done, nephew!" Chimalli exclaimed as he turned just in time to see Ohtli's first kill.

Ohtli emitted a half-hearted smile and nocked another arrow as Kelia returned to help Chimalli with the increasing number of soldiers that rushed over the walls.

The downpour of rain continued to slam against the fighters on the walls of the fortress, and the dim light of a half-moon provided the only illumination for the battlefield.

Acalan's loud and dominating commands echoed across the defensive perimeter that the Blooded men, women, and children of Machu Picchu protected with their lives. The Grandmaster was calm and confident, showing his prowess as a leader along with his skills as a warrior.

"On your left, little dove!" Sahagun yelled a few paces from where Chimalli, Kelia, and Ohtli fought. Erandi dodged an incoming surge from two Chanka warriors that had snuck up a ladder unnoticed behind her. The weight of their charge thrust the Aztec woman to the ground, and the Chankas closed in to finish her.

Sahagun bolted into action, leaping across the dead warriors that littered the walls and piercing his sword through the chest of one of Erandi's attackers. The man collapsed to the ground, but his companion caught Sahagun off guard by slashing his club straight through the former conquistador's guard. Sahagun's sword fell from his hand, and he careened against the stone ramparts. Just as the warrior shouted and swung his club towards Sahagun's head, an arrow soared through the air and penetrated the center of the man's back. Sahagun, still dazed and attempting to regain his composure, glanced over to see a smiling Ohtli readying another arrow after saving the Spaniard's life.

"God still watches over you!" the young boy hollered to Sahagun, both of whom had found common ground in their Christian beliefs.

"So it would seem!" Sahagun grinned at Ohtli as Erandi lifted herself off the ground to defend against an incoming assault.

Meanwhile, Chasca fought like a goddess, single-handedly holding off an entire wave of Chanka troops that flooded the walls. The Blooded fighters around her had mostly perished, but the young Inca battled with the strength of ten warriors, weaving her axe in and out of the flesh of dozens of Chankas and Spaniards.

Despite the vicious line of defense displayed by the Blooded, their numbers slowly began to dwindle across the line. Conquistadors and Chanka warriors laid dead in droves along the walls, but their vast numbers continued to weigh heavy on the defenders.

Acalan, having just sent an arrow into another Spanish neck, peered at his surroundings and analyzed the chaos that ensued. The ramparts were no longer defensible as Pizarro's soldiers poured into the breach. Kelia and Erandi retreated to Ohtli's side, Chimalli and Sahagun stood back-to-back, and Chasca began to waver despite creating a mountain of bodies with every swing of her axe.

"Warriors!" Acalan hollered loud enough so that every remaining Blooded fighter could hear. "Fall back to the Great Hall! Fall back, men! The line is broken!"

Acalan's command echoed across the battlements, and the realization of impending defeat sunk into the hearts of the Blooded warriors. In mass, the defenders retreated off the walls and back down the steps to the pathway leading to the fortress.

"Chasca, let's go!" Kelia shouted. "Fall back!"

Chasca gave no response and continued killing at will with an expression of hatred on her face, a look that indicated her bloodlust and disregard for Acalan's order to retreat. Witnessing the severed heads of her mother and father had placed her in a trance, one that removed the trivial thoughts of pain or danger from her mind. It was simply Chasca, her axe, and the enemy. Nothing else mattered in that moment.

"Erandi, get Ohtli back to the Great Hall!" Kelia shouted.

"Where are you going?!" Erandi replied anxiously as Kelia sprinted towards Chasca. "Shit! Chimalli!" Erandi continued. "Get Kelia! She's going back for Chasca!"

Chimalli sprang into action, leaving Sahagun's side and bolting forward to follow Kelia.

Erandi, Sahagun, and Ohtli all retreated to the pathway below as Acalan led his men back to the next level of the fortress.

"Fight, warriors of the blood!" Acalan shouted as the Spanish and Chanka fighters pursued them off the walls and down the path. "Fight to the last man!"

Death and chaos littered the streets leading through the residential section of the Blooded stronghold. Men, women, and children alike fled and defended themselves from the Spanish onslaught in the narrow corridors of the fortress.

Back on the wall, Chasca continued striking down attackers on her section of the ramparts like a crazed berserker, but even in her trance-like state, her strength began to diminish.

"Chasca! We must fall back!" Kelia shouted as she and Chimalli reached the Inca's side.

"Leave me," Chasca said calmly after slaying another Chanka foe and glancing down at the cloth that contained her parents' heads. She had placed them nearby to watch over them and keep them safe from further degradation by the dishonorable conquistadors. "My place is here, with my mother and father."

"You're not thinking straight!" Kelia pleaded to the woman who she fought to near-death at the High Temple of the Apus but had now become a trusted friend. "Snap out of it! We must get back to the Great Hall! It's our only chance!"

"Chance?" Chasca chuckled softly. "This world is lost to me. I've failed my family and my people. My only chance at redemption is to die by the sword."

The three warriors fought off an approaching wave of attackers and dropped them to the ground with lethal blows, but their ability to defend the wall was quickly deteriorating.

"We must go!" Chimalli exclaimed to Kelia. "If she wants to stay, it's her choice!"

Kelia heard Chimalli's plea and knew his words to be true. The Spanish and Chankas already pillaged the fortress behind them, and it was only a matter of time before their position was overrun. Kelia and Chimalli gave one final glance of respect towards their fellow Blooded warrior.

Chasca nodded to the Aztecs before placing her hand on Kelia's shoulder and emitting the last words she would ever speak to them. "Fly, my friends."

Chasca's words entered the Aztecs' hearts just as another wave of enemies approached. Chimalli took Kelia by the arm and leapt from the top of the wall, rolling through the mud by the stone gateway that had been pried open.

The Spaniards that had just entered the gates swung at the falling Aztecs, but Kelia and Chimalli dodged the attacks and made their escape up the pathway to the residential section. When they were finally clear of enemies, both peered back to the wall one final time.

Chasca, daughter of the deceased emperor and defender of her people, slumped to her knees as a Spanish sword sliced through the back of her leg. While she fought off the attack and killed the conquistador, a Chanka warrior charged and planted his spear in her back. The tip of the spear pierced her body and exited her stomach, and the Inca's eyes widened at the feeling of her flesh being torn asunder. Even with a spear now protruding through her torso, Chasca still found the strength to pivot around and slay her Chanka adversary.

Chasca's world became dark, but the pain she felt paled in comparison to the release that enveloped her soul, like the burden of life had been lifted from her shoulders. The Inca slouched backwards while remaining on her knees. The base of the spear that impaled her stomach contacted the ground behind her and propped her waning body up while the tip pointed to the sky. The falling rain splashed upon Chasca's weary face as her lips formed a wide smile, a beaming absolution that wiped away the pain of existing in her mortal body.

"Strange time to be joyous, princess," Pizarro proclaimed while approaching with his guards. "We'll see how wide that smile gets when your head is placed on a spike next to all your little savage friends."

Chasca said nothing in response. She would not dignify the crude Spanish leader by giving in to his attempts to provoke her. Instead, she widened her smile even further and glared into Pizarro's eyes. In her final moments, Chasca invoked a terrible curse upon the Spaniard. She never broke her glance, even as Pizarro's dagger pierced the flesh of her chest and neck. The fire that remained in Chasca's persistent stare horrified the Spaniard, and he frantically stabbed the Inca's body to get the sight of her blood-stained eyes out of his mind. It took Pizarro cutting Chasca's eyes from her skull to cease her glare, but the curse she planted never left his soul.

Chasca ascended and took Rumi's hand as he ushered her forward to the next life. She took a seat next to her mother and father, leaving the mortal realm behind for all eternity. The eagles wept for her death but rejoiced for the beautiful soul that now soared in the clouds amongst them.

Volume V, Part V
Fall of the Blood

What can mere mortals do when pitted against a hatred so vile that it stains the ground red and curses every blade of grass that grows for a thousand years? Every man, every woman, every soul in this realm faces a choice in life, a crossroads that will dictate their eternal presence in the afterlife.

If I've learned anything in my life as a warrior, lover, scribe, and friend, amongst other titles, it's that coincidence is nonexistent. Even in the darkest of times, the moments that seem hopeless, the phases of life that reveal one's character to their core, it's all a test. An examination. A cruel and calculated assessment, if you will, conjured by the Creator to evaluate a creation. Like one would fire a new musket at a target to test its accuracy, or how a sword freshly forged would be sliced through an animal's hide to gauge its strength and durability, life itself is no different. We are all tried in a court of celestial existence, each of us, perhaps in different ways, but tested all the same.

Will God look upon my actions and smile on the day of my judgment? Will He accept that I have taken the lives of so many of His creations, both wicked and righteous. Is it up to us mortals to place that judgment upon others? To evaluate one's degree of righteousness before taking their life? Or are we doomed to the fires of eternal damnation for seeking to control that which cannot be controlled, stripped of redemption for all time?

Surely these thoughts coursed through the minds of every Blooded soul that remained inside the fortress of Machu Picchu as the wicked cast their shadow upon the mountain.

"Barricade the entrance!" Acalan shouted to the last of his warriors. The sounds of death echoed beyond the walls of the Great Hall, the building that was said to be the closest manmade structure to the realm of the Inca gods. Anyone still trapped outside, fighter or not, was overwhelmed and slaughtered.

"Make way!" Sahagun hollered while removing a section of the barriers that led to the inner sanctum. "Chimalli! Kelia! Come quickly!"

The two Aztecs rushed into the chamber where they had been inducted into the order, panting from the long sprint to the top of the mountain.

"Where's Chasca?" Acalan questioned, staring down the hallway to witness the Inca's arrival, one that would never come to pass.

Chimalli remained silent and turned his head in sadness while Kelia peered at the crimson-stained floor where Chasca had washed them in the Blood.

"She fell," Kelia finally muttered, projecting a sadness that swallowed the energy of the sanctum. Sahagun and Erandi both stopped for a moment and soaked in the grave news. Chasca's death hit Ohtli the hardest, though, as his mind raced to the memories he shared with her.

"She was always kind to me," Ohtli stated, his eyes filling with tears, "even when she knew nothing about me, not even my name. She was one of the bravest souls I've ever known."

"An honorable death, no doubt," Acalan uttered after absorbing the moment into his conscience, "a loss that even the gods will mourn."

"She now dines with those she has loved and lost, reunited once more," said Chimalli, "as is the case with all that have fallen to the sword on this night."

"I fear we will join them soon," Erandi added. "The Spaniards will offer no mercy."

"Perhaps we should take our own lives and rid them of the satisfaction," one of the other Blooded members expressed as his words were met with a few confirming nods.

"Take your own lives if you must," Sahagun asserted, "but I will do no such thing. My God will take his vengeance upon me for committing such an act. I will stay and die by the sword of my enemies."

"As will I," agreed Chimalli.

"And I," Acalan added.

A subsequent confirmation of Sahagun's declaration sounded from Kelia, Erandi, and Ohtli. Even the Blooded that suggested death by their own hands were swayed against it.

"It is settled then," Acalan proclaimed, prompting a nod from the others. "We will defend this chamber to our last breath, and we will fall to our enemies' blades, not our own."

The shouts of approaching Spaniards and Chankas echoed from the entrance to the Great Hall while its defenders grabbed their weapons and held tight to their loved ones.

"Whatever happens," Sahagun declared to Erandi after placing his codex into the pack that secured around his shoulders, "loving you has been my life's honor, an even greater one than writing my codex."

Erandi smiled and caressed his coarse, bloody hands with her own. "I never imagined I would hear those words from you," she said.

"Nor I," Sahagun admitted with a slight chuckle. "For so long, this codex has been everything to me, my purpose in life, but I've now found another purpose, my little dove, one that transcends the earthly boundaries of reason and logic. My heart aches, quite literally, with the thought of losing you or being separated by death."

Chimalli laughed as he held Kelia and Ohtli in his arms and overheard Sahagun's words. "I thought you were writing a tale of greed and power on those pages, my friend," he remarked. "Sounds more like a love story to me."

"Love is more powerful than all the wealth and land in the world," Sahagun confessed. "It molds us, shapes us, gives us a sense of direction."

Kelia peered into Chimalli's eyes as Sahagun concluded his poetic speech. Chimalli kissed her on the forehead and pulled her tight against his body.

"If this is to be our end, the end for the Blooded, the end for our world as we know it," Acalan proclaimed loud enough so that the last remaining Blooded in the chamber could hear him, "let it be such an end that the world will have no choice but to take notice of our sacrifice. Let the eagles fly us to the halls of our ancestors with pride, if that is our fate. Where there is death, there is also life. This is the balance. This is the way of the Blood."

"This is the way of the Blood," the members of the order repeated together, hearing the Grandmaster's words and absorbing them with honor.

The clamor of Spanish and Chanka cries grew even louder now as the enemy soldiers were mere moments from turning the corner and entering the inner sanctum.

"Any man, woman, and child capable of wielding a blade, step forward and let your wrath be felt!" Acalan continued. "Let the fury of the gods course through your veins!"

A war cry erupted amongst the Blooded, matching the approaching shouts of the Spanish. Chimalli and Sahagun pounded their chests, Kelia and Erandi slashed their blades through the air, and Acalan vocalized a call to the gods. Even Ohtli shouted and cursed while gripping the bow that Kelia had given him. The boy took a deep breath and placed an arrow against the strings.

A screaming conquistador then emerged into their sights and charged ahead. Before the man could come close to the barricade that separated the two forces, Acalan strung an arrow and released it so rapidly, Apollo himself would have blushed. The tip of the arrow pierced the conquistador's eye and exited the back of his skull. The Grandmaster and several other Blooded archers then let loose a barrage of arrows on a swarm of soldiers that flooded into the breach.

"For the Blood of this land!" Chimalli shouted in Nahuatl. "Fight!"

The conquistadors and their Chanka allies, at least the ones who survived the arrow volley, smashed against the barricade that led into the inner sanctum.

Time seemed to slow for the defenders.

Each warrior Chimalli cut down produced another.

Each arrow Acalan released sunk into an endless horde of enemies.

It is written in the pages of the codex that the defense of the Great Hall of Machu Picchu would go down as one of the greatest stands ever taken in the realm of men. Akin to the fields of Agincourt or the narrow pass of Thermopylae, the halls of Machu Picchu served as a historic battleground of defensive prowess that was matched by few battles throughout antiquity.

Alas, like many tales before it, the Battle of Machu Picchu and the epic defense of the Great Hall would not come to a joyful conclusion. After hours of fighting, spilling blood, and defending the stones of the sanctum, the defenders were undone by a weak spot in the barricade.

Conquistadors flooded through the opening, backing the few remaining Blooded warriors to the steps where the Blood Council seats rested. A place considered to be a divine and sacred conduit of the gods was now reduced to a battlefield of anarchy and destruction.

"Muskets to the front!" Pizarro shouted as he stomped his boots into the inner sanctum and peered around the room, marveling at its heigh ceilings and majestic columns.

Before him stood the exhausted, panting figures of the Blooded heroes that had fought so bravely to defend the people of Machu Picchu. The women and children who were unable to fight huddled amongst the seats of the council and prayed for a release from their inevitable doom.

Chimalli barely possessed the strength to hold his obsidian tipped club anymore, but he mustered every bit of energy left in his body to step forward and glare into the Spanish leader's eyes.

"Chimalli! Stop!" Kelia shouted while pulling at his arm.

"Don't do anything foolish, kid!" Sahagun warned. "These men will kill you!"

Chimalli shook off the pleas of his fellow Blooded warriors, including those of the woman he loved the most in this world. The young Aztec, with blood and determination plastered across his face, stumbled forward to meet the Spanish musket line.

"Pizarro, fight me!" Chimalli demanded with a roar that resounded through the chamber. "Fight me like a man and leave these people alone!"

Pizarro brushed past his soldiers and stared at the battered Chimalli, pursing his lips into a smug expression. "Fight you, you say? Man to man? And why would I do that?"

"To show your men they're not being led by a coward!"

Pizarro chuckled and paced across the front line of his men as each of their muskets aimed in the direction of the Blooded defenders. "So if you kill me and win, my men lay down their arms and walk away? Is that right?"

"Right," Chimalli confirmed. "Never to return to this place."

"Such a tempting offer. I would relish the opportunity to place your head on a pike just like I did to the one that attacked me at Moray," Pizarro said with a grin, referring to his triumph over Tullu. The Spanish leader stroked his beard in thought and contemplated the young Aztec's challenge. "But do you really think I would risk everything I've built in a sword duel with you? The savage mind is inferior, sure, but I've seen you fight. You're one of the most talented warriors I've ever seen. I like to put myself in a position of advantage over my opponent, as I've already done, and fighting you would only prove to negate that advantage."

"I figured you would make an excuse to avoid a fair fight," Chimalli scoffed. "Typical of men such as yourself."

"Men such as I," Pizarro retorted with anger, "will go down in history. You think anyone will think twice about you and your friends? Just more dead savages. You think the words that traitor over there puts down on his dirty parchment will ever see the light of day?"

Sahagun giggled softly at the mention of his codex. "You've heard of my work?" he asked with a lighthearted and pompous smile.

"That's all I've heard ever since you people arrived here," Pizarro answered with a sneer. "The Spaniard who betrayed his own people and writes tales of the savages that he keeps in his backpack. It's become rather exhausting."

Sahagun's smile widened a bit more as the thought of his codex reaching the ears of the people excited him.

"I wouldn't get too cheerful over there, traitor," Pizarro continued. "The first thing I shall do when you're all dead is burn those pages and piss on the ashes."

Pizarro's aggressive words caused Sahagun's smile to fade as he held tight to the straps that held his pack in place.

"With that said," Pizarro said as he redirected his attention back to Chimalli, "I decline your offer and sentence you and your savage friends to death."

"Muskets! Prepare to fire!" the Spaniard ordered as he marched to the edge of the firing line.

Ohtli gasped at the command given by his former father and held tight to Kelia's arm. Sahagun and Erandi locked their fingers together once more, and Acalan stood resolute in the face of impending death. All of them, including Chimalli, relaxed their defensive postures and awaited the release that would come from the Spanish musket balls.

"Muskets! F—"

"Wait!" Chimalli shouted, interrupting the Spaniard's orders.

"What now, barbarian?!" Pizarro pressed in frustration. "Face your death like a man!"

"I ask only for one pistol," Chimalli requested. "Just one, against twenty of your rifles. At least let us die with that honor."

Pizarro chuckled once more and reached for the pistol in his holster, the same one used to put a musket ball in Tullu's gut. "You want a pistol?!" the impatient Spaniard hollered. "Here!"

It all happened so fast. Pizarro flung his pistol towards Chimalli, and before the Aztec could even catch it, the Spaniard commenced his order to unleash the muskets. The thing about Chimalli of Tenochtitlan, though, was that he was a man led by his gods, safeguarded by a swarm of vigilant eagles, and driven by the will to protect those he loved at all costs. All of these qualities, and more, guided his hand as he grasped the handle of Pizarro's pistol. Without hesitation and in one fluid motion, Chimalli fired the Spanish weapon at the crate of gunpowder that had been loaded into the chamber by Sahagun and Chasca after the failed assault on Cuzco.

The resulting explosion rocked the stones of the inner sanctum and blasted a gaping hole in the side wall of the structure. The force of the detonation careened the Spanish and Chanka fighters across the room and slammed them against the walls and floors. Pizarro, who was on the opposite side from the gunpowder crate, crashed to the ground with just enough force to smash his head on a nearby stone without killing him.

Chimalli and the rest of the Blooded were jolted backwards but remained far enough away not to be affected much by the blast.

Stones rolled across the ground and settled.

Debris fluttered through the air and clouded the room in a haze.

The Blooded warriors, still shocked at the explosion that saved their lives, held tight to their weapons and marched towards the enemy line of wounded soldiers. Erandi was the first to jam her blade into an injured conquistador, and the others followed behind her. The slaughter that commenced covered the stones in yet another flowing stream of crimson.

Chimalli and Kelia, both coated from head to toe with their own blood and that of their enemies, ominously approached Pizarro, who crawled and whimpered on the ground in front of them.

The Spanish leader backed into a corner and stumbled to his feet while the Aztecs stared at him with vengeance in their eyes.

"I believe I will accept that challenge now, b-boy," Pizarro muttered while wavering in his stance. The realization of his situation crept into the Spaniard's soul as he attempted to save himself. "What will it be? Pistols? Swords? Bare knuckles?"

Pizarro chuckled and spit blood from his mouth, grimacing from the pain of his wounds.

"Bare knuckles sound good to me. I think you'll find this much more difficult than the last time you fought me when I was a child," Chimalli answered, dropping his club and bolting forward at the Spaniard before he could react.

Pizarro attempted to swing his sword at Chimalli and break the fair terms of the fight, but the Aztec dodged the attack and disarmed his battered opponent. Chimalli slung Pizarro's sword to the ground and planted his fist into the Spanish leader's nose. Over and over, he pummeled the helpless man's face while Kelia and the others did nothing to stop him.

Years of rage came out in one moment. Like Rodrigo had done to Javier on the causeway at Tenochtitlan, Chimalli now did the same to Pizarro in the Great Hall of Machu Picchu.

The threat of Pizarro and his aura of invincibility diminished with each successive strike. When Chimalli finally ceased his assault on the Spaniard, Pizarro clung to life and grinned through the bloody mess that used to be his face. His teeth had been jarred loose by Chimalli's fists, and his eyes could barely stay open due to the immense swelling around them.

"My love, the honor of the kill is yours," the panting Chimalli declared to Kelia as he dismounted Pizarro.

Kelia formed her lips into an expression of anger and strode over to the Spaniard with her dagger drawn. "This is for my mother," she proclaimed.

"To h-hell with y-your whore m—"

Pizarro's final words were interrupted by the squelching sounds of Kelia's dagger entering his neck. She ripped out the Spaniard's throat with a continuous thrust of her blade, emitting a deafening shout with each stab.

Chimalli finally pulled her back after several seconds had passed. He and Kelia were both covered in the Spaniard's blood, which was a welcome feeling for the two Aztecs who Pizarro had tormented for so long.

"What now?" Erandi asked. "The rest of the Spaniards will come after they've finished pillaging the fortress."

Sahagun nodded and wiped the blood from his sword. "Even without their leader, they'll still overtake us," he added. "We won't be able to hold them back again."

"There's another way out," Acalan replied, "thanks to that hole that was just blown in the wall. That corridor leads to a passage out of the Great Hall and down the backside of the mountain."

"Make for the mountain pass, Acalan," Chimalli said. "Get the women and children to safety."

"What about you?" Acalan asked. "Will you join us?"

"I will, but there's something Kelia and I must do first."

■■■■■■■■■

A red sun settled behind the clouds and nestled its way below the tree line. The sky lit up with a dark shade of crimson, a lament from the heavens of the blood that was spilt that night at Machu Picchu.

Acalan and Ohtli stared out at the crimson sky with hope; hope for God or the gods to guide their path, hope for a better world. Beside them, Sahagun and Erandi glanced towards the horizon as well, soaking in the rays of the setting sun.

A trotting of hooves clamored on the mountainside, and only Ohtli turned to face the sound of horses approaching. The young boy smiled as Chimalli and Kelia dismounted the two Spanish mares, Lilly and Lyla, to join their friends in awe of the sunset.

"Where does this path lead?" Chimalli asked Acalan as the rays of the red sun struck his face and filled him with a divine clairvoyance.

"Do you mean this path?" Acalan responded, motioning towards the literal path of dirt and rocks beside them. "Or this one?" he questioned, gesturing his hand towards the open valley below that stretched as far as the eye could see.

Chimalli chuckled as he clasped his fingers around Kelia's, inducing a smile from both Aztec lovers. "This one," he replied while still staring towards the horizon.

Kelia shuffled in her stance and glanced at the others. "Cuzco is lost. Machu Picchu, burning. I fear the Incas have been undone, their empire collapsing beneath the Spanish boot, just like Tenochtitlan."

"You're right, my love," Chimalli confirmed. "It's time to move on from this land, to find a new home for the Blooded."

"I've heard rumors of a city many moons from here," Acalan claimed. "Outside the confines of the Inca lands. A city made of solid gold, enough gold to make the gods themselves jealous."

"A city of gold?" Sahagun prodded with a laugh of his own. "Sounds like a fiction."

"Perhaps, but there's only one way to find out." Acalan grinned and turned a watchful eye towards the others, and they all reciprocated his excitement.

"Here's to more bloody adventures!" Sahagun shouted as he unsheathed his sword and pointed it towards the sky.

Chimalli, Kelia, Ohtli, Erandi, and Acalan all circled around and raised their weapons to meet the Spaniard's.

"For Chasca!" Kelia declared.

"For the people!" bellowed Chimalli.

"For the Blooded!" Acalan yelled.

The crew of Aztecs and Spaniards all emitted a glorious shout that echoed across the valley.

"By the way," Sahagun probed once the group lowered their weapons, "what do they call this mythical city of gold?"

Acalan looked to the sky and peered upon the eagles that circled overhead, absorbing their divine energy. "I have heard no name for this place in the tongues of the native tribes, but in your language, my Spanish friend, it is simply called–"

Acalan paused as every eye and ear fixed upon him.

"–El Dorado."

Made in the USA
Columbia, SC
25 September 2024